STRONG OPI

STRONG OPINIONS

J. M. Coetzee and the Authority of Contemporary Fiction

EDITED BY CHRIS DANTA, SUE KOSSEW AND JULIAN MURPHET

BLOOMSBURY
NEW YORK • LONDON • NEW DELHI • SYDNEY

Bloomsbury Academic

An imprint of Bloomsbury Publishing Plc

175 Fifth Avenue
New York
NY 10010
USA

50 Bedford Square
London
WC1B 3DP
UK

www.bloomsbury.com

First published by Continuum International Publishing Group 2011
Paperback edition first published 2013

Library of Congress Cataloging-in-Publication Data
A catalog record for this book is available from the Library of Congress

ISBN: HB: 978-1-4411-0530-1
PB: 978-1-6235-6958-7

Typeset by Pindar NZ, Auckland, New Zealand

Contents

Acknowledgements

Most of the essays in this volume were originally presented at a conference hosted at the University of New South Wales on 23–24 January 2009 on the topic of "Coetzee in Australia." The editors of this volume, who were also the organizers of that conference, would like to acknowledge the kind support of the School of English, Media and Performing Arts and the Faculty of Arts and Social Sciences at UNSW. We would like to thank Riccardo Vecchio for his beautiful design work on the cover of this book. Bill Ashcroft and Paul Patton helped to nurture the volume when it was at the proposal phase. Haaris Naqvi at Continuum supported the project from the outset and has been not just a consummate professional but also an absolute joy to work with.

Contributors

Bill Ashcroft is an Australian Professorial Fellow at the University of New South Wales, Sydney. A founding exponent of post-colonial theory, co-author of *The Empire Writes Back* (Routledge, 1989, 2002), the first text to examine systematically the field of "post-colonial studies." He is author and co-author of sixteen books, variously translated into five languages, including *Post-colonial Transformation* (Routledge, 2001); *On Post-colonial Futures* (Continuum, 2001); *Caliban's Voice* (Routledge, 2008), and over 150 chapters and papers.

Elleke Boehmer is the author of the world bestseller *Colonial and Postcolonial Literature: Migrant Metaphors* (Oxford University Press, 1995, 2005), of the non-fiction studies *Empire, the National and the Postcolonial, 1890–1920* (Oxford University Press, 2002) and *Stories of Women: Gender and Narrative in the Postcolonial Nation* (Manchester University Press, 2005), and the biography *Nelson Mandela* (Oxford University Press, 2008). She has published four widely praised novels, *Screens Against the Sky* (short-listed David Higham Prize, Bloosmbury, 1990), *An Immaculate Figure* (Bloomsbury, 1993), *Bloodlines* (short-listed Sanlam Prize, David Philip, 2000), and *Nile Baby* (Ayebia, 2008). She is the Professor of World Literature in English at the University of Oxford and General Editor of the Oxford Studies in Postcolonial Literatures Series.

Chris Danta is an Australian Research Council Postdoctoral Fellow in the School of English, Media and Performing Arts at the University of New South Wales. He is the author of *Literature Suspends Death: Sacrifice and Storytelling in Kierkegaard, Kafka and Blanchot* (Continuum, 2011) and has published essays in *New Literary History*, *Textual Practice*, *Modernism/Modernity*, *Sub-Stance* and *Literature and Theology*. His postdoctoral project tracks how the animal fable changes after Darwin in writers such as Robert Louis Stevenson, H. G. Wells, Franz Kafka, David Garnett and Coetzee.

Melinda Harvey is Lecturer in English at Monash University, Melbourne. Her article "Re-educating the Romantic: Sex and the Nature-Poet in J. M. Coetzee's *Disgrace*" appeared in *Sydney Studies in English* in 2005. She is currently working on an essay that explores Coetzee's relationship with Russian novelists of the nineteenth century, especially Dostoevsky.

Sue Kossew is Professor of English at Monash University. Her publications include *Pen and Power: A Post-colonial Reading of J. M. Coetzee and André Brink* (Rodopi, 1996), *Critical Essays on J. M. Coetzee* (G. K. Hall, 1998), *Re-Imagining Africa: New Critical Perspectives* (edited with Dianne Schwerdt, Nova, 2001) and *Writing Woman, Writing Place: Australian and South African Fiction* (Routledge, 2004). She has recently edited a book of critical essays entitled *Lighting Dark Places: Essays on Kate Grenville* published by Rodopi in 2010.

Maria López is Lecturer in the English Department at the University of Córdoba, Spain. She has written on J. M. Coetzee and other postcolonial writers, and her monograph on Coetzee, *Acts of Visitation: The Narrative of J. M. Coetzee*, is forthcoming from Rodopi. Her current research interests deal with the intersection between literature and ethics, exploration narratives, and forms of community in South African literature.

Mike Marais, who teaches in the Department of English at Rhodes University, has published widely on J. M. Coetzee and contemporary South African fiction. His monograph on Coetzee, entitled *Secretary of the Invisible: The Idea of Hospitality in the Fiction of J. M. Coetzee*, was published by Rodopi in 2009.

Julian Murphet is Professor of Modern Film and Literature at the University of New South Wales. He is the author of *Multimedia Modernism* (Cambridge, 2009), *Literature and Race in Los Angeles* (Cambridge, 2001), co-author of *Narrative and Media* (Cambridge, 2005), and co-editor of *Literature and Visual Technologies* (Palgrave, 2003). He has authored numerous articles and book chapters on topics ranging from postmodernism, film history, literary and cultural theory, and race studies.

Paul Patton is Professor of Philosophy at the University of New South Wales. He is the author of *Deleuze and the Political* (Routledge, 2000) and *Deleuzian Concepts: Philosophy, Colonization, Politics* (Stanford, 2010). He is co-editor (with John Protevi) of *Between Deleuze and Derrida* (Continuum, 2003) and (with Simon Bignall) of *Deleuze and the Postcolonial* (Edinburgh, 2010).

Anthony Uhlmann is Professor of Literature in the Writing and Society Research Group at the University of Western Sydney. He is the editor of the *Journal of Beckett Studies* and the author of *Beckett and Poststructuralism* (Cambridge University Press, 1999) and *Samuel Beckett and the Philosophical Image* (Cambridge University Press, 2006). His most recent book is *Thinking in Literature: Joyce, Woolf, Nabokov* (Continuum, 2011).

INTRODUCTION

J. M. Coetzee

The Janus Face of Authority

Chris Danta

An innately philosophical author, J. M. Coetzee remains fascinated by the question of what grants the literary text the right to begin. For this reason, the beginnings of Coetzee's novels are often overdetermined. His 2003 novel *Elizabeth Costello: Eight Lessons*, for example, starts with a kind of metafictional stutter: "There is first of all the problem of the opening, namely, how to get us from where we are, which is, as yet, nowhere, to the far bank."[1] Rather than simply beginning to tell us a story, Coetzee's third-person narrator here reflects on the problem of beginning to tell a story. The narrator recognizes that the literary work should transport its readers from where they are to the far shore of fiction, but demurs at the point of having to carry out this imaginative act of bridging. He or she continues: "Let us assume that, however it may have been done, it is done . . . We have left behind the territory in which we were. We are in the far territory, where we want to be."[2] Rather than a story, this is the mere desire for a story. Here is an act of narration that paradoxically teaches its readers the meaning of the unusual word *velleity*: "The fact or quality of merely willing, wishing, or desiring, without any effort or advance towards action or realization."[3]

The opening few sentences of *Elizabeth Costello* leave us feeling dislocated: neither entirely in a story, nor entirely out of one. Indeed, so acute is our sense of dislocation that we might even decide that we are not in fact reading a novel. So why does Coetzee choose to begin in this testy and overdetermined way, with such apparently slack or half-hearted narration?

It might be to underscore a point his initial-sake, JC, makes in *Diary of a Bad Year*. JC begins his "strong opinion" on authority in fiction by noting: "In the novel, the voice that speaks the first sentence, then the second and so onward — call it the voice of the narrator — has, to begin with, no authority at all. Authority must be earned; on the novelist author lies the onus to build up, out of nothing, such authority."[4] The narrator of *Elizabeth Costello* makes us realize that the storyteller initially lacks authority by unnaturally prolonging the threshold moment that we experience before the story properly begins. "Let us suppose that literature begins at the moment when literature becomes a question,"[5] writes the French critic Maurice Blanchot in his essay "Literature and the Right to Death." What is happening at the beginning of *Elizabeth Costello* is that literature is becoming a question for the reader. Rather than being transported anywhere, we are here being put back on our heels for a moment and made to reflect upon the nature of the literary enterprise.

Coetzee betrays his modernist roots — the influence of Beckett and of Kafka upon his writing — when he makes the advent of the literary coincide with the scrupulous eschewal of authority. Coetzee willfully shuns authority not just in his fiction but also in his more autobiographical writings. In a discussion with David Attwell at the end of *Doubling the Point: Essays and Interviews,* he starts to tell his own story from 1970 to 1990 in the third-person present tense.

> In the first half of this story — a story spoken in a wavering voice, for the speaker is not only blind, but written as he is as a white South African into the latter half of the twentieth century, disabled, disqualified — a man-who-writes reacts to the situation he finds himself in of being without authority, writing without authority.[6]

Blind, disabled, disqualified, without authority: just as he does at the beginning of *Elizabeth Costello*, Coetzee here almost qualifies his narrator (in this case, himself) out of existence. Coetzee's self-conscious desire to speak or write without authority is clearly a response to his political situation as a white South African writer living and working under the apartheid regime. But it is not just that, since it persists in Coetzee's Australian novels. Not simply a political use of the literary, the withdrawal of authority is also for Coetzee constitutional to the act of writing itself. The nineteenth-century Danish philosopher Søren Kierkegaard once observed, "as a writer I am a peculiar sort of genius neither more nor less — absolutely without authority and therefore completely dependent on his own liquidation so as never to become, for anyone, an authority."[7] We might well say the same thing of Coetzee — that as a writer he is a peculiar sort of genius bent on never becoming, for anyone, an authority.

But what does it mean to write without authority?

It certainly doesn't mean to write badly — Coetzee is nothing if not a master prose stylist. To write without authority is rather to make authority a question in and through one's writing. The claim of this new collection of essays on Coetzee's work is that, if Coetzee allows us to pose the question "What is literature?" more forcefully and fruitfully than any other living author, it is because of the various ways in which he exposes his readers to the paradox of literary authority. JC spells out the terms of this paradox for us in *Diary*:

> What is the source of authority, or of what the formalists called the authority-effect? If authority could be achieved simply by tricks of rhetoric, then Plato was surely justified

> in expelling poets from his ideal republic. But what if authority can be attained only by opening the poet-self to some higher force, by ceasing to be oneself and beginning to speak vatically?
>
> The god can be invoked, but does not necessarily come. *Learn to speak without authority*, says Kierkegaard. By copying Kierkegaard's words here, I make Kierkegaard into an authority. Authority cannot be taught, cannot be learned. The paradox is a true one.[8]

JC here rails against the pronouncements of French theorists Roland Barthes and Michel Foucault about the death of the author (or the displacement of the writer as the primary agent of the writing).[9] Authority cannot simply be an effect of the text or a rhetorical trick, he thinks. There must be something more transcendental to it — at least, if the writer is to avoid being expelled from the philosopher's ideal republic. To the notion of the death of the author JC thus opposes the Romantic idea of the writer as a kind of prophet: literature as the opening of the author's poet-self to some higher force.

Insofar as JC can be read as a lyrical abbreviation of JMC, then we can see that for Coetzee to write without authority is to cede one's authority to some higher force and, in so doing, to cease being oneself. Eliding JC with JMC on this point might seem wrongheaded to those who identify Coetzee as an arch secularist and Postmodernist. But the fact is there has always been a transcendental aspect to Coetzee's postmodernism. Coetzee has never shied away in his narratives from using words like *truth*, *soul* and *grace*. To take just one of many possible examples, when President Garrard asks Elizabeth Costello in the novel of that name whether her vegetarianism arises out of moral conviction, she answers him in all earnestness, "'No, I don't think so. . . It comes out of a desire to save my soul.'"[10]

Something that Coetzee says to Attwell in *Doubling the Point* helps to explain these kinds of sincere appeals to the metaphysical. Here, Coetzee speaks of the writer as having not just a social duty but also a transcendental duty:

> To me, duty can be of two kinds: it can be an obligation imposed on the writer by society, by the soul of the society, by society in its hopes and dreams; or it can be something constitutional to the writer, what one might loosely call conscience but what I would tentatively prefer to call an imperative, a transcendental imperative.[11]

Coetzee here isolates the writer's poet-self from the rest of the community. The writer has a duty to his or her fellows, he thinks, but also a duty to his or her own conscience. It is at this level of conscience or purely personal scruple that the writer's duty stops being social and starts becoming transcendental and even quasi-religious.

JC's and Coetzee's appeals to the transcendental imperative of the writer help us to understand why Coetzee has utilized some of his public appearances over the past decade or so to stage the problem of literary authority in the most reflexive and ascetic ways. Most famously, on 15 October 1997, Coetzee stood up to give the first of his two Tanner Lectures on Human Values at Princeton University and instead began to read out his fictional narrative involving Elizabeth Costello, *The Lives of Animals*. The Tanner Lectures are a distinguished multi-university scholarly lecture series. As it states on the Princeton University website advertising them, "Appointment as a Tanner lecturer is recognition for uncommon achievement and outstanding abilities in the field of human values." The purpose of the lectures is "to advance and reflect upon the scholarly and scientific learning related to human values."[12] How must it have felt, then, to be in the audience that night, expecting to hear a scholarly lecture from one of the world's leading novelists and Professor of General Literature at the University of Cape Town, but instead receiving a reading from a piece of fiction?

Derek Attridge was there that night at Princeton and reflects on Coetzee's performance in his 2004 book *J. M. Coetzee and the Ethics of Reading*. As Attridge points out, there was no attempt to prepare the audience for Coetzee's literary stunt: Coetzee simply got up and starting reading "in his quiet, grave voice: 'He is waiting at the gate when her plane comes in.'"[13] A further disquieting feature of Coetzee's Princeton performance was that he preferred to answer the questions asked of him after his lecture/reading for his fictional character, that is, in the mode: "'I think what Elizabeth Costello would say is that. . . .'"[14] In some sense, Coetzee does give the members of his audience what they want in *The Lives of Animals*. Elizabeth Costello is (like Coetzee) a distinguished author of fiction who is invited to give lectures at an American university and decides to speak about the ways humans treat and mistreat non-human animals. Her topic is precisely human values as these are exposed by our treatment of other animals. But in another sense Coetzee must have frustrated a number of those who attended his two Tanner Lectures — "The Philosophers and the Animals" and "The Poets and the Animals" — because what he appears to do in these lectures is to shelter behind fiction. Why, some might have asked, did Coetzee choose to broach the topic of human values through the indirection of fiction? Why didn't he speak more directly, in his own voice, with the authority, that is, of an acclaimed novelist and academic?

The immediate problem with Coetzee reading out a piece of fiction rather than speaking in his own voice is that it makes it impossible for the audience to distinguish between the author's views and his character's views. The philosopher Peter Singer, one of the academics invited to respond to Coetzee's Princeton lectures, marks this problem at the end of his response in *The Lives of Animals* when he writes: "But *are* they Coetzee's arguments? That's just the point — that's why I don't know how to go about responding to this so-called lecture. They are *Costello's* arguments. Coetzee's fictional device enables him to distance himself from them."[15] Singer cannot see a point to Coetzee's reflexive fictioneering. For him, it only serves to excuse Coetzee from taking full responsibility for Costello's strong opinions about the human–animal relation. Singer casts his response in the form of a dialogue between himself and his daughter Naomi over breakfast. But he does so only in order to invoke the authority of Plato and to indict Coetzee for speaking fictionally. Here, then, more than two millennia after Plato's

Republic, we find the poet once again being excluded from the philosopher's ideal community.[16]

How might one defend Coetzee against this ancient charge of using fiction irresponsibly? One way is to say that in his Tanner Lectures (and subsequently in *The Lives of Animals* and *Elizabeth Costello*) Coetzee is trying to fulfill the two duties of the writer that he identifies in *Doubling the Point*. In this case, one might read Elizabeth Costello as a fictional embodiment of the social and the transcendental imperative of the writer. Costello fulfils the writer's public duty through Costello's trenchant lectures on the lives of animals. Here, as Singer notes, she develops arguments about humans and animals, literature and philosophy to which we can respond. But Costello is not merely a rhetorical cipher through which Coetzee expresses various strong opinions for which he is reluctant to take full responsibility. She also encapsulates the more privative and metaphysical aspect of writing — as when, borrowing from the Polish poet Czeslaw Milosz, she describes the writer as "secretary of the invisible."[17] Immediately after saying this to her panel of judges in the gently Kafkaesque penultimate chapter of *Elizabeth Costello*, Coetzee's heroine pauses: "This is where she expects them to interrupt. *Dictated to by whom?* she expects them to ask. And she has her answer ready: *By powers beyond us*. But there is no interruption, no question."[18] Here, then, in *Elizabeth Costello* we find a lyrical anticipation of JC's strong opinion in *Diary* about the transcendental nature of authority in fiction.

As I see it, Elizabeth Costello is an experiment in incarnation through which Coetzee expresses the Janus face of literary authority: the sense in which the writer is paradoxically turned outward towards his or her community, but also inward towards the higher authority of his or her own conscience. Singer fails to come to terms with Coetzee's Tanner Lectures because he fails to come to terms with the transcendental duty of the literary author to which they respond. According to this transcendental imperative, the writer gains authority — in a highly Kierkegaardian way — by losing it, by opening his or her poet-self to some higher authority in order to speak vatically, by becoming secretary of the invisible. Rather than seeing Coetzee as irresponsibly sheltering behind fiction in his Tanner Lectures, as if fiction were something merely negative or defensive, it is possible to see him instead as exposing himself and his audience to what we might call the "bare life" of literature — or literature degree zero.

Coetzee neatly defines this notion of the bare life of literature for us in those opening sentences of *Elizabeth Costello*, which I first pronounced as instances of slack or half-hearted narration — the very embodiment of postmodern velleity. As we have seen, these sentences place us awkwardly between the realm of the social and the realm of the transcendental. According to their narration, we have not yet left our own reality, nor are we yet in a fully fictional world. Rather, we find ourselves suspended between reality and fiction in a quasi-social, quasi-transcendental space. We are turned towards the prospective story, and yet are also somehow turning away from it. My claim here is that we never stop experiencing *Elizabeth Costello* in this Janus-faced way. For this quasi-social, quasi-transcendental space we have entered into is for Coetzee the very space — and bare life — of literature.

As David Attwell points out in a recent article:

> The overriding subject of *Elizabeth Costello* (2003), *Slow Man* (2005) and *Diary* (2007) is really the practice of authorship itself, a question always in the background of earlier work, but it has now become the fabric and substance. Beyond Roland Barthes' death of the author, the ontology of the writer as agent of the writing has begun to return, though in some reconstructed and still rather opaque sense.[19]

The ontology of the writer as agent of the writing returns once again in Coetzee's latest novel *Summertime: Scenes from Provincial Life* (2009) — though in a ghostly sort of way. The central conceit of Coetzee's third fictional memoir (after *Boyhood* and *Youth*) is that the author is literally dead. An English academic, Mr. Vincent, is writing a biography of the deceased author John Coetzee and interviewing some of those who knew Coetzee between the years 1972 and 1975, when he lived in Cape Town and was working on his second novel, *In the Heart of the Country*. Like Coetzee's other two fictionalized memoirs, *Summertime* makes the point in sometimes brutal terms that literary authority does not reside in the life or the being of the writer. One of the interviewees, Sophie Denoël, comments on Coetzee towards the end of the novel: "As a writer he knew what he was doing, he had a certain style, and style is the beginning of distinction. But he had no special sensitivity that I could detect, no original insight into the human condition. He was just a man, a man of his time, talented, maybe even gifted, but, frankly, not a giant."[20]

One of ways in which Coetzee eschews authority in his fiction is to pillory his characters, including himself as a character. As Bill Ashcroft notes in his contribution to this volume: "There is no writer I know who is harder on his characters [than Coetzee], particularly those characters whom we might associate with the author — Jacobus Coetzee in *Dusklands*, David Lurie in *Disgrace*, the central characters of *Boyhood, Youth* and *Summertime*, the testy narrator in *Diary of a Bad Year*, or even Elizabeth Costello, both tired and tiresome in those moments when she is most clearly ventriloquising Coetzee's beliefs." *Summertime* certainly works to divest Coetzee of his aura as a Nobel Prize-winning author by presenting him as "just a man." But it also works in the opposite way to establish literary authority as having an irreducibly transcendental or metaphysical aspect. At another point in the interview between Sophie and Mr. Vincent, she asks him if he has authorization to write his biography and he replies: "Does one need authorization to write a book? From whom would one seek it? I certainly don't know."[21] There are odd moments in Coetzee's fiction, characterized by a kind of philosophical lyricism, in which one feels oneself to be directly addressed by the author, who through his characters poses the philosophical questions that are driving the narrative. This is just one of these moments. Here we feel Mr. Vincent suddenly becoming secretary of the invisible as he turns literature into a question for us that we cannot answer by appealing either to Coetzee's text or to Coetzee's person. On the latest evidence of *Summertime*, the death of the author in Coetzee points in two directions at once:

not just to the author becoming an ordinary (or even less-than-ordinary) man but also to the author opening his poet-self to some higher force in order to begin to speak vatically.

Coetzee says to Attwell in *Doubling the Point* that "all autobiography is storytelling, all writing is autobiography."[22] Later in the same interview he uses the portmanteau term "*autre*biography"[23] — which we might translate as biography of the other, biography of the self as another — to describe his process of relating his life in the third person. How does one write without authority? In a sense, it is by writing *autre*biography, by othering oneself through one's writing, by speaking in the third rather than in the first person. Kierkegaard achieved this goal of othering himself in his writing by adopting pseudonyms that evoked the themes of his books: Johannes de Silentio is the pseudonym that writes *Fear and Trembling*, a book about Abraham's silence in Genesis 22; Constantin Constantius is the pseudonym that writes *Repetition*, a book about the impossibility of repeating one's experience of something. Coetzee's pseudonyms are more tightly focused than Kierkegaard's on the ontology of the author and of literary authority. Elizabeth Curren, Elizabeth Costello and JC are all writers who turn literature into a question by presenting writing as a Janus-faced vocation: at once social and personal-transcendental.

Strong Opinions: J. M. Coetzee and the Authority of Contemporary Fiction examines how Coetzee's novels create and unsettle literary authority by performing, in sometimes painfully direct ways, literature's construction of authority out of nothing. As we've seen, Coetzee shows authority to be most acutely a problem in that semi-metamorphic moment before the literary narrative properly begins. At the beginning of *Elizabeth Costello* we find ourselves in the "waiting room" of narrative, that is, in a quasi-social and quasi-transcendental place in which we expect a story but are not yet given one. The questions we might ask at this moment of the text in order to orient ourselves are the same questions that the contributors to this volume ask of Coetzee's fiction more generally: How should we relate to place? How should we understand literary form? What limits are being called into question by this strangely self-conscious act of storytelling?

The collection is divided into three sections that correspond to these three modes of question I have identified: "Place", "Form" and "Limits." The first section — Place — engages with the problem of how Coetzee's decision to immigrate to Australia in 2002 and become an Australian citizen in 2003 has affected his fiction. Australia has figured prominently in Coetzee's recent work. Even before he took up residence in Adelaide, South Australia, Coetzee presents Elizabeth Costello as an Australian writer in *The Lives of Animals* (1999). *Slow Man* and *Diary of a Bad Year* are both set in Australia — Adelaide and Sydney, respectively. The first three essays of the volume debate whether Coetzee presents his newly adopted country more realistically or more schematically. Despite taking up significantly different positions on this question, these essays all find in Coetzee's fiction (whether the earlier South African or the later Australian) what Elleke Boehmer calls in Chapter 1 "a philosophical meditation on the real." While Boehmer sees Coetzee as engaging with Australia realistically, she also makes the important qualification that Coetzee's Australia is, like his South Africa, a country of the mind. For Melinda Harvey, the relative thinness of Coetzee's representation of Australia shows him to be following the examples of his two Russian idols, Tolstoy and Dostoevsky, by whittling the real into ever-more pedagogic and vatic shapes. For Maria López, Coetzee develops in his novels an ethic of the non-proprietorial consciousness, according to which his characters of European descent eschew the traditional role of owners or settlers in order to perceive themselves instead as temporary visitors or guests.

Coetzee's characters — like Kafka's characters — also eschew authority by displacing it onto some other person or thing. In *Diary of a Bad Year*, JC's strong opinions become gentler as a result of his erotic encounter with his young amanuensis, Anya. Opinions are precisely what put us in relation to others and to other things. And the essays in the second section of the volume — Form — are all concerned with how the deconstruction of authority in Coetzee takes place via the inter-subjective and the intertextual. At issue here is the effectiveness and coherence of Coetzee's project of literary mirroring. For Paul Patton, Coetzee's formal innovation in *Diary*, which is to separate his text into three typographically distinct bands, works to humanize JC's bookish opinions by allowing them to be diffused by the contextualizing narrative. For Julian Murphet, the form of *Diary* remains too friable to forge its own aesthetic truth and, rather than transcending the realm of opinion, as the form of the novel should, *Diary* banally eroticizes this realm. In his reading of *Foe*, Anthony Uhlmann defends Coetzee's project of literary mirroring by showing how intertextuality is a productive form of symbolic doubling that enables the secondary text (*Foe*) to expose the formal workings of the absent original text (*Robinson Crusoe*) in a manner akin to negative theology.

Literature may be thought to lack authority because it follows — and is secondary to — reality. As Blanchot puts the paradox in "Literature and the Right to Death": "How can I recover it, how can I turn around and look at what exists *before*, if all my power consists of making it into what exists *after*? The language of literature is a search for this moment which precedes literature. Literature usually calls it existence."[24] How does literature overcome the problem of its own belatedness? One way is to emphasize potentiality, to fix upon those moments in our experience in which what happened might also have happened otherwise. Coetzee's literature constantly burrows into the interstices of history or reality or existence in order to expose and interrupt the colonizing work these notions perform if taken to be a priori determiners of human identity. "I am someone who has intimations of freedom (as every chained prisoner has)," says Coetzee to Attwell in *Doubling the Point*, "and constructs representations — which are shadows themselves — of people slipping their chains and turning their faces to the light."[25] The essays in the third section of the volume — Limits — all show how Coetzee uses the paradoxical potentiality of the figure of the "chained prisoner" to rethink notions such as history, humanity and reality. As Mike Marais demonstrates in his reading of *Slow Man*, the author Elizabeth Costello follows her character Paul Rayment, whose autonomy from her is precisely his unrealized potential as a character. In another reading of this text and of *Diary of a Bad Year*, Sue Kossew shows how Coetzee uses his exilic identity in Australia to undo the false triumphalism of national belonging. Amplifying the biographical moment of Coetzee's near-death by drowning in *Boyhood*, Chris Danta sees Coetzee's fiction as circumscribing a melancholy space between the thought of (his) imminent death and death itself. In a reading of *Foe*, Bill Ashcroft identifies silence — in particular, Friday's silence — as a site of utopian possibility through which Coetzee resists the empire of the author's voice.

In his recent essay, "Creation and Salvation," the Italian philosopher Giorgio Agamben writes, "redemption is nothing other than a potentiality to create that remains pending, that turns on itself and 'saves' itself."[26] In Coetzee's recent fiction we see him paying greater attention to this idea of a potentiality to create that remains pending. In this sense, we might read Coetzee's postmodern reflexivity as expressing not arch-secularism but rather a desire for redemption, a desire to secrete in the book a moment of ineliminable or unrealizable — and therefore redemptive — potential.

One might explain Coetzee's fascination with the beginning of the text by pointing out that it is the moment of greatest potential.

Since I have made so much of Coetzee's beginnings, it is perhaps fitting that I conclude this introduction by examining the momentous opening scene of *Slow Man* in which Paul Rayment is suddenly knocked off his bicycle by Wayne Blight's car in a near-fatal accident.

> The blow catches him from the right, sharp and surprising and painful, like a bolt of electricity, lifting him up off the bicycle. *Relax!* he tells himself as he flies through the air (*flies through the air with the greatest of ease!*), and indeed he can feel his limbs go obediently slack. *Like a cat* he tells himself: *roll, then spring to your feet, ready for what comes next*. The unusual word *limber* or *limbre* is on the horizon too.[27]

Like the reader in the opening sentences of *Elizabeth Costello* (for whom the unusual word *velleity* is on the horizon), Paul Rayment is here caught somewhere between the real world and the far shore of fiction. Rayment's accident, in other words, is that semi-metamorphic moment that takes place before the narrative properly begins and in which desire and reality comingle. As Elleke Boehmer shows in her analysis of this opening scene, having exposed his character to the "sharp and surprising and painful" blow of the real, Coetzee just as quickly shows the pure event lapsing into language. As he flies through the air with the greatest of ease, Rayment is well on his way to becoming a character in a story. But what makes this opening so forceful is that, in a certain sense, he is not yet one. For a split second, or the blink of an eye, he is redeemed by the fact that he is like us as we read: pinioned between reality and its metamorphic shadow, which is language or literature.

NOTES

1 J. M. Coetzee, *Elizabeth Costello: Eight Lessons* (Sydney: Vintage, 2003), 1.
2 Coetzee, *Elizabeth Costello*, 1.
3 *Oxford English Dictionary*, 2nd ed., s.v. "velleity," def. 1.
4 J. M. Coetzee, *Diary of a Bad Year* (Melbourne: Text, 2007), 122.
5 Maurice Blanchot, *The Work of Fire*, trans. Charlotte Mandell (Stanford, California: Stanford University Press, 1995), 300.
6 J. M. Coetzee, *Doubling the Point: Essays and Interviews*, ed. David Attwell (Cambridge, Massachusetts, and London: Harvard University Press, 1992), 392.
7 Søren Kierkegaard, *Crisis in the Life of an Actress*, cited in Theodor W. Adorno, *Kierkegaard: Construction of the Aesthetic*, trans. and ed. Robert Hullot-Kentor (Minneapolis: University of Minnesota Press, 1989), 5.
8 Coetzee, *Diary of a Bad Year*, 123–4, original emphasis.
9 As David Attwell notes in "Mastering Authority: J. M. Coetzee's *Diary of a Bad Year*": "This rejection of the Barthesian credo is an abjuration on Coetzee's part, because he has often implicitly positioned himself in the tradition it represents, the tradition of anti-illusionism which culminates for Coetzee in Samuel Beckett." (*Social Dynamics* 36:1 [2010]: 220).
10 Coetzee, *Elizabeth Costello*, 89.
11 Coetzee, *Doubling the Point*, 340.
12 "About this Series," http://lectures.princeton.edu/?cat=13 (accessed 10 December 2010).
13 Derek Attridge, *J. M. Coetzee and the Ethics of Reading: Literature in the Event* (Chicago and London: University of Chicago Press, 2004), 192.
14 Attridge, *J. M. Coetzee and the Ethics of Reading*, 193.
15 J. M. Coetzee et al., *The Lives of Animals* (Princeton, New Jersey: Princeton University Press, 1999), 91, original emphasis.
16 For a discussion of how Coetzee's *The Lives of Animals* invokes the ancient quarrel between philosophy and literature see Stephen Mulhall, *The Wounded Animal: J. M. Coetzee & the Difficulty of Reality in Literature & Philosophy* (Princeton and Oxford: Princeton University Press, 2009), 1–18.
17 Coetzee, *Elizabeth Costello*, 199.
18 Coetzee, *Elizabeth Costello*, 199–200, original emphasis.
19 Attwell, "Mastering Authority: J. M. Coetzee's *Diary of a Bad Year*," 217.
20 J. M. Coetzee, *Summertime: Scenes from Provincial Life* (North Sydney: Knopf, 2009), 242.
21 Coetzee, *Summertime*, 225.
22 Coetzee, *Doubling the Point*, 391.
23 Coetzee, *Doubling the Point*, 394.
24 Blanchot, *The Work of Fire*, 327, original emphasis.
25 Coetzee, *Doubling the Point*, 341.
26 Giorgio Agamben, "Creation and Salvation," in *Nudities*, trans. David Kishik and Stefan Pedatella (Stanford, California: Stanford University Press, 2011), 7.
27 J. M. Coetzee, *Slow Man* (London: Viking, 2005), 1, original emphasis.

PART ONE

PLACE

CHAPTER 1

J. M. Coetzee's Australian Realism

Elleke Boehmer

AUSTRALIAS OF THE MIND

The heading to this first section of the essay is taken from Seamus Heaney's 1976 "Englands of the Mind," in which he discusses the different approaches of his then contemporaries Hughes, Hill and Larkin to the matter of England-approaches forced, Heaney writes, by their concern additionally to ask what the matter is with England.[1] For Heaney, in that essay a writer's country of the mind refers to the relationship in their work between their language, that is, their articulate noise, and their sense of their deep history as poets. It refers to a conjunction of voice and worldview, which is to say, the foundation of the writer's vision in tradition and myth, combined with the territorial, regional or national memories and emotional attachments important to them. In Heaney's pen-portrait of Ted Hughes's "England of the mind," a mix of Northern dialect, oral tradition, pagan myth, and rocky, mineral landscape is traced, whereas, by contrast, Geoffrey Hill's world is medieval and dynastic, Latinate though determinedly also of the matter of England.

My discussion of South African-born J. M. Coetzee's Australian-phase oeuvre begins by adapting Heaney's formulation of the English poets' combined voice and worldview to inaugurate a critical treatment of Coetzee's representation of his new land Australia, that is, of his Australia as an imaginative prospect, a complex of tradition, myth, and territorial and national memory. The analysis will be sharpened by reading this work alongside the influential representation of the matter of Australia by two of Coetzee's prominent Australian contemporaries, Peter Carey and Tim Winton – their post-2000 work in particular, which coincides with Coetzee's Australian phase. The comparative investigation of Coetzee's formal approaches to Australia will, it is hoped, encourage a broad, even stereoscopic, investigation of how in Coetzee the choices of and allusions to certain genres and forms have produced, or have made an attempt at producing, even if in a jobbing or perfunctory way, a recognizably Australian world. Tim Winton's work (in particular here his 2004 novel *Dirt Music* and in 2008's *Breath*) might be characterized in terms drawn from Heaney as matching a vigorous, colloquial, masculine, yet plangent language to the lone male figures who dominate his plots, and the bleak and deserted Western Australian seascapes and landscapes in which they find themselves and attempt to make a life. Peter Carey's voice, as in his post-2000 novels *My Life as a Fake* (2003) and *Theft* (2006), is more knowing, aphoristic, self-referential and transnational than Winton's, and though his social vision is as pessimistic it is without Winton's hope for transcendence through immersion in the natural world. In the case of both writers, the relationship of land and voice, of (Australian) context and language, is definitive: it is taken by both to be as central to Australian writing as to the English writing that interests Heaney (as Carey forcefully demonstrates with his ventriloquism of folk hero Ned Kelly's voice in his 2000 *True History of the Kelly Gang*). Indeed, observes Heaney, the defensive love of territory, the awareness of Englishness, which now defines English poetry, was once a quality possessed "only by those poets whom we might call colonial."[2] His formulation can be refracted to venture the proposition that an awareness of being Australian, of both writing Australia and writing as an Australian, in Australian vernacular, is a quality possessed if not indeed strenuously taken hold of by writers like Winton and Carey who, despite the transnational dimensions to their careers, both consciously self-define as Australian.

Seen from this point of view, the decision to adopt the identity of Australian writer, first through his alter ego Elizabeth Costello, before he physically settled in Australia, and then in his own person, was a testing challenge for the writer J. M. Coetzee. For, after all, Coetzee is a writer who — to transliterate from Heaney commenting on Larkin, the third poet in his essay — has tended across the greater part of his career, from *In the Heart of the Country* (1976) onwards, to write at a distance from region, local context and vernacular. He adopts a "scrupulous meanness"; his work definitively takes as read a gap between the writer and their subject. "Alienation," he writes, is required for the activity of "appreciation."[3] The "secretary of the invisible," he suggests in *Elizabeth Costello*, by definition writes from a distance.[4] Coetzee's is a famously stripped-down, standardized yet globalized English voice — one that assumes a broadly secular, humanist position. In becoming an Australia-located writer, the demand to write Australia as an Australian, to "make up" Australia, as Elizabeth Costello says, may have seemed to Coetzee a tall imaginative order, equivalent to the assertion of a particularly "strong opinion" with respect to national allegiance.[5]

Yet, this essay submits, Coetzee has perceptibly grasped this challenge, though, as is to be expected of his work, he has done so in subtle, incremental, often less-than-obvious (even partially unconvinced) ways, though arguably with a greater directness of reference than he has shown with respect to the imagining of South Africa. If in novels like *Life and Times of Michael K* (1983) or *Age of Iron* (1990) — as in *White Writing* (1988) — Coetzee was concerned with the "imaginative schemas" through which the arid South African hinterland could be represented, his Australia, I suggest, is similarly conceived as a land of the mind, a space relayed through intellectual schemas. Paradoxically, however, the *reality* of this new country is in relative terms the more strongly registered and perceived than the imaginary construct of South Africa in Coetzee's oeuvre generally has been. Yet this is a paradox that reduces in magnitude if it is remembered that Coetzee has always been preoccupied with the codes through which realism is at once established and undermined: in fiction after fiction, whether set in South Africa or Australia or Petersburg, he involves his reader in scrutinizing the operation of these codes of, as Elizabeth Costello has it, "embodying" afresh.[6] The difference is that in Australia, a country that he has acquired by conscious adoption rather than through the accidents of birth, he has been more noticeably concerned not only to establish the country fictionally as a space, but also to *realize* or embody it as an actual, recognizable location.

"Here no elsewhere underwrites my existence," Larkin said about living in England, comparing this with his brief experience of living in Belfast, as an outsider.[7] For Coetzee, one of the more important elements of his relationship to Australia, his interest in embracing Australia intellectually, is how that relationship is brought into the consciousness of his novels — from *Elizabeth Costello* onwards — in notational, realist-seeming ways, though also with a certain sense of correctness and obligation, what might be called the politeness of the naturalized citizen. Up until its fictionalized yet realistically conceived Dulgannon frogs episode, Australia insinuates itself into *Elizabeth Costello*, for example, either in the form of journalistic outline or sketchy reportage, or as a metonymic visual shorthand, where single precisely conceived images or scenes are made to designate a wider social world. "So real," opines Elizabeth Costello metatextually of Marijana's domestic interior in *Slow Man*, which is described via the shorthand referents of white leather furniture, lurid abstract painting and ceiling fan.[8] What this sharply defined, "real-life" interest in Australia signifies, it would seem, is that in writing Australia Coetzee has kicked away some of the more abstract metafictional schemas that in South Africa underwrote his visual imagination, and has resorted to a referential vocabulary that at least superficially has a more immediate or less mediated relationship to the world that is being described.

There are two interlocking forces at work in this matrix of representation. First, Coetzee appears to be broadly concerned that the South African "elsewhere" not simply be adapted to provide imaginative scaffolding for his Australian existence. This interest is bound up with his concern openly to take on Australian citizenship, publicly to profess Australianness, to seek a single-minded, full-hearted commitment. But he is also concerned — and this is something that the greater part of this essay will explore — with how the reality or context of Australia might be evoked in his work; he is even, to take this a stage further, concerned with the quality of the real in Australia and hence also with how it is experienced and evoked. This interest in grappling with the real in Australia, and with the reality of Australia, relates to other interests that have grown in prominence in his more recent, Australian-phase work — the interest in living from the heart, and in the full-blooded body, and not only through the simulacra of the literary, to cite from Elizabeth Costello's eighth lesson.[9] In relation to this, it is worth noticing that the preoccupation with understanding "real-life" through the medium of the body is something that is important to Australian writing also, as is palpable for example, in the harsh Western Australian realism of Tim Winton in which the human is repeatedly reduced to pre-verbal, "forked creature" states of being.

The concern to grapple with the real is arguably central in South African white writing, too, but there, at least in Coetzee's account, reality perhaps is less accessible, more resistant to representation. More so than his Australia, Coetzee's South Africa is overwritten by rival dream topographies and imported, inauthentic languages. It is, in his view, striated by race, by the historical struggle of white writing with black presence, more intensively than his Australia appears to be, his reference to the Tasmanians in *Elizabeth Costello* notwithstanding. As Coetzee writes in *White Writing*: "The [South African] poet scans the landscape with his hermeneutic gaze, but it remains trackless, refuses to emerge into meaningfulness as a landscape of signs."[10]

In short, Coetzee in Australia, when compared to his writing in and of South Africa, is interested not just in the operations of embodied realism, as that is a perennial concern, but is interested also in the quality of reality, even in the quality of the real, and hence of its boundaries and breaking points, as these pertain in Australia, as well as more universally. As a symptom of this preoccupation, *Diary of a Bad Year*, especially the more candid second section, is virtually overwritten with words signifying the real or the true: "really," "truth," "truly," "authority effect," as well as of course "love," the "truth" of "the heart," the "thing itself," "love itself."[11] In the passage towards the end of *Diary* where JC considers whether Tolstoy's characters *really* feel and inspire fellow feeling, he repeatedly returns to the "indisputable certainty"[12] or authority invoked by a realist writer like Tolstoy.

As if to drive the preoccupation home, Coetzee's interest in the real, and the representation of the real in Australia, is not so much conveyed as reinforced, from *Slow Man* on, through what might be termed appropriate, bespoke media; the relative realism of the first part of *Slow Man*, at least up until its self-reflexive chiasmus; the essayistic and diaristic, as if "real," commentaries of *Diary of a Bad Year*. When I say this I am aware of course, to cite Derek Attridge once again, that "for all his experimentation" Coetzee "has always drawn on the stubborn power of realism, on the vivid representation of a world, external and internal, into which the reader is invited."[13] It is an observation that relates directly to *Slow Man* where, in spite of the questions about novelistic convention that are raised through the introduction of Elizabeth Costello as writer-character, the novel is nonetheless unequivocal in finding that the power of communicating the impact of the real is of primary importance to fiction. What then makes up this real to Coetzee? What form does it take? Drawing on Lacan, Slavoj Žižek in *Welcome to the Desert of the Real* and *Violence* provocatively suggests that the desert of the real is that which exceeds the reality effects of language even though language is ceaselessly preoccupied with it. The real for Žižek, and by extension also for Coetzee, is that which cannot be produced by, or contained within, verbal artifice, yet, paradoxically, can only be approached through it.

Coetzee's writing the Australian real (or, at least, the reality of Australia, however obliquely so) is, this essay further submits, an interestingly engaged act, perhaps even an Australian act, for so nationally disaffected a writer. How the nation is embodied and secured through myth and metaphor has of course been a widespread issue in post-colonial or new national literatures, as also in post-colonial criticism, across several decades. But, whereas Coetzee as a South African writer assumed a circumspect critical position in relation to that process of imaginative embodiment, in Australia his stance is seemingly less objectifying, less concerned to negate what lies before him. Although his coolly rational narrative personae do not go so far as to seek that close intercalation of land and language that Heaney finds in Hughes, or that Tim Winton's *Breath*, for example, yearns towards, Coetzee himself appears to be aware that in literature Australian reality conventionally finds expression in, or comes into being through, certain figures, in the form of a certain national imaginary, and he visibly adopts a less-than-distant position in relation to these. Paul Rayment says of himself:

> I can pass among Australians. I cannot pass among the French. That, as far as I am concerned, is all there is to it, to the national-identity business: where one passes and where one does not.[14]

In Australia, I submit, Coetzee wishes for his imagination, or for his constructions of Australian reality, to pass as something resembling the real thing.

Several ironies straightaway encroach upon these observations. An obvious one is that, as Australian literary history shows, Australian white writing has long been as preoccupied with the elusiveness of the Australian real, as South African white writing has been with its alienation from southern African land. It has been as concerned with the impenetrability of the landscape to European names; with the unavailability of reciprocity between poet and space; with the violence of founding societies and identities upon the alien land. Marcus Clarke writing about the poetry of his nineteenth-century compatriot Adam Lindsay Gordon famously regretted the lack of a perceptual framework, a "language of the barren and the uncouth," through which to interpret "the hieroglyphs of haggard gum trees, blown into odd shapes."[15] From this anxiety over inadequate signification and flawed simulacra, as is well known, emerges Australia's fascination with hoaxes and the ersatz. The "peculiar susceptibility of the Australian literary establishment to fraudulence and fakery," stands to reason when the hunger is for an unobtainable authenticity, in relation to which confections and imitations, "beautiful lies," produce a temporary prophylaxis or passing relief.[16] The propensity to produce fakes, opines hoaxer Christopher Chubb in Peter Carey's *My Life as a Fake*, is forced by "the terror of being out of date,"[17] the tyranny of distance from the place where authenticity resides. In his later *Theft*, talented provincials self-consciously act out the lifestyles of famous cosmopolitans. The pivot that both novels turn on is this paradox: the faker understands nothing so closely, and hates nothing so much, as a lie. Coetzee's photograph collector Paul Rayment, too, suggestively hates all fakes and despises prostheses.[18] Another, related, irony is that, as my earlier quotation anticipated, Coetzee has himself in *White Writing* powerfully theorized the condition of colonial anomie, what he describes there as the colonial's uneasy and never entirely successful imaginative appropriation of the resistant so-called settled land. At any number of points in *White Writing*, and almost continuously in its introduction, it could be the nineteenth-century poet in Australia, too, that he is addressing. The intellectual schemas of dystopic South Africa apply equally to Australia's similarly wide, brown land, as can be illustrated with the following adapted quotation from *White Writing*, in which references to "South Africa" have been replaced with the word "Australia": "In the words he throws out to the landscape, in the echoes he listens for, he is seeking a dialogue with [Australia], a reciprocity with [Australia], that will allow him an identity better than that of visitor, stranger, transient."[19] Elsewhere he describes the "self-defeating process of naming [Australia] by defining it as non-Europe–self-defeating because in each particular in which [Australia] is identified to be non-European, it remains Europe, not [Australia], that is named."[20] As in South Africa, so in Australia, the white writer is enclosed within the hermeneutic circle imposed by the foreign, imported tropes through which he attempts to think his new and allegedly "empty" land.

That South Africa and Australia were, for all their differences, white settler colonies within the British Empire, goes some way towards explaining these strong parallels. So, too, does the fact that in imaginative terms they formed part of the dystopian colonial south, as it was constructed in triangulated contrast with the enlightened north on the one hand, and the brave new world of America on the other.[21] This dystopic southernness, too, Coetzee explores and analyses in *White Writing*; and its intriguing intellectual resistances and challenges to the imagination are aspects that may have informed and subtended his interest in immigrating to Australia in the first place. Commenting on contemporary Australia's pitiless treatment of asylum-seekers, JC in *Diary of a Bad Year* explicitly observes of the country's unpromising mythographic condition: "Australia was never a promised land, a new world, an island paradise offering its bounty to the new arrival . . . Life in the Antipodes was meant to be a punishment."[22]

The point these intersecting ironies are making is that the enigma of Coetzee's arrival in Australia, this "land of whiteness,"[23] as a white writer, as a writer, he had to a significant degree scripted in advance. He had in broad strokes, as if by design, mapped its imaginative topography, its hermeneutic non-visibility, beforehand. The déjà vu of the process, the inevitable always-already, must have been palpable to him, almost too obvious, possibly even laughable, full of the repeats and predictable prat-falls of situation comedy, even before his move. Or as Elizabeth Costello's sister Blanche tells her when referring to false humanist ideals introduced to Africa: "It is not just in Zululand that it happened. It happened in

Australia too. It happened all over the colonized world, just not in so neat a form."[24] With its imaginative topoi prescribed in advance, Australia, to a Coetzee interested in the limitations of representing the real, entailed in some ways as difficult a case as did Zululand. The ennui of the always-already, of that which cannot be said because too many attempts have already been made to say it, gives an interesting gloss to the language through which Coetzee refers to Australia in the line-up of his writing from *Elizabeth Costello* through to *Diary of a Bad Year*.

In those places where Australia is designated in *Elizabeth Costello*, a functional, even minimalist, referential language is deployed — not so much stripped-down, as Coetzee's language in *Disgrace* and elsewhere has been described, as less-than-literary, ennuyé, perfunctory. It is a language that is, as it were, impatient with the task of description yet concerned with it even so, out of a sense of writerly duty to context. So Elizabeth Costello refers, in passing, merely to the "Irish-Catholic Melbourne of her childhood," assuming that this code is sufficient to invoke an entire context.[25] Though Elizabeth resists Australia's being described as the "far edge,"[26] it is in the novel still something of a place apart, not only from the rest of the world, as it is often described, but also from the international cross-border realm of the novel, of Elizabeth Costello's transnational peregrinations. Interestingly, none of the lessons is set in Australia. She has led, Elizabeth reflects, "an antipodean life, removed from the worst of history," "quiet" and "protected."[27] "History happened elsewhere," Kate Grenville makes a related though also feminist point, in *Joan Makes History* (1988).[28]

In *Slow Man*, the language of minimalist denotation in respect of Australia persists, and is spun out in the form of the thin strand of scene-setting that runs through the novel. The vocabulary designating South Australia is dominated by street names, basic topographical features and the urban commonplaces of Adelaide: "He will never stride up Black Hill again, never pedal off to the market to do his shopping, much less come swooping on his bicycle down the curves of Montacute." "Years ago he used to cycle through Munno Para on the way to Gawler. Then it was just a few houses dotted around a filling station, with bare scrub behind."[29] Magill Road, repeatedly cited, is built up not only as a metonym for Paul's accident, but also, following on, as a sign of the real, the intrusion of the inconceivable real into the world of the everyday.[30]

The language of sere reportage insinuates itself also into the quasi-academic prose of the essays that make up *Diary of a Bad Year*; in particular into the uppermost strand of the first part, "Strong Opinions," JC's jaded pronouncements on public life. Here Australia, specifically Sydney, post-2001, post–Iraq War, is a land of compromised liberal idealism, reduced moral decency, and withering national pride; incorporated into the global economy, yet also marginal to it, increasingly given to exhibiting "the bullying, authoritarian, militaristic strain" to which "western political life" has become susceptible.[31] Australia is thus in several ways a perfect backdrop and foil for protagonist JC's exposition of his "pessimistic anarchistic quietism" as against the "hurly-burly of politics."[32] Impelled by his interest in speaking a greater truth about public affairs to "ordinary people" than that supplied by politicians, JC's essays or *ansichten* for the book *Strong Opinions* have shifted him from being a novelist given to dispensing lessons, to being "a pedant who dabbles in fiction."[33] Even so, throughout the novel it is the evocation of the real in the manner especially of Tolstoy — how it is done, why it is important, how it is trammeled, what its absolute conditions are — that motivates the narrative, as the real of the emotions also does Anya's story.[34]

REALITY EFFECTS

Yet Coetzee is not merely concerned with incorporating contemporary Australia, or the real in Australia, into his writing by referencing it, by marking its presence or here-ness in denotative terms. He is also, as this section will further enlarge, concerned to induce even more powerful reality effects than those supplied as part of his vocabulary, by seeming to engage with some of Australia's foundational stories — and by doing so in informed, pre-emptive ways, as well as with his habitual cool correctness. In other words, even before he fully arrived in Australia, and then ever more intensively following his arrival, Coetzee participated as if presciently in its ongoing commonplaces or defining intellectual schemas; he contributed after his own fashion to the composition of an Australia of the mind.

To illustrate, the following paragraphs outline four of the foundational stories to which Coetzee has arguably responded, two of which are closely interlinked, all of which would merit further expansion in a longer version of this discussion. There may of course be others. Analyzed in any number of cultural historical studies, severally or together, these stories Coetzee has adopted concern the maimed white hero; the fake or forgery; the made-up monster figure who becomes a type of doppelganger; and the tale of new immigration.[35] They are surveyed in that order.

Dead white males

Australian literature is famously well populated with flawed, maimed and dying white heroes, double-sided figures who gesture back at colonial nostalgia for Europe, yet also signify a desire to regenerate as Australian through their suffering and dying.[36] (The dead white male tale is of course closely bound up with the denial of, or unwillingness to represent, the black or Aboriginal presence.) Paul Rayment of *Slow Man* makes up one of this category of maimed heroes-manqué. He is a not-quite-dead, old, white male bearing various characteristic features: a sense of homelessness and hollowness; an interest in the elusiveness of truth; a tendency to procrastinate; an acceptance of Australia as a place of residence that is comfortable but not a true home. Although *Slow Man*-Paul resists getting a move on, to his creator Elizabeth Costello's frustration, he recalls both the eponymous delusional explorer-figure Voss of Patrick White's 1957 myth-infused novel (who incidentally is name-checked in Coetzee's *Dusklands*), as well as the damaged, disillusioned sub-heroes of Tim Winton's work, such as Luther Fox of *Dirt Music*. Not least among the features he shares with these others is his wound — his severed leg with its "angry colour and swollen look." There is also his overweening pride, and his sense of living a borrowed life, which he holds in common in particular with Fox, that is, of living through other people and other people's children.[37] Yet, as any reader of Coetzee will know, Paul Rayment also of course shows certain resemblances with other of Coetzee's childless male characters — the magistrate of *Waiting for the Barbarians*, Michael K, even perhaps Friday in *Foe*.

Fraudulence, real fakes, monster figures

As is clear from both Peter Carey's *My Life as a Fake* and his *Theft*, Australian culture's preoccupation with copies of the real is one side of the same coin as its fascination for copies becoming real, and for creations coming back to dog their creators with often fatal effects.[38]

As also in his *True History of the Kelly Gang*, Carey has made a career of remaking his country's definitive stories, so the prevalence of the fraud, the copy and the doppelganger monster in his later work is perhaps predictable. Yet it is also, for all that, an interesting sign of his continuing interest in writing under the banner of Australia, despite his move over two decades ago to New York. In *My Life as a Fake* the so-called fake, the Ern Malley equivalent, Bob McCorkle, turns out to be a real person, another human. The novel turns on the conceit that the hoax in fact coincides with the life and work of a real man and poet who then proceeds to haunt and overwhelm the life of his creator, Christopher Chubb, in true *Frankenstein*-ian fashion. So McCorkle not only steals his child from him and brings her up as his own, but also succeeds in writing more innovative and accomplished poetry than Chubb's, though, gallingly to Chubb, in the manner of the mocking modernist pastiche he first initiated. *Theft* represents a further development of this to-Carey-fascinating theme of true frauds and fraudulent truths. The tale of Butcher Bones and his recreation of a lost Jacques Liebowitz, which is eventually passed off as an original, is narrated by the twin voices of Butcher and his so-called "damaged" brother Hugh, another monstrous figure. Hugh, who is in many ways as involved in the making of the artist's art, and his life, as the artist is, functions in the novel as an imperfect copy of his brother, though he bears a clear eye for the grey area that separates the true from the fake.

To introduce Coetzee to the theme, he too, of course, has always had an interest in what differentiates the real thing from the copy; therefore, what is particularly interesting about *Slow Man*, his first fully Australian novel, is that he feels obliged overtly to assert his interest in "fictional truths and truthful fictions."[39] In a novel preoccupied with how Paul Rayment's life becomes Elizabeth Costello's creation, and she, as his creator, his doppelganger, he if anything overdetermines our reading by stamping the novel with the sign of the fake, with the sign of Australian literary construction, in the near-homonymic Fauchery forgery incident. When Paul Rayment allows Drako Jokić to make free with his photograph collection, Drako abuses his hospitality, though largely benignly, by making amusing photoshopped copies of Paul's precious prints and replacing the real thing with the fakes. Intriguingly, as the fakes replace the faces of the people in the photos with the faces of his family members, the fakes come to bear the features of immediate contemporary reality.

The tale of new immigration

Post–World War II immigration to Australia (as against nineteenth-century immigration), that development of which the Jokić family's move from Croatia via Germany to South Australia forms a small part, has for decades involved the country ever more deeply in networks of transnational connection and cross-ocean contact.[40] From Brian Castro's *Birds of Passage* (1983), through to Yasmine Gooneratne's *A Change of Skies* (1994), to Christos Tsiolkas's *Dead Europe* (2005), novels by Australian writers of immigrant background have repeatedly dealt in and critically reflected upon such connections. As far back as *Illywhacker* (1988), and vividly in recent work, like *My Life as a Fake* and *Theft*, Peter Carey, too, traces and retraces the pathways of travel, commerce and migration that connect Australia to Asia (in particular Malaya in *Fake*) and to the United States in *Theft*. Even within the more circumscribed geographical domain of Tim Winton's work, several of his characters disappear from their native Western Australia on surfing or sailing holidays to Indonesia. And Coetzee, himself a white immigrant to Australia, is visibly concerned in his post-2003 fiction with light, white or less-visible migration, most obviously so in *Slow Man*.

Certainly from the vantage point of Paul Rayment as narrative consciousness, *Slow Man* is a story about the white immigrant experience; about how a respect for long cultural traditions and European antiquity translates in a context where an awareness of history appears less deeply embedded. Their immigrant background is what he feels he has in common with Marijana Jokić and her family; a feeling animated by the belief that this experience, though begun abroad (in France in his case), can be grafted on to the Australian national imaginary, as one of its legitimate, tributary stories. The first serious conversation he has with Marijana, conducted while she is carefully dusting his books, deals with Australia's "zero history" as seen from the new immigrant point of view, and with the importance of "showing Australia has history too."[41] *Diary of a Bad Year* maintains this immigrant awareness insofar as JC refers several times to his former identity as a South African and now South-African-born writer, and comments on Australia in his *ansichten* as a "man outside"[42] (to quote Peter Carey quoting Max Harris of the Ern Malley affair). *Diary*, too, is in this respect a tale told by an immigrant or, more accurately, two immigrants. JC's young friend Anya, though she is in various ways comfortably at home in Australia, if not in her relationship with white Australian male Alan, marks herself out as "just the little Filipina,"[43] and has been educated in international schools.

The purpose of this "Cook's tour" of Australia's imaginative topography and its coverage by Coetzee, was to elaborate my earlier assertion that he came to the country with many of the definitive preoccupations of its white writing readymade, as if carried in his own portable myth-kitty, and that he was not concerned to hide the fact. Moreover, even if some or all of these seemingly borrowed or copied definitive stories were not in fact formally pre-emptive, remembering his South African settler-writer background, they nonetheless have the appearance in his Australian fiction of the readymade, the as-if-by-design, as is self-reflexively underlined in the made-to-measure Fauchery forgery incident in *Slow Man*. The readymade or anticipatory quality of the country's definitive literary tropes in Coetzee is, this essay submits, crucial for an understanding of how he has come to an interested though always still intellectualized engagement with Australia in his work. He was concerned to cite these conventions, and to do so faithfully, I suggest, in order to declare an involvement as a writer from outside with the matter of Australia. And he did so in a way that bears only a limited resemblance to his evocation of generic Cape space, which is at once everywhere and nowhere, in his South African fiction. So, no matter how generic some of his Australian topographical and cultural references are, they are by contrast noticeably denotative and directed, and recognizably Australian.

Unlike in Coetzee's South African situation, where his reticence vis-à-vis his nation of birth and matters of national belonging was legendary, though he was consistently identified as South African, no Australian writer worthy of the name since the 1960s has deigned not to talk about Australia in their work, to take up positions vis-à-vis Australian history, culture or geography. To write Australia, to engage with its iconic stories and embellish its myths, to engage knowingly in its troubled past, in short, to imagine its reality, is the mark of the Australian writer. This would apply even to those well-known literary exports of Australia, the works of Thomas Keneally and Clive James. The tug of the real is something that Tim Winton characteristically evokes, as in the earth humming with the impact of the sea in *Breath*, or in Pikelet's first-person narrative voice loaded with Australian vernacular.[44] In that novel the boys Pikelet and Loonie spend their entire days as boy surfers in quest of those dangerous "flickering" moments — riding giant waves and feeling, momentarily, supremely alive — that will both define and deform the rest of their lives.[45] But the tug of the real is something that even Postmodernist master Carey registers, as in *My Life as a Fake*.

In his Australian fiction, this essay has proposed, Coetzee is concerned to reference the standard Australian representational conventions, the commonplace reality effects, in order to declare, first, that he subscribes as a writer of this place, as an Australian writer. He seeks to do justice to Australia as it is most typically and elusively defined, as hard, sere reality, yet he also seeks to do so, I further suggest, in deliberately knowing, even paradoxically distancing, ways. Beginning to write Australia, first in *Elizabeth Costello*, then in *Slow Man* and *Diary of a Bad Year*,

Coetzee laid out the basic "intellectual schemas," the furniture of the settled Australia mind, in order both to register an allegiance, and at the same time to move beyond it. Though these schemas conventionally signify aspects of reality in Australia, they also signal their own constructedness, their artifice. They point to the real, yet mask it at the same time, which is why they were useful to Coetzee both compositionally and in theoretical terms for his engagement with Australian reality. Indeed, it may be that the citation of the standard tropes worked ultimately not as a recognition preparatory to an underwriting of an Australia "somewhere," or not only, but as a polite but firm retreat, as if to say: I note an interest, but I choose finally to withdraw from full participation. The possibility has become particularly pointed with the 2009 appearance of *Summertime*, the third volume in his part-autobiographical trilogy *Scenes from Provincial Life*, a novel which returns to South Africa as the setting and in which Australia has no significant place. Is South Africa then, one wonders with the benefit of retrospect, the ultimate site of Coetzee's real?

Although on one level Coetzee has appeared to embrace Australian reality effects in order to embrace Australia in his work, to identify as Australian, on another level his involvement is chiefly by way of a philosophical meditation on the real, as is evident from two key scenes, which I will touch upon in closing. Coetzee, the writer of *White Writing*, evidently knows what makes Australian white writing. Indeed, he knows it so well that he ostentatiously communicates his interest to his readers. The opening of *Slow Man* is unequivocal on the tug or the impact of the real, on cutting life to the quick: Coetzee begins, and Paul Rayment begins, in medias res, with a seemingly intransitive action, a man flying through the air, the cause of the accident at this point non-specific. And the novel wishes from that moment of opening to retrieve its impact if not its pain, to engage with and relive its reality-effects, though throughout it must remain tantalizingly out of reach. From *Slow Man* to *Diary of a Bad Year* therefore the trajectory is clear. Coetzee, I suggest, is involved in rounding up the various circus animals of the colonial dystopia, the haunt of dying white males, both in Australia and beyond Australia. He exhibits these creatures, demonstrates that he manipulates and understands them, but then pushes on to think about what really constitutes the real, what is the thing itself, whether in Australia or beyond it. Writing Australia within Australia, Coetzee ultimately declines to deal only in the readymade, the conventional, the imaginary.

The first sign we get of this, the first of my two key scenes, comes in the form of the Dulgannon frogs episode in *Elizabeth Costello*'s eighth lesson, where she presents to those at the portals to the next life a demonstration of what, ultimately, is meaningful to her. She is speaking as a writer, and what she wants to prove to her judges is, as Derek Attridge has explained, not her beliefs, as she feels as a writer she does not have these, but the process of believing, the seeking of the meaningful.[46] Her illustration of the frogs who lie buried, as if dead, in the dry riverbed and revive in the wet season, she presents at the end of a series of meditations across the novel on questions of suffering, humanness, value and the writer's life. So it is offered as a final submission, more a last breath than a climax, not so much an afterthought as an after-belief — something that becomes particularly poignant when it is remembered, as Melinda Harvey has noted, that the Dulgannon River, said to be in the state of Victoria, does not in fact exist.[47] The frogs story, Elizabeth is careful to emphasize, is not an allegory. Rather, it is an illustration of existence, of life, and hence, I would venture to add, of reality; of that which continues, eluding and resisting language, of that which *is* "whether or not I believe in them,"[48] as Elizabeth says, and whether or not the Dulgannon River exists also. What most fixes her mind about the frogs is not only their separateness, but how they *appear* to bear meaning, given their particular ability to revive after hibernation, to accept, and re-accept, "returning life." "There is something about them that obscurely engages her, something about their mud tombs and the fingers of their hands, fingers that end in little ball, soft wet mucous. She thinks of the frog beneath the earth, spread out as if flying, as if parachuting through the darkness."[49]

"Spread out as if flying" — it is an anticipation. As already suggested, to me the most eloquent sign of Coetzee's desire to acknowledge the real in Australia is that his first fully Australian novel, where South Africa is nowhere mentioned, opens with that hit of the real of Paul's accident. This pure event is my second closing scene. In the first paragraph, "he," "him," the narrative consciousness, is rendered the object of an action; "the blow," administered by, what is it?— Wayne Blight, Magill Road, the physical world, a quantity of light? "You took quite a blow," the doctor explains, though again there is no subject to the action; what happened is something that has "befallen" him; and again, in a later stream of thought, it is "an accident, something that befalls one," which brings only pain ("the real thing") and exposure.[50] In this sense what befalls Paul is not unlike the light that befalls the group of people in Fauchery's photograph. Wayne Blight himself, Paul later explains, may not have seen him on his bike through being "dazzled by the sun."[51] So the accident becomes, as Elizabeth Costello later says, a bringing to life for Paul, though not as a flying creature but as "a lump of all too solid flesh."[52] The blow, the light, the pain, Magill Road, the hard Australian earth that is the medium of the dead-alive frogs — all these, severally and together, underwrite Paul's reality — a reality that inevitably lapses into language, into standard signifying practices, the very moment after he strikes the ground.

NOTES

1 Seamus Heaney, "Englands of the Mind," in *Preoccupations: Selected Prose 1968–1978* (London: Faber, 1980), 151–2.

2 Heaney, "Englands of the Mind," 150–1.

3 J. M. Coetzee, *White Writing: On the Culture of Letters in South Africa* (Chicago: University of Chicago Press, 1988), 7–8.

4 J. M. Coetzee, *Elizabeth Costello: Eight Lessons* (London: Secker & Warburg, 2003), 199–200.

5 Coetzee, *Elizabeth Costello*, 12.

6 Derek Attridge, *J. M. Coetzee and the Ethics of Reading* (Pietermaritzburg: University of Kwazulu Natal Press, 2005), 102; Coetzee, *Elizabeth Costello*, 9.

7 Heaney, "Englands of the Mind," 151–69.
8 J. M. Coetzee, *Slow Man* (London: Secker & Warburg, 2005), 241–2.
9 Coetzee, *Elizabeth Costello*, 193–226.
10 Coetzee, *White Writing*, 9.
11 J. M. Coetzee, *Diary of a Bad Year* (London: Secker & Warburg, 2007), 234, 119, 126, 196, 198, 149–51, 185.
12 Coetzee, *Diary of a Bad Year*, 235.
13 Attridge, *J. M. Coetzee and the Ethics of Reading*, 201.
14 Coetzee, *Slow Man*, 197.
15 See Marcus Clarke, "Preface to Adam Lindsay Gordon's *Poems*," in *Empire Writing*, ed. Elleke Boehmer (Oxford and New York: Oxford University Press, 1998), 50–2.
16 Graham Huggan, *Australian Literature: Postcolonialism, Racism, Transnationalism* (Oxford and New York: Oxford University Press, 2007), 101.
17 Peter Carey, *My Life as a Fake* (London: Faber, 2003), 29.
18 Coetzee, *Slow Man*, 255.
19 Coetzee, *White Writing*, 8.
20 Coetzee, *White Writing*, 164.
21 The historical and imaginative links between these southern colonial spaces were widely explored in Kate Darian-Smith, Liz Gunner and Sarah Nuttall, eds. *Text, Theory, Space: Land, Literature and History in South African and Australia* (London: Routledge 1993), in which Coetzee's formulations predictably featured prominently. See also Christopher Miller's *Blank Darkness: Africanist Discourse in French* (Chicago: University of Chicago Press, 1985).
22 Coetzee, *Diary of a Bad Year*, 112.
23 Coetzee, *Slow Man*, 13.
24 Coetzee, *Elizabeth Costello*, 141.
25 Coetzee, *Elizabeth Costello*, 179, also 125.
26 Coetzee, *Elizabeth Costello*, 15.
27 Coetzee, *Elizabeth Costello*, 215.
28 See Huggan, *Australian Literature*, 66.
29 Coetzee, *Slow Man*, 25, 241; also 151.
30 On the novel's multiple metafictional turns, see Sue Kossew, "Border Crossings," in *J. M. Coetzee in Context and Theory*, eds. Elleke Boehmer, Katy Iddiols and Robert Eaglestone (London: Continuum, 2009): 60–7.
31 Coetzee, *Diary of a Bad Year*, 120.
32 Coetzee, *Diary of a Bad Year*, 203, 171.
33 Coetzee, *Diary of a Bad Year*, 125–6, 191.
34 Coetzee, *Diary of a Bad Year*, 192.
35 Reference is to the cultural, historical and literary studies of, amongst others, Paul Carter, *The Road to Botany Bay* (London: Faber, 1987); Andrew Hassan, *Sailing to Australia: Shipboard Diaries by Nineteenth-Century British Emigrants* (Manchester: Manchester University Press, 1994); Chris Healy, *From the Ruins of Colonialism* (Cambridge: Cambridge University Press, 1997); Graham Huggan, *Australian Literature*; Kay Schaffer, *Women and the Bush: Forces of Desire in the Australian Cultural Tradition* (Cambridge: Cambridge University Press, 1988); and Richard White, *Inventing Australia: Images and Identity 1688–1980* (Sydney: Allen and Unwin, 1981).
36 Huggan, *Australian Literature*, 88–9.
37 Coetzee, *Slow Man*, 35; Tim Winton, *Dirt Music* (London: Picador 2004), 380–1
38 Huggan, *Australian Literature*, 101.
39 Attridge, *J. M. Coetzee and the Ethics of Reading*, 199.
40 Huggan, *Australian Literature*, 111, 113.
41 Coetzee, *Slow Man*, 49.
42 Carey, *My Life as a Fake*, 268.
43 Coetzee, *Diary of a Bad Year*, 70.

44 Tim Winton, *Breath* (London: Picador, 2008), 9.
45 Winton, *Breath*, 95.
46 Attridge, *J. M. Coetzee and the Ethics of Reading*, 201ff.
47 See the essay in this volume.
48 Coetzee, *Elizabeth Costello*, 217, 219.
49 Coetzee, *Elizabeth Costello*, 219.
50 Coetzee, *Slow Man*, 5, 4, 12.
51 Coetzee, *Slow Man*, 68.
52 Coetzee, *Slow Man*, 159, 198.

CHAPTER 2

"In Australia you start zero"

The Escape from Place in J. M. Coetzee's Late Novels

Melinda Harvey

By his own admission, J. M. Coetzee has always been a creator of "spare, thrifty world[s]."[1] In a 1983 interview with Tony Morphet, Coetzee confessed: "I don't have much interest in, or can't seriously engage myself with, the kind of realism that takes pride in copying the 'real' world."[2] *Disgrace*'s David Lurie tells his student Melanie that Wordsworth is "one of [his] masters"; among Coetzee's masters are Kafka and Beckett, writers whose settings are perfunctory, archetypal, decorticated.[3] In *Elizabeth Costello*, it is Kafka who is named responsible for breaking "the word-mirror . . . irreparably" — that is, for questioning the facility of words to reflect reality exactly.[4] As for Beckett, Coetzee celebrates his loaves-and-fishes approach to conjuring the world in a 1973 essay called "Samuel Beckett and the Temptations of Style": "Beckett is mathematician enough to appreciate this lesson: make a single sure affirmation, and from it the whole contingent world of bicycles and greatcoats can, with a little patience, a little diligence, be deduced."[5] It is a formula *Elizabeth Costello*'s narrator self-consciously employs: "Supply the particulars, allow the significations to emerge of themselves."[6]

That the sense of Australian place in Coetzee's three novels since emigration to Australia in 2002 is slight, even compared with the skinflint world-making that we have come to expect from him since *Dusklands*, has often been remarked upon by the books' reviewers. Reviewing *Diary of a Bad Year* for *Slate*, Judith Shulevitz notes that Coetzee's "settings are as barren as deserts, even if they're in cities."[7] Siddhartha Deb in *Bookforum* notes that "not since *Disgrace*, his farewell to South Africa, has [Coetzee] written a novel that offers the comforting illusion of realism."[8] An anonymous reviewer in the *New Yorker* had this to say about *Elizabeth Costello*: the "heroine's journey takes place almost entirely in the realm of the mind, and the effect is that of exploring a cold, depopulated planet."[9]

Ian Watt notes that a key imperative of the novel from its beginning has been to give readers, in immediacy and transparency, the real world.[10] Coetzee has questioned the novel's claims to be able to do this for the entirety of his career. His resistance to a detailed rendering of place in his own writing has been motivated by a number of things over the years, notably:

1 *An awareness that the postmodern crisis of representation has problematized forever the relationship between text and world.* In interview, Coetzee has called realism "illusionism," echoing Maupassant.[11] He has also insisted upon the dissimilitude between life and art, noting that "making sense of life inside a book is different from making sense of real life — not more difficult or less difficult, just different."[12]

2 *A refusal to meet the demand that fiction engage with place so that its problems emerge and an activist imperative pervades.* As David Attwell has explained, realism was "the unquestioned means of bearing witness to, and telling the truth about, South Africa" from Olive Schreiner to Nadine Gordimer, but Coetzee's attitude to realism "when pressed . . . waver[ed] between embattled defensiveness and incisive critique."[13] The majority of his South African novels employ allegory and metafiction in order to sidestep this understanding of the realist novel's intent and purpose. The abjuration of realism on these grounds amounts to a counter-protest; the production of fiction, Coetzee seems to be saying, should not have its meaning pre-coded and interpretation shut down in this way.

3 *A distaste for taking possession of places by delineating them in language.* In *White Writing*, Coetzee shows his sensitivity to appropriation through fictional narratives in particular by examining the South African *plaasroman* (or "farm novel") and shows how literature participates in the attempt to establish a relationship with and lay claim to land.[14]

4 *A natural unreceptivity of the pictorial eye.* In his autobiographical essay "Homage" (1993) — very much the Urtext for *Youth* (2002) — Coetzee talks of his "predominating sensory orientation" being "aural," not visual.[15]

The difficulties of describing a new country in fiction were anticipated by Coetzee back in 1984:

> One can appreciate and enjoy many geographies, but there is only one that one feels in one's bones. And I certainly know from experience that I don't respond to Europe or the United States in the same way as I do to South Africa. And I would probably feel a certain sense of artificial background construction if I were to write fiction set in another environment.[16]

This essay takes a close look at Australia as it emerges — or, rather, fails to emerge — in *Elizabeth Costello*, *Slow Man* and *Diary of a Bad Year*. Coetzee's presentment of Australian people, locations and politics — the things that can be usually counted upon to make place vivid and particular in fiction — actually achieves the very opposite in these novels; Coetzee's Australia becomes a kind of "non-place" because it is an "every-where" as he writes it.

ELIZABETH COSTELLO

We are told on the opening page of *Elizabeth Costello* that Elizabeth "was born in Melbourne and still lives there."[17] But the novel never describes Melbourne, or Australia, for that matter. The near-entirety of its action is set overseas — in the United States, South Africa, the Netherlands and on the waters between Christchurch (New Zealand) and Cape Town. Elizabeth is nominally "at home, settled back into her own life" a couple of times in the novel — she writes her letter to Blanche about Mr Phillips there, for example, but there is no accompanying scene-setting.[18] The two most significant renderings of Australian place in the novel are generated by Elizabeth when she recollects her childhood. Both renderings are severely compromised by the brevity of the recollection as well as its dubious truth-value.

The most striking of these two glimpses of Australia comes in the novel's concluding pages. In her revised statement to what she has come to know as "the board," Elizabeth speaks of her childhood in rural Victoria, "a region of climactic extremes: of scorching droughts followed by torrential rains that swelled the rivers with the carcasses of drowned animals." She elaborates upon one particular river, the Dulgannon, whose muddy bed delivered "tens of thousands of little frogs rejoicing in the largesse of the heavens,"[19] as if from nowhere, after the rains. Despite Elizabeth's assurances to one of the more unbelieving of the board's judges that the Dulgannon is a real river — "It is not negligible. You will find it on most maps."[20] — it does not, in actual fact, exist. There is no Dulgannon River listed in the *Gazetteer of Australia*, a register of nearly 300,000 geographical names in Australia.[21] No one — not even *Elizabeth Costello*'s Australian reviewers and critics — has questioned the Dulgannon's existence, though the frogs are frequently and enthusiastically discussed.[22]

The meaning of these "little frogs" and Elizabeth's professed "belief" in them later on in the chapter is no straightforward matter — especially given we must now also take into account the fact that this particular image of frogs returns in *Diary of a Bad Year*; JC's neighbour Bella Saunders is concerned for the welfare of the frogs along the old creek bed near Sydenham Towers: "Will they not be baked alive in their little earthern chambers?" she asks him.[23] At the very least, Elizabeth's story about the frogs is a canard. Balzac explains the term *canard* in his novel, *Lost Illusions*: Says newspaperman Hector Merlin, "That's our word for a scrap of fiction told for true."[24] Elizabeth's Dulgannon River and its mud frogs are a scrap of fiction told as truth. That it is a scrap of fiction told as truth *inside a fiction* seems to be at the heart of what Coetzee is getting at. We are clearly meant to hear in Elizabeth's statement an echo of Marianne Moore's famous lines from the 1921 version of her poem, "Poetry": The poet's task is to "present / for inspection 'imaginary gardens with real toads in them.'"[25] *Elizabeth Costello* is full of "'imaginary gardens with real toads in them'": imaginary colleges in real cities, imaginary people in real cities, imaginary writers talking about real writers and imaginary lectures presented as real lectures. In a novel that makes a passing parade of its realist tricks, Elizabeth's revised statement to the board — "The river exists. The frogs exist. I exist. What more do you want?"[26] — upholds the possibility of discussing truths in fiction, of speaking about real issues in invented places.

This account of a childhood spent on the Dulgannon River stands in direct opposition to another evocation of Australian place in *Elizabeth Costello*. At the beginning of the novel Elizabeth gives an interview at a college radio station. Elizabeth's son John, the focalizer of this scene at the radio station, watches on as she offers what he feels is a rather pat rendition of "[her] childhood in the suburbs of Melbourne (cockatoos screeching at the bottom of the garden)."[27] This hackneyed Australian reminiscence isn't fleshed out any more than this, but it puts the lie to, or at least contests, the Dulgannon River memory without us having to resort to consulting the *Gazetteer of Australia*. With the unbelieving judge at the gates in Lesson 8 readers also ask, having overheard the suburban Melbourne version in Lesson 1, "And you spent your childhood there, on the Dulgannon? Because it says nothing here, in your docket, about a childhood on the Dulgannon."[28] John sinks the boot in further. He notes that his mother's "strategy with interviewers is to take control of the exchange, presenting them with blocks of dialogue that have been rehearsed so often he wonders if they have not solidified in her mind and become some kind of truth."[29] The reality of the childhood in suburban Melbourne becomes as dubious as the childhood in rural Victoria. This chimes with Elizabeth's account of what she is doing in her books — that is, "making up an Australia."[30] But "making up an Australia" is *not* what Coetzee is doing in *Elizabeth Costello*. We spend the majority of our time in the no-man's-lands of hotels, cruise-ships, lecture halls and even on what appears to be the outer perimeter of a secularized version of heaven. After Marc Augé, we might call these spaces "non-places," spaces of physical, intellectual or indeed spiritual transience and exchange that function outside history and politics.[31] Their antithesis might well be a place like apartheid South Africa.

SLOW MAN

There is an abundance of toponyms in *Slow Man* and they are real; you can find Magill Road, Pulteney Street, North Terrace, Coniston Terrace, Rundle Mall, Norwood, North Adelaide, the river Torrens and Munno Para on any map of Adelaide. The phone number that Paul Rayment includes in his letter to Miroslav Jokić is a real Adelaide phone number (though I can report that when you dial it the man who picks up does not answer to the name of Paul).[32] Unlike *Elizabeth Costello*, which delights in pseudoisms and genericisms, *Slow Man* insists on its

Australian location through nomenclatorial specificity. Despite the preponderance of proper names, however, an Australian reality doesn't really emerge for a local, much less an overseas, readership: Adelaide, after all, is not Sydney or Melbourne — it is not as well-known or oft-visited as either of these cities. As D. J. Taylor in his review of the novel for London's *The Independent* newspaper wrote: "The setting is the Adelaide suburbs, but it might as well be Copenhagen for all the attention paid to the backdrop."[33]

Typically, post-colonial national literatures luxuriate in place names. The motivation is at once oppositional and commercial: these literary works use toponyms to make present particular locations that have been marginalized or obscured, but also to exude a touristic kind of readerly appeal. For Graham Huggan, this rather schizophrenic logic — anti-imperial but market-driven — is the hallmark of the "postcolonial exotic."[34] There is nothing exotic about *Slow Man*'s toponyms, however. To the English-speaking eye they do not look strange; most of the mentioned places are eponyms, named after British people and places. The most exotic of the place names — Munno Para — means "golden wattle creek" in the dialect of the indigenous Kaurna people upon whose lands Adelaide sits,[35] but it connotes post–World War II migration and working-class suburbia on the outskirts for contemporary Adelaideans. It is likely that Seven Narrapinga Close, Munno Para was selected as the home of the Jokić family because of its proximity to Elizabeth — a suburb that shares its name with the seventy-two-year-old Australian author of *The House of Eccles Street* who descends upon Paul, an unwanted guest, one-third of the way through *Slow Man*. Coetzee's use of toponyms, thus, doesn't signal an imperative to render the Australian real. Instead, they stand in the place of rendering the Australian real. They work, if at all, like a miraculous shorthand for the place-shy writer, anchoring the novel in the real world but transmitting very little sense of that real world in the doing so. J. Hillis Miller has noted that, typically, "literature exploits th[e] extraordinary power of words to go on signifying in the total absence of any phenomenal referent."[36] In *Slow Man*, Coetzee exploits the extraordinary power of toponyms to insist that a phenomenal referent exists without actually making a world out of words. The novel's toponyms are signs that transcend the places to which they refer. The surname of Paul — born in Lourdes, the site of modern-day miracles — gives the game away: as he tells us himself, "Rayment" rhymes not with "payment" but with "*vraiment*," French for "truly" or "really."[37] Throw around a few place names and a nominal setting, as opposed to a sense of place, emerges.

Interstate and overseas places are mentioned — Tunkalilla, Coober Pedy, Carlton, Northcote, Ballarat, Canberra and Brisbane as well as Dubrovnik, Zadar, Toulouse and the river Seine — but the overwhelming feeling *Slow Man* produces is one of constriction. The reader is stuck in Paul's "gloomy" and "stuffy" flat for nearly the entirety of the novel — a flat described for us by Elizabeth towards the end of *Slow Man* as a "Bavarian funeral parlour."[38] Elizabeth's is a surrealist "word-mirror," and the surrealist bent of the novel is presaged long before her arrival in the novel by the rather more conventionally realist indirect narrative of Paul's time in hospital in its early pages:

> This — this strange bed, this bare room, this smell both antiseptic and faintly ruinous — this is clearly no dream, it is the real thing, as real as things get. Yet the whole of today, if it is all the same day, if time still means anything, has the feel of the dream. Certainly this thing . . . this monstrous object swathed in white and attached to his hip, comes straight out of the land of dreams. And what about the other thing, the thing that the young man with the madly flashing glasses spoke of with such enthusiasm — when will that make its appearance? . . . The picture that comes to mind is of a wooden shaft with a barb at its head like a harpoon and rubber suckers on its three little feet. It is out of Surrealism. It is out of Dali.[39]

Even when we escape the "bare room" at the hospital and the "Bavarian funeral parlour" of a flat, we encounter a surrealist world. The taxi drops off Paul and Elizabeth at Seven Narrapinga Close, Munno Para, and we are presented with "a colonial-style house with a green lawn around an austere little rectangular Japanese garden: a slab of black marble with water trickling down its face, rushes, grey pebbles." "So real!. . . So authentic!" exclaims Elizabeth, getting out of the car. This, of course, draws our attention to the fact of its being the very opposite, an ersatz reality.[40] A similar note is struck earlier on in the novel when Paul tracks down Elizabeth in city parkland. The bareness of the setting — and the vibe — is Beckettian, who is name-checked in the novel,[41] with a touch of Dali: a river, a bench, some ducks, two tramps (one amputee, one old lady on death's doorstep) and, for a moment, "[a] young couple in a pedal-boat in the shape of a giant swan . . . smiling cheerily."[42] The unreality of the scene, and the unsatisfactoriness of its fictive rendering, is pointed out inside the text itself. Towards the end of the chapter Elizabeth quotes to Paul the words that began the chapter for us, its readers:

> Let me tell you what you see, or what you tell yourself you are seeing. An old woman by the side of the River Torrens feeding the ducks . . . But the reality is more complicated than that, Paul. In reality you see a great deal more — see it and then block it out . . . *He finds her by the riverside, sitting on a bench, clustered around by ducks that she seems to be feeding* — it may be simple, as an account, its simplicity may even beguile one, but it is not good enough. It does not bring me to life . . . Or the ducks, for that matter, if you prefer not to have me at the centre of the picture.[43]

What scant realist world-making there is in *Slow Man* is undone by Elizabeth Costello — metafiction undermines mimesis.

Slow Man is a novel that seems to be a type of self-testing on Coetzee's part, post–Nobel Prize: Can I write a novel that has a protagonist who can't move, who won't act, who's getting old, who knows practically no one and who's boring as all hell? Can I write a novel set in Adelaide, a city on the edge of one of the most arid regions in Australia with very little fiction of note written about it,[44] that makes no claims about Adelaide or Australia at all? Paul, who frequently acknowledges that he is dull and unresponsive, is a dream protagonist for the place-shy Coetzee. No legs means no setting; Paul's bicycle accident on the first page of the novel activates a waiver suspending the need to render what Zola called "the solid earth on which [the writer's] characters are to tread" for the rest.[45]

DIARY OF A BAD YEAR

The most recent of Coetzee's Australian novels, *Diary of a Bad Year*, is set in Sydney. JC, Anya and Alan live in the North Tower of Sydenham Towers. The precise location of this apartment complex is never disclosed; one is tempted to situate Sydenham Towers in inner-city Pyrmont but it really could be in any number of locations north or south of the Sydney Harbour Bridge. Anya says the unit she shares with her partner Alan is twenty-five floors up and has "a view of the harbour, if you squint."[46] Later, she tells us they can see "the traffic on the sliver of Darling Harbour . . . between the high-rises" from their sun-porch.[47] "Sliver," "squint" — these are words apropos to describe Coetzee's oblique world-making in this novel. One is also reminded of JC himself, coming up with his "Strong Opinions" on "what's wrong with today's world" in a flat fitted with slat blinds, his failing eyes requiring him to "squint at what [he has] just written, barely able to decipher it [himself]."[48] These words, what is more, go some way to describing the design of the novel's body matter. *Diary of a Bad Year* diverges from the usual layout of Western scripts, which have readers move from the top-left to the bottom-right of a page and then from the top-left to the bottom-right of the next one. Instead, its pages are split into two (three from page 25) by a horizontal bar. What we get, in essence, are three thin belts or slivers of text that run horizontally instead of vertically. Reading to the bottom-right-hand corner of each page, then, becomes a choice rather than a convention. The reader is always necessarily squinting or looking askance.

Elizabeth Lowry has described Coetzee's prose as "stripped or blanched: the literary equivalent of furniture from IKEA."[49] In *Diary of a Bad Year*, IKEA words prop an IKEA world. Political buzzwords stand in the place of physical description — John Howard, the Anti-Terrorist Act of 2005, Work Choices, the Coalition of the Willing. But on closer inspection only a minority of these buzzwords are Australian-made; most come from abroad — George W. Bush, Shock and Awe, Guantanamo Bay, Al-Qaeda, the Pentagon. Even more come from a different time as well as a different place — the Trojan War, Thomas Hobbes, the Third Reich, Mutually Assured Destruction. Anya is unconvinced these words have anything much to do with the real: "Write about the world around you," she urges JC.[50] By the start of the "Second Diary" the politics has all but disappeared. Instead, JC discourses on a combination of pet topics and perennial themes — birds, dreams, Eros, family, ageing, cricket and, crucially, Russian literature. Deep into this section of *Diary of a Bad Year*, JC, musing about Tolstoy, writes:

> I read the work of other writers, read the passages of dense description they have with care and labour composed with the purpose of evoking imaginary spectacles before the inner eye, and my heart sinks. I was never much good at evocation of the real, and have even less stomach for the task now. The truth is, I have never taken much pleasure in the visible world, don't feel with much conviction the urge to recreate it in words.[51]

JC makes a number of statements in the novel that even the most circumspect Coetzee reader itches to pin to the author himself. This is one of them.

As in *Slow Man*, there is a sense of constriction. I have already mentioned JC's shuttered ground-floor apartment. Also visited are Sydenham Towers' laundry room and the public park across the street. These locations are nondescript. Like the hotels, cruise-ships and lecture halls of *Elizabeth Costello* they bear some of the usual stamps of non-places — transience, functionality and a listless ambience: JC and Anya accidentally cross paths "watching the washing go around" "at eleven in the morning on a weekday"; Anya settles on sunning herself and "browsing through a magazine" in the park "between jobs."[52] For what one can only assume is a densely populated building in a densely populated part of the inner-city it seems rather empty. There appear to be more birds and frogs about than people. "I live on the ground floor and have since 1995 and still I don't know all my neighbours," JC tells Anya when they meet in the laundry for the first time.[53] "Felicitous coincidences" are required for neighbours to meet.[54] JC writes in his diary: "A week passed before I saw [Anya] again — in a well-designed apartment block like this, tracking one's neighbours is not easy — and then only fleetingly as she passed through the front door in a flash of white slacks . . ."[55] To find out about Anya, JC must question the caretaker of the North Tower. To find out about JC, Anya looks him up on the internet. As Anya puts it, JC and she "are neighbours of a kind, distant neighbours."[56]

JC and Anya's "distant neighbours[hip]" is replicated on the page; JC's diary sits atop Anya's diary, a horizontal line keeping their thoughts apart. Like the floors of a high-rise, the tripartite layout of the page intensifies the sense of social isolation. Rootlessness is the norm in Coetzee's Australian novels, literalized by Anya and Alan's penthouse on the twenty-fifth floor, Paul's missing foot and Elizabeth's peripatetic existence in *Elizabeth Costello* and her vagrancy in *Slow Man*. Contrast the depiction of some of the characters from the South African fiction, for example, *Disgrace*'s Lucy Lurie "comfortably barefoot" in the Eastern Cape, with "fingernails . . . none too clean" with "country dirt," or Michael K, municipal gardener in Cape Town, "cultivator" of pumpkins and melons from seed in the veld, eating insects and roots lying belly flat on the ground.[57] Elizabeth explains to Paul in *Slow Man*, "You know, there are those whom I call the chthonic, the ones who stand with their feet planted in their native earth; and then there are the butterflies, creatures of light and air, temporary residents, alighting here, alighting there."[58] If Coetzee's South African characters tend toward the chthonic, then his Australian characters are certainly "butterflies," deracinated and fugitive.

Nations are constructed in opposition to an Other, but otherness defines

Australia in *Diary of a Bad Year*. Its characters are marked by an unassailable foreignness. JC is a South African who's long been mistaken for a Columbian by residents of Sydenham Towers, which prompts Alan to call him "Juan" and Anya to call him "El Señor" and "Señor C," punning on the word "senior."[59] His "Strong Opinions," written in English, are slated only to be read in German and French. Anya — the Russian diminutive of Anna — grew up in France, Egypt and the United States, was educated in Geneva and enjoys playing "the little Filipina" though she has never lived in the Philippines. JC privately calls Alan "Mr Aberdeen," because of his "Celtic pallor."[60] Foreignness also marks Coetzee's Australians in the other novels. Elizabeth Costello is an Australian whose work demands she lead a peripatetic existence, roaming the lands and waters of the world, with no opinions on "Aboriginal rights" or "the Australian novel today."[61] In *Slow Man* Elizabeth is at home, but time and again she is rendered Irish.[62] Her pawn Paul was born in France and brought to Australia by his Dutch stepfather as a child. When Elizabeth accuses him of "speak[ing] English like a foreigner" he retorts, "I speak English because I am a foreigner. I am a foreigner by nature and I have been a foreigner all my life."[63] This is interesting when we recall how many times Paul corrects the Croatian-born Marijana's speech. This is a leitmotif of the late novels: foreigners correcting other foreigners' English, and native English speakers correcting other native English speakers' English. JC is dismayed by Anya's poor word recognition skills, which have her transcribe "somewhere in the Urals" as "somewhere in the urinals."[64] Meanwhile, Anya sees herself as much more than a typist, "fix[ing]...up" JC's sentences "here and there where [she] can, where they lack a certain something, a certain oomph" and dishing out the occasional compliment when she feels it is deserved: "Your English is very good, considering . . . it isn't your mother tongue."[65]

THE ESCAPE FROM PLACE

Coetzee's late novels do not set themselves the task of summoning a sense of Australian place; in fact, they set themselves the task of testing and proving treacherous the usual methods by which a sense of place is summoned in novels. The late novels draw on Australian identities, locations and politics but a distinctive Australia is nowhere to be found. In these novels place is less artificially constructed than systematically erased. To understand how deeply subversive this is, we must consider *Elizabeth Costello*, *Slow Man* and *Diary of a Bad Year* in the context of a national literature that established itself and thrives on a belief in Australia's exceptionality as a place; Australia has a landscape utterly unlike anywhere else on earth, and from that real and essential uniqueness has sprung nativeness in terms of fictional characters and action. Here we might recall Henry Lawson's famous lines from his 1892 short story called "The Bush Undertaker": "The grand Australian bush — the nurse and tutor of eccentric minds, the home of the weird, and of much that is different from things in other lands."[66]

Coetzee disobliges another of Australian literature's staple means of engendering a sense of place — an appeal to the past. In *Slow Man*, images recording Australia's Gold Rush history by the French photographer Antoine Fauchery lie dormant in Paul's filing cabinet. They are something to look at, Paul says to Drago when he comes to stay, "if you get bored, if you have nothing to do." It is yet to be seen if these "distribution[s] of particles of silver" will one day solder, "like a mystical charm," a sense of national identity.[67] For now, they are material merely for private mischief. When Drago and a friend from school decide to doctor one of the photographs, substituting a fiercely moustached Jokić grandfather for one of the Ballarat diggers and little sister Ljuba for one of the digger's children, Marijana brushes it off as "just a joke." Elizabeth goes much further, claiming that falsification of the historical record in general "is of the utmost insignificance." When Paul asks her to consider the consequences of "this so-called joke" going unnoticed at the State Library where he intends to donate his collection of Faucherys she says, "Then it would become part of our folklore that brigand moustaches were in fashion in 1850s Victoria. That's all. This is really not a matter worth going on about."[68] In *Diary of a Bad Year*, the only place to be reflected upon with a sense of the past is the small park across the road from Sydenham Towers. But the history that is told predates both the arrival of indigenous Australians, let alone European Australians, by over a million years. In fact it is an account of the past that pointedly excludes the life of human beings — it is a history of the local birds. A cockatoo is imagined to offer a new perspective on Australian place and its ownership: "This is a public garden. You are as much a visitor as I . . . It's a free world, he says."[69] In his 1987 *Weekly Mail* Book Week address Coetzee defined history as "nothing but a certain kind of story that people agree to tell each other" and proposed a novel of "rivalry" that would "show up the mythic status of history."[70] The late novels demythologize history in a general sense but go one step further — they seem to quibble with the whole idea that Australia has a history even in this lightweight sense of a discourse that commands consensus to begin with.

Marijana says to Paul in *Slow Man*: "In Europe people say Australia have no history because in Australia everyone is new. Don't mind if you come with this history or that history, in Australia you start zero. Zero history, you understand?"[71] The consequence of "zero history" can been seen in the plotting of Coetzee's Australian novels compared with the South African novels. The episodic nature of *Elizabeth Costello* appears to be determined by Elizabeth's travels abroad; there is a story to tell, it seems, when Elizabeth is anywhere bar Australia. The plots of *Slow Man* and *Diary of a Bad Year* are very creaky. Connections between people are tenuous and formed on the basis of whim rather than necessity. Elizabeth arrives unwanted and unwarranted on Paul's doorstep, Paul offers to pay for Drago's schooling to become a kind of "co-husband" to Marijana and JC manufactures a need for a typist for his "Strong Opinions" in order to see more of Anya: "I too am in need of a secretary, I said, grasping the nettle."[72] There is the clunkiness and implausibility of the porn film about the plots of these two novels: patient falls for nurse with "prideful" breasts, old man meets sexy neighbour in "tomato-red shift

. . . startling in its brevity" in the laundry room.[73] In *Diary of a Bad Year* JC tells Anya that after a "lifetime of working with stories" he now knows that "[s]tories tell themselves, they don't get told."[74] But this statement doesn't seem to hold in Australia, a place where stories don't tell themselves and don't come quickly. JC hasn't written a novel for years and one is tempted to think that this isn't simply due to old age and a lack of patience. Only 79 pages of stolid storytelling occur in *Slow Man* before Coetzee admits the advent, *deus ex machina*-like, of the meddling author Elizabeth Costello to hurry Paul on and make something happen. It is Elizabeth who urges Paul to "push the mortal envelope" — to meet up with Marianna, the woman in the lift with the dark glasses at the hospital, and to do something with his love for Marijana before regret casts over his days "with a grey monotone."[75] Elizabeth may well insist that she isn't interfering but the mere fact of her presence in Paul's flat is an intervention in the same way that the observer of an electron changes the movement of that electron in particle physics.

Plotting is very different in the South African novels. Characters are locked into hierarchical power relations or ties of responsibility and obligation, be they loath to them or not, and the plots are, as if accordingly, wound as tightly as springs. For example, one thinks of how inevitably Elizabeth Curren in *Age of Iron* is imbricated in the lives of Florence and her son Bheki, how porous her house is to strangers like Verceuil and John due to history and politics. "Power is power, after all," she tells Verceuil. "It invades. That is its nature. It invades one's life."[76] Contrast *Diary of a Bad Year*, with its bi- and trifurcated narrative, suggesting that history and politics are hermetic discourses in Australia that have little to do with the private affairs of its citizens. The "Strong Opinions" sit on the page, atop the personal diaries, like liquids with different specific gravity, having nothing to do with one another. Anya — something of a holy fool in *Diary of a Bad Year* — is on to something when she writes in her letter to JC that "maybe there is no story in politics."[77]

The listless plots of the late novels are a symptom of the fact that neither the depiction of landscape, history nor the current political reality conjures a sense of place when Coetzee writes Australia. This is, in part, because Australia has never been settled in the strict sense of that word; constant waves of migration and the newer uniformities enforced by globalization have seen to it that Australia as a nation doesn't exist. In *Diary of a Bad Year*, JC proposes that a Finn might have felt a sense of pride hearing Sibelius's Fifth Symphony for the first time nearly a century ago and that an American today might commit suicide "rather than live in disgrace" for the crimes committed by her government in her name. But an individual Australian, it seems, is denied purchase on either pride or disgrace through a sense of communal belonging. With no nation to negotiate, Coetzee in Australia transcends place without needing to resort to allegory, without engaging in the "immense labour" of "invent[ing] a world out of place and time and situat[ing] the action there, as [he] did in *Waiting for the Barbarians*."[78] There's no reason to suppose Coetzee's reasons for moving to Australia were different than the ones that would have any of us move countries — a relationship, a job, a change of scene. Nonetheless it is true that for Coetzee in Australia rendering place becomes an option, not an obligation — something he had always dreamed of. Ethical dilemmas stemming from historical and political responsibility no longer attach themselves like burrs to fiction writing as they did in South Africa. In the memoir *Youth*, published the year Coetzee moved to Australia, John asks, "What kind of world is this in which he lives? Where can one turn to be free of the fury of politics?"[79] The answer is in tracking Coetzee's own pattern of migration: Australia.

To date, Coetzee has cast place aside in order to take up a different, less-embedded conversation. If there is a sense of duty in the Australian novels, it is to something bigger, wider, older than Australia — it is a duty to Western literature. Emigration means that a writer's homeland can become the books and writers that have preceded him, and as Coetzee said in a 2003 interview, his own "intellectual allegiances are clearly European, not African."[80] At this point it is worth recalling a discussion that occurs between Elizabeth and her son John in the opening pages of *Elizabeth Costello*. Mother and son have returned to their hotel after dinner with the jurors of the Stowe Award, and some representatives from Altona College. Elizabeth Costello says:

> "As a group, don't they strike you as rather . . ."
>
> "Rather lightweight?"
>
> She nods.
>
> "Well, they are. The heavyweights don't involve themselves in this kind of show. The heavyweights are wrestling with the heavyweight problems."
>
> "I am not heavyweight enough for them?"
>
> "No, you're heavyweight all right . . . But for the present you're not a problem, just an example."
>
> "An example of what?"
>
> "An example of writing. An example of how someone of your station and your generation and your origins writes. An instance."
>
> "An instance? Am I allowed a word of protest? After all the effort I put into not writing like anyone else?"[81]

The escape from place enabled by Australia allows Coetzee to be more of a "heavyweight" and less of an "instance." Ernest Hemingway used to talk of the writer — himself, especially — as a prizefighter, successively challenging and defeating dead writers — Maupassant, Stendhal, Turgenev — in a struggle to become literary champion of the world. In the late novels Coetzee is sparring with the greats in part-tribute, part-contestation, and increasingly (this is a term JC uses in *Diary of a Bad Year*) part-"metaphysical ache."[82] Here is *Elizabeth Costello*'s John again, this time to Susan Moebius:

> "Have you considered the possibility that my mother may have got beyond the man-woman thing? That she may have explored it as far as it goes, and is now after bigger game?"

"Such as?"

. . .

"Such as measuring herself against the illustrious dead. Such as paying tribute to the powers that animate her. For instance."

"Is that what she says?"

"Don't you think that that is what she has been doing all her life: measuring herself against the masters? Does no one in your profession recognize it?"[83]

Many people in our profession have recognized that Coetzee has always written books conscious of other books. But in the late novels we are witnessing a change in the way books are used in his books. We might characterize this shift as a move from the allusive, the derivative, from the revisionist to the interlocutive, the discursive, the polyphonic. Instead of conjuring a sense of place and all that entails in the late novels we find a kind of transhistorical inquiry, fuelled by Coetzee's own touchstone texts. Literature once helped Coetzee escape place, as in the case of his novel *Foe*, which uses the world created by Daniel Defoe's *Robinson Crusoe* in order to avoid the obligation to represent South Africa. Now that literature doesn't have to offer recourse to realism for Coetzee because Australia obviates the need for an alternative reality to substitute for the real world, a more wholesale dialogue can be opened up with other books on the level of ideas, most crucially about how one should live. As in the novels of Dostoevsky, another of Coetzee's "masters," conversation results in a dropping-away or shedding of the external world. In Dostoevsky's novels — and increasingly in Coetzee's — people "come together in infinity," as Ivan Shatov's says to Stavrogin in Part II of *Demons*, to talk about the important things.[84]

In this shift from literary revisionism to metaphysical colloquy Coetzee's progress as a writer parallels that of Elizabeth Costello. Her fourth novel, the novel that "made her name," was a rewriting of James Joyce's *Ulysses* called *The House on Eccles Street* with Molly not Leopold Bloom as its main character. In Susan Moebius' words, Elizabeth "take[s] Molly out of the house . . . where her husband and her lover and in a certain sense her author have confined her . . . and turned her loose on the streets of Dublin." But three decades on Elizabeth tells Moebius in an interview that she is no longer interested in using literature in that way: "But, seriously, we can't go on parasitizing the classics for ever." It's significant that the narrator, focalized through Elizabeth's son John again, asks us to pay attention to this statement: "This is not in the script at all. A new departure. Where will it lead? But alas, the Moebius woman . . . does not pick up on it."[85]

This isn't the place to embark upon a study of where Coetzee's "new departure" has led him in his late novels. Suffice to say, there is an intensification of Coetzee's engagement in what scholars have called the "Great Conversation." The mettle of ideas that have accompanied us throughout human history are tested, ideas that have helped us how to live and how to die — Eros, agape, care, duty, the soul, and so on. The late novels are preoccupied with a nagging sense there is an onus on the writer to opine or teach. This is why there are so many scenes of instruction, so many scenes constructed around pedagogical moments in the late novels: the lecture halls of *Elizabeth Costello*, the "godfatherly" advice on bike-riding and offer of money for Wellington College in *Slow Man*, the book of "Strong Opinions" in *Diary of a Bad Year*. This also accounts for an increasing fascination for — and possibly even a yearning for — the vatic voice. What we see in the late novels is a Modernist leave-taking, which, with hindsight, was signaled in *Youth*; as Stephen Mulhall has noted, Coetzee's project in his fiction has chimed with Modernism's "driving desire" to problematize the realist project of creating "a convincing appearance of reality itself."[86] This project has now taken another turn. It is not enough to expose place-making in fiction as a fiction. There is a driving desire now to go after what William Faulkner called in his 1950 Nobel Prize Banquet Speech "the old verities."[87] This focus on the "old verities" accounts for the utterly sincere return to the Russian novelists of the nineteenth century, Tolstoy and Dostoevsky. If Coetzee's emigration to Australia points us in the direction of any place at all it is Russia. *The Master of Petersburg* (1995), so long the odd novel out in Coetzee's oeuvre, now looks of the essence. In *Diary of a Bad Year*, JC ponders Tolstoy's career, his turn from a writer of "dense description" of the "visual world" to his "growing detachment from the world" and "cleaning of the mind to take on more important tasks":

> No one is more alive to the real world than the young Leo Tolstoy, the Tolstoy of *War and Peace*. After *War and Peace*, if we follow the standard account, Tolstoy entered upon a long decline into didacticism that culminated in the aridity of the late short fiction. Yet to the older Tolstoy the evolution must have seemed quite different. Far from declining, he must have felt, he was ridding himself of the shackles that had enslaved him to appearances, enabling him to face directly the one question that truly engaged his soul: how to live.[88]

Coetzee's late novels embody a self-conscious "cleaning of the mind" in an attempt "to face directly the one question that truly engage[s] his soul: how to live," and this project is *en train* thanks to the escape from place that Australia has made possible.

NOTES

1 J. M. Coetzee, *Doubling the Point: Essays and Interviews* (Cambridge: Harvard University Press, 1992), 20.
2 Tony Morphet, "Two Interviews with J. M. Coetzee, 1983 and 1987," *TriQuarterly* 69 (1987), 455.
3 J. M. Coetzee, *Disgrace* (London: Secker & Warburg, 1999), 13.
4 J. M. Coetzee, *Elizabeth Costello* (London: Viking, 2003), 19.
5 J. M. Coetzee, "Samuel Beckett and the Temptations of Style" (1973), in *Doubling the Point*, 43.
6 Coetzee, *Elizabeth Costello*, 4.
7 Judith Shulevitz, "Who Cares?" review of *Diary of a Bad Year*, *Slate*, 10 December 2007, www.slate.com/id/2179374/pagenum/all/ (accessed 11 January 2010).
8 Siddhartha Deb, "Señor Year," review of *Diary of a Bad Year*, *Bookforum*, December/January 2008, www.bookforum.com/inprint/014_04/1385 (accessed 11 January 2010).

9 Anonymous review of *Elizabeth Costello*, in *The New Yorker*, 27 October 2003, http://www.newyorker.com/archive/2003/10/27/031027crbn_brieflynoted2 (accessed 11 January 2010).
10 Ian Watt, *The Rise of the Novel* (Berkeley: University of California Press, 1957), 17–18.
11 Coetzee, *Doubling the Point*, 27; Guy de Maupassant, "*Le Roman*" [Introduction to *Pierre et Jean* (1888)], in *Novelists on the Novel*, ed. Miriam Allott (London: Routledge & Kegan Paul, 1959), 71.
12 A. Thorold and R. Wicksteed, "Grubbing for the Ideological Implications: A Clash (More or Less) with J. M. Coetzee," *Sjambok*, n.d., 4.
13 David Attwell, *South Africa and the Politics of Writing* (Berkeley: University of California Press, 1993), 11.
14 J. M. Coetzee, *White Writing: On the Culture of Letters in South Africa* (New Haven CT: Yale University Press, 1988).
15 J. M. Coetzee, "Homage," *Threepenny Review* 53 (Spring 1993): 5.
16 Folke Rhedin, "J. M. Coetzee: Interview," *Kunapipi* 6:1 (1984): 10.
17 Coetzee, *Elizabeth Costello*, 1.
18 Coetzee, *Elizabeth Costello*, 145.
19 Coetzee, *Elizabeth Costello*, 216.
20 Coetzee, *Elizabeth Costello*, 218.
21 *Gazetteer of Australia* (2008), www.ga.gov.au/map/names/ (accessed 11 January 2010). I wish to thank Julieanne Lamond for pointing me in the direction of this database.
22 See, for example, James Wood, "A Frog's Life," review of *Elizabeth Costello*, in *London Review of Books* 25:20, 23 October 2003, www.lrb.co.uk/v25/n20/james-wood/a-frogs-life (accessed 11 January 2010).
23 Coetzee, *Diary of a Bad Year*, 211.
24 Honoré de Balzac, *Lost Illusions*, trans. Herbert J. Hunt (London: Penguin, 1971), 349.
25 Marianne Moore, "Poetry," *Marianne Moore: Complete Poems* (London: Faber, 1984), 267.
26 Coetzee, *Elizabeth Costello*, 218.
27 Coetzee, *Elizabeth Costello*, 9.
28 Coetzee, *Elizabeth Costello*, 218.
29 Coetzee, *Elizabeth Costello*, 9.
30 Coetzee, *Elizabeth Costello*, 12.
31 Marc Augé, *Non-Places: Introduction to an Anthropology of Supermodernity*, trans. John Howe (London: Verso, 2008; 1992).
32 J. M. Coetzee, *Slow Man* (London: Viking, 2005), 225.
33 D. J. Taylor, "Codes for the enigma of survival," review of *Slow Man*, in *The Independent*, 2 September 2005, www.independent.co.uk/arts-entertainment/books/reviews/slow-man-by-j-m-coetzee-505074.html (accessed 11 January 2010).
34 Graham Huggan, *The Postcolonial Exotic: Marketing the Margins* (London: Routledge, 2001).
35 *The Manning Index of South Australian History*, State Library of South Australia, www.slsa.sa.gov.au/manning/ (accessed 11 January 2010).
36 J. Hillis Miller, *On Literature* (London: Routledge, 2002), 16.
37 Coetzee, *Slow Man*, 192.
38 Coetzee, *Slow Man*, 85, 100, 227.
39 Coetzee, *Slow Man*, 9.
40 Coetzee, *Slow Man*, 242.
41 Says Elizabeth of the novel's *dramatis personae*, "Four people in four corners, moping, like tramps in Beckett, and myself in the middle, being wasted by time." Coetzee, *Slow Man*, 141.
42 Coetzee, *Slow Man*, 154.
43 Coetzee, *Slow Man*, 158–9.
44 Murray Bail's *Holden's Performance* (1987) is, of course, one example of an Adelaide novel of significance.
45 Emile Zola, "The Experimental Novel" (1880), in *The Nineteenth Century Novel: A Critical Reader*, ed. Stephen Regan (London: Routledge, 2001), 108.

46 J. M. Coetzee, *Diary of a Bad Year* (London: Harvill Secker, 2007), 32.
47 Coetzee, *Diary of a Bad Year*, 100.
48 Coetzee, *Diary of a Bad Year*, 20, 26, 28, 32, 42.
49 Elizabeth Lowry, "J. M. Coetzee's ruffled mirrors," in *TLS*, 22 August 2007, http://entertainment.timesonline.co.uk/tol/arts_and_entertainment/the_tls/article2322205.ece (accessed 11 January 2010).
50 Coetzee, *Diary of a Bad Year*, 35.
51 Coetzee, *Diary of a Bad Year*, 192.
52 Coetzee, *Diary of a Bad Year*, 6, 12.
53 Coetzee, *Diary of a Bad Year*, 5.
54 Coetzee, *Diary of a Bad Year*, 12.
55 Coetzee, *Diary of a Bad Year*, 8.
56 Coetzee, *Diary of a Bad Year*, 32.
57 Coetzee, *Disgrace*, 59, 61; J. M. Coetzee, *Life & Times of Michael K* (London: Vintage, 1998), 59, 102.
58 Coetzee, *Slow Man*, 198.
59 Coetzee, *Diary of a Bad Year*, 26.
60 Coetzee, *Diary of a Bad Year*, 6, 11.
61 Coetzee, *Elizabeth Costello*, 10.
62 For example, "He never knows, with the Costello woman, when he is being treated seriously and when he is being taken for a ride. He can cope with the English, that is to say the Anglo-Australians. It is the Irish who have always given him trouble, and the Irish strain in Australia." Coetzee, *Slow Man*, 230.
63 Coetzee, *Slow Man*, 231.
64 Coetzee, *Diary of a Bad Year*, 25.
65 Coetzee, *Diary of a Bad Year*, 29, 51.
66 Henry Lawson, "The Bush Undertaker" (1892), in *The Anthology of Colonial Australian Gothic Fiction*, eds. Ken Gelder and Rachael Weaver (Melbourne: Melbourne University Press, 2007), 146.
67 Coetzee, *Slow Man*, 177.
68 Coetzee, *Slow Man*, 249, 259.
69 Coetzee, *Diary of a Bad Year*, 209.
70 J. M. Coetzee, "The Novel Today", *Upstream* 6.1 (Summer 1988): 2–5.
71 Coetzee, *Slow Man*, 49.
72 Coetzee, *Diary of a Bad Year*, 15.
73 Coetzee, *Diary of a Bad Year*, 3.
74 Coetzee, *Diary of a Bad Year*, 55.
75 Coetzee, *Slow Man*, 139.
76 J. M. Coetzee, *Age of Iron* (London: Secker & Warburg, 1990), 107.
77 Coetzee, *Diary of a Bad Year*, 222.
78 Morphet, "Two Interviews with J. M. Coetzee, 1983 and 1987," 455.
79 J. M. Coetzee, *Youth* (London: Vintage, 2002), 85.
80 David Attwell, "An Exclusive Interview with J. M. Coetzee," *Dagens Nyeter*, 8 December, 2003, www.dn.se/kultur-noje/an-exclusive-interview-with-j-m-coetzee-1.227254 (accessed 10 January 2010).
81 Coetzee, *Elizabeth Costello*, 7–8.
82 Coetzee, *Diary of a Bad Year*, 7.
83 Coetzee, *Elizabeth Costello*, 25–6.
84 Fyodor Dostoevsky, *Demons*, trans. Richard Pevear and Larissa Volokhonsky (London: Vintage, 1994), 252.
85 Coetzee, *Elizabeth Costello*, 15.
86 Stephen Mulhall, *The Wounded Animal: J. M. Coetzee & the Difficulty of Reality in Literature & Philosophy* (Princeton and Oxford: Princeton University Press, 2009), 140.
87 William Faulkner, Nobel Prize Banquet Speech, 10 December 1950, http://nobelprize.org/nobel_prizes/literature/laureates/1949/faulkner-speech.html (accessed 10 January 2010).
88 Coetzee, *Diary of a Bad Year*, 192–3.

CHAPTER 3

J. M. Coetzee and Patrick White

Explorers, Settlers, Guests

Maria López

In the Introduction to *White Writing: On the Culture of Letters in South Africa* (1988), J. M. Coetzee asserts that he is concerned "with certain of the ideas, the great intellectual schemas, through which South Africa has been thought by Europe; and with the land itself, South Africa as landscape and landed property."[1] These concerns actually traverse a great deal of Coetzee's literary production, in which the question of the land is approached from the two perspectives alluded to in the sentence quoted above: a rather intellectual and aesthetic one — as Sarah Nuttall has argued, "historically, the land in white English South African fiction has raised hermeneutic questions: how to read it and how to find a language to speak about it"[2] — but also a more historical and political perspective, related to the ownership, occupation and distribution of the land, and to the power relations associated with them.

This essay will focus on the explicit rejection of certain ways of reading and appropriating the land, together with the quest for an alternative and ethical mode of relating to the South African land that we find from the very beginning of Coetzee's literary career. In this sense, I would like to argue that in order to understand the figure of the explorer Jacobus Coetzee — probably the character that most fully embodies the violent "proprietorial consciousness" in southern Africa rejected by Coetzee — it may prove most fruitful to turn to Patrick White. In White's novel, *Voss* (1957), we find a similar depiction of the relation between the European exploring consciousness, the surrounding land and its native inhabitants, this time, in the Australian context. The analogies between these two territories, both once part of the British Empire, have been repeatedly remarked. Thus, the editors of *Text, Theory, Space: Land, Literature and History in South Africa and Australia* (1996) point to "the similar latitudes, their arid, fragile interiors, and their shared settler myths of the 'empty land' and policies of white racial domination."[3] But in their concern with the physical and epistemological confrontation between the European psyche and the colonial landscape, the link between Coetzee and White goes beyond the specificities of their respective contexts. As Glenn Hooper puts it, "from the long list of almost endless variables that constituted imperial experience there was always one, fairly constant, element for colonists to consider: how to physically combat and control the environment," an environment that "confront[ed] the viewer with epistemological difficulties that destabilized meaning and certainty."[4] The fact that Coetzee has ended up migrating to Australia, and setting some of his fiction in this context, makes us wonder whether there is some kind of correlation between his initial depictions of the relation between the European person and the southern African land, so similar to those of his Australian counterpart, Patrick White, and his later treatment of the Australian context in novels such as *Elizabeth Costello* (2003), *Slow Man* (2005) and *Diary of a Bad Year* (2007). This is certainly not the case, and the answer probably does not only lie in the obvious fact that the concerns and the literary language of his recent fiction considerably differ from those of his early fiction. If the Australian landscape is notably absent in Coetzee's "Australian" novels, the reason may lie in the powerful sense of attachment to the South African land that keeps emerging from *In the Heart of the Country* (1977) onwards. This tender and loving attachment to the land, however and paradoxically, will tend to be accompanied by a sense of geographical transience and provisionality. And this provisional attachment, as experienced by Magda and other characters, such as the child of *Boyhood* (1997), is going to be dependent upon a "non-proprietorial conciousness" towards the South African land. In his (anti)pastoral narratives, Coetzee dismantles the central features that, in "The Great South African Novel" (1983), he identified in the traditional Afrikaans novel: "an 'official' view of South Africa as a settled land;" and a "proprietorial consciousness" according to which "the South African earth *belongs* to certain people and not to others."[5] In the light of his complete narrative production, Coetzee's critique may be expanded to the whole process of European exploration and settlement on the South African land, and to the way it has denied ownership to its original owners.

Hence, the critique of "proprietorial consciousness" that we find in *Dusklands* turns, in subsequent texts such as *Boyhood* or *Summertime* (2009), into the ethical proposal of a "non-proprietorial consciousness," according to which Coetzee's characters of European descent reject the traditional role of owners or settlers, perceiving themselves, instead, as temporary visitors or guests. The implication is a rejection of the history of dispossession and violence, and of unequal power relations, brought about by European settlement in southern Africa. And this vulnerable geographical position cannot be seen as separate from a vulnerable narrative position from which the limits of authority are fully exposed. Thus, Magda's experience of settlement on the South African Karoo as an unfulfilling and partly meaningless one is linked with her inability to tell a coherent and comprehensible story of the land surrounding her. Throughout his literary career, Coetzee has told the story of the South African land in a tentative and fragmentary voice, calling attention to the provisionality and even illegitimacy of his narrative position. And this vacillating narrative position goes hand in hand with a non-rooted, non-native geographical position, which becomes even more accentuated in his "Australian" novels, in which telling the story of an immense land where the late settler is, as put by Costello, no more than a "flea" or a "butterfly," looks like a preposterous task.

DUSKLANDS AND *VOSS*: EXPLORERS AND PENETRATIVE VISION

In "Homage" (1993), Coetzee explains that in the 1960s, there was no South African writer he felt he could follow in order to write about his homeland: the few "versions of *the land*" that had been written in South Africa were "false and corrupt." On the contrary, Australia had thrown up Patrick White, "a writer who could go into the heart of the country and return with a version of that country powerful enough for his readers to believe in and take a lead from (I am thinking particularly of *Voss*, and in it of Heinrich Voss's meditations)."[6] Coetzee begins his literary career with a ferocious attack on the way in which the southern African land has been articulated and appropriated by European thought as embodied by European explorers. Patrick White must have exerted some influence on the way this project was conceived, and certainly in "The Narrative of Jacobus Coetzee" — the second novella making up *Dusklands* (1974) and Coetzee's particular *version* of early European exploration in southern Africa — the figure of the Dutch explorer bears much resemblance to his Australian predecessor.

Since the accounts of the expeditions of Ludwig Leichhardt — the German explorer and naturalist who came to Australia in 1842 and whose party disappeared when trying to travel from Moreton Bay (Brisbane) to Perth — are behind the composition of *Voss*,[7] the German origin of the main character must be due to the Prussian nationality of the historical character of Leichhardt. However, we also find in Voss the creative and irrational powers of the German romantic genius, which may fully expand in the infinite distances of the Australian landscape: "Every man has a genius, though it is not always discoverable. Least of all when choked by the trivialities of daily existence. But in this disturbing country . . . it is possible more easily to discard the inessential and to attempt the infinite."[8] Voss is, then, endowed with a temperament that is not far from the Nietzschean willpower of the superman. For him, "future . . . is will" (V, 68), and his will is "his royal instrument" (V, 297).

At a certain point, Laura Trevelyan rightly asserts: "this expedition of yours is pure will" (V, 69). And she understands that in his project to "cross the continent from one end to the other" (V, 33), Voss is driven by motivations and objectives different from those of her fellow countrymen: "he does not intend to make a fortune out of this country, like other men" (V, 28). In fact, throughout the novel, his personality is repeatedly posed against the materialist character of Mr. Bonner, the patron of the expedition. As Mark Williams has argued, whereas the merchant sees the country as "a totality of material facts and things, a whole that can be mapped, carved up and turned to profit," for Voss, the continent is "a metaphysical totality, a pure idea which his will imposes on reality."[9] Voss is not interested in the domestication and ownership of the land, which constitutes the main concern of the Australian colonial land-owning classes, as the young landowner, Ralph Angus, makes clear when he explains why he will not continue any farther into wilderness: "I have enough land"; "there is land enough along the coast for anyone to stake a reasonable claim" (V, 347).

However, if Voss is not driven by the desire for material possession, he is motivated by a different kind of possessiveness: what we could call *imaginative* or *metaphysical possessiveness*,[10] and it is in this sense that his Romantic affinities most fully emerge. He intends to possess the country with his will, to contain the infinite Australian interior within his immense willpower. Early in the novel he already thinks of Australia as the "country of which he had become possessed by implicit right" (V, 27), and when he actually penetrates it in physical terms, he experiences it as a "vast, expectant country, whether of stone deserts, veiled mountains, or voluptuous, fleshy forests. But his" (V, 137). In his sense, Voss's visionary mind very much resembles William Blake's,[11] especially in the passage in which Voss contemplates a sunrise that is presented as his own creation: he is "the creator" (V, 282), for whom, "each morning is, like the creative act, the first." With his genius and aspirations to divinity, Voss does not only possess nature, but even creates it, just as "in Blake the criterion or standard of reality is the genius,"[12] as Northrop Frye argued in his classic study, *Fearful Symmetry* (1947).

Imaginative and creative possession is achieved by vision, and in relation to Voss, Laura asserts that this country "is his by right of vision" (V, 29). Thus, on leaving Rhine Towers, Voss is presented as "possessing the whole country with his eyes. In those eyes the hills and valleys lay still, but expectant, or responded in ripples of leaf and grass" (V, 155). His relation to the surrounding reality depends, then, upon Blake's "double vision," in which the sight of the "outward eye" gains power and clarity through the vision of the "inward eye."' And Jacobus Coetzee, like Voss, appropriates the land around him through his eyes: "I meditated upon the acres of new ground I had eaten up with my eyes" (V, 77). But unlike Voss, his motivations are tied to the materialistic search for useful land for colonial settlement and trading purposes: "commerce with the wild is a tireless enterprise of turning it into orchard and farm"; he is "a hunter, a domesticator of the wilderness, a hero of enumeration" (V, 80).

In the final chapter of *White Writing*, Coetzee focuses on "the poetry of topographic description" written by poets of European provenance in South Africa, and whose central concern is "whether the African landscape can be articulated in a European language, whether the European can be at home in Africa."[13] For Coetzee, in "colonial pictorial art" — associated with "conquest and domination" — the "poet's penetrating gaze" is an "imperial gaze," keen on discovering "the true story of the land . . . that lies buried . . . beneath the surface."[14] Just as Frye, in *The Bush Garden: Essays on the Canadian Imagination* (1971), identifies the

Canadian literary sensibility with "the sense of probing into the distance," with the "faraway look,"[15] Coetzee detects in poets and explorers in southern Africa a penetrating gaze. Thus, for the poet Sydney Clouts, "the organ of mastery" is the eye, just as for Wordsworth — Coetzee quotes from the *Prelude* — vision is "the most despotic of our senses."[16] For Jacobus, eyes are certainly his "organs of mastery," as in the wild, he experiences that "only the eyes have power . . . I become a spherical reflecting eye moving through wilderness and ingesting it . . . There is nothing from which my eye turns, I am all that I see" (V, 79). What we find in this passage is "the metaphor of an unimpeded excursion of the eye,"[17] through which the colonial self tries to accommodate to the unfamiliarity of the new context.

In Jacobus's description of himself as "a spherical reflecting eye," there is a clear allusion to the American Transcendentalist Ralph Waldo Emerson, who in his 1836 seminal essay "Nature," asserts that in the woods, he becomes "a transparent eye-ball; I am nothing; I see all."[18] For Emerson, the poet, thanks to his vision, is the indisputable owner of the landscape: "Miller owns this field, Locke that, and Manning the woodland beyond. But none of them owns the landscape. There is a property in the horizon which no man has but he *whose eye* can integrate all the parts, that is, the poet."[19] My point is that both White and Coetzee, in order to depict a colonizing and exploring consciousness that aims at possessing an alienating surrounding landscape, appeal to an aesthetic sensibility in which the struggle or communion between poetic consciousness and nature is central; namely, the sensibility of the Romantic and American Transcendentalist writers. The following acknowledgement by Coetzee to David Attwell in a 2003 interview seems to confirm this idea: "Wordsworth is a constant presence when I write about human beings and their relations to the natural world."[20]

Coetzee argues that in the poetry of Clouts, the eye, "the principal organ of penetration and takeover," achieves "entry into nature . . . after a hard struggle with the resistance of the world."[21] Jacobus and Voss experience the resistance of their surrounding world in different ways, which seem to be directly related to the geographical features of either the South African or the Australian land. This could be related to the fact that both Coetzee and White, in personal statements, have spoken of their special connection with a certain kind of landscape. In "Remembering Texas," Coetzee refers to the alienness with which he regarded the green hills of Texas and the Surrey downs; what he missed in them "seemed to be a certain emptiness, empty earth and empty sky, to which South Africa had accustomed [him]."[22] Similarly, in "The Prodigal Son" (1958), White explains that during the time he spent in the Middle East and in Greece in the 1940s, he felt a "terrible nostalgia of the desert landscapes."[23] In "The Narrative of Jacobus Coetzee," geographical conditioning is seen in the role played by stones, which highlight the aridity and impenetrability of the southwestern African terrain, and question Jacobus's exploring career, based on a "life of penetration": "How then, asked the stone, can the hammer-wielder who seeks to penetrate the heart of the universe be sure that there exist any interiors? Are they not perhaps fictions, these lures of interiors for rape which the universe uses to draw out its explorers?"[24]

Voss's confidence in his capacity for penetration and possession, on the other hand, is so intense that he feels even able to turn the hardness of stones into softness: "New hope convinced him that he would interpret the needs of all men, the souls of rock, even. In that more tender light the bare flesh of rocks was promisingly gentle" (V, 191). His "obsession," on the contrary, is "to overcome distance" (V, 167). In fact, after leaving Jildra, the last post of civilization, "his new kingdom" (V, 191) materializes as he begins to cover "the infinite distances of that dun country of which he was taking possession" (V, 190). However, as they begin to penetrate a "devilish country" (V, 336) with "winding gullies," "it was as if the whole landscape had been thrown up into great earthworks defending the distance" (V, 363). And whereas the European cavalcade finds it more and more difficult to advance, and half of the party actually decides to return, Aborigines are shown as moving across the hellish land with "the inexorability of confidence" (V, 363). At several points, the fact that Voss cannot overcome the distance that separates him from his Aboriginal guides, Dugald and Jackie, "the subjects of his new kingdom [who] preferred to keep their distance" (V, 191), is emphasized. Voss realizes that "their eyes were open, he could see, upon some great activity of their minds. If only he could have penetrated to that distance, he would have felt more satisfied" (V, 201). Black people are at home in the "infinite distances" that will finally defeat Voss: like his historical counterpart, Ludwig Leichhardt, he and his men will forever remain lost in them.

Just as Voss feels impotent, as he cannot penetrate into the Aborigines' mental eye, Jacobus Coetzee feels that his capacity of vision is threatened when he perceives in the Hottentots the same capacity of vision: the savage is "representative of that out there which my eye once enfolded and ingested and which now promises to enfold, ingest, and project me through itself" (D, 81). In the Afterword, S. J. Coetzee also pays attention to "the European eye" (D, 115). And although he acknowledges that "we can never be sure with respect to an indigenous phenomenon that indigenous eyes were not the first eyes laid on it" (D, 115–16), he does not ascribe to "indigenous eyes" the capacity to discover: "Who discovered this? or, to be more precise, Which European discovered this?" (D, 115). There is here a strong critique of *ocularcentrism*, the "vision-generated, vision-centered interpretation of knowledge, truth, and reality"[25] that has dominated Western culture, presented as linked with the colonial and imperial enterprise.

About Voss's eyes we know that they were "of that pale, pure blue" and "the clearer for this confirmation of vision by fact" (V, 210). Similarly, Jacobus tells himself that "the Hottentots knew nothing of penetration. For penetration you need blue eyes" (D, 97). However, immediately afterwards, he asserts, thus contradicting himself, that he has been "violated by the cackling heathen": "they had violated my privacy, all my privacies, from the privacy of my property to the privacy of my body," alluding to his humiliating illness and sojourn in the Nama village. In his final annihilation of it, his victory is only partial: "If the Hottentots comprise an immense world of delight, it is an impenetrable world, impenetrable to men like me, who must either skirt it, which is to evade our mission, or clear it out of the way" (D, 106). Since he has not managed to penetrate the Hottentot world — having, thus, failed in his exploring enterprise — he must obliterate it. But as he proceeds to its extermination, he feels that there was "no resistance to my power and no limit to its projection . . . I was undergoing nothing less than a failure of imagination before the void (D, 101–2).

For the Romantics, the biggest failure was the failure of the imagination. Voss will butt his head "at whatsoever darkness of earth" (V, 44), in order to follow a "strange, seemingly inconceivable idea" (V, 44); an "Idea" that "was not possible really." For him, "the future of great areas of sand is a purely metaphysical one" (V, 62). Jacobus's final deed is a victory in physical terms, but a defeat in metaphysical terms. His power needs "resistance" in order to assert itself; as his imaginative penetrating acts encounter a "void," there is no content to be penetrated and no depth to be reached. Probably the stone was right: the "interiors" that explorers seek are, after all, only "fictions." "The Narrative of Jacobus Coetzee" depicts the failure of European proprietorial consciousness in southern Africa, together with its devastating and violent consequences. As they remain trapped in a solipsistic disjuncture or gap between their outward and inward vision, and between their physical and metaphysical worlds, Jacobus and Voss are defeated in their craving for possession. In the contest between the land and the exploring European imagination, Australian desert distances and African impenetrable stoniness have finally won.

IN THE HEART OF THE COUNTRY AND *THE TREE OF MAN*: SETTLERS AND POSSESSION

In the Heart of the Country (1977) and *The Tree of Man* (1955) deal with a later stage in the colonial history of Coetzee's and White's respective countries, namely, the stage of the settling experience. *The Tree of Man* traces the story of three generations of a family of settler-farmers in the bush outside Sydney. If *Voss* is haunted by the impossibility of ever coming to fully possess the Australian land — "I believe I have begun to understand this great country, which we have been presumptuous enough to call *ours*" (V, 239), Laura Trevelyan asserts — the struggle for the possession of the land, both at a physical and spiritual level, is also central in *The Tree of Man*. The main actor in this struggle is Alan Parker, with whom the narrative begins, as he drives his cart into the solitude of the bush: "A cart drove between the two big stringybarks and stopped. These were the dominant trees in that part of the bush, rising above the involved scrub with the simplicity of true grandeur."[26] In these lines, and in the paragraphs that follow, the natural space is presented as characterized by a sacred quality that is somehow violated by this foreign human presence that will begin to appropriate the surrounding nature as it strikes a tree with an axe in order to make a fire: "that particular part of the bush has been made his by the entwining fire" (TM, 9). Stan Parker will build a shack in the clearing and bring his wife, Amy, to share his life with him, and the crucial stages of their life together will be marked by their having to come to terms with different natural phenomena and disasters, such as storms, floods, droughts and bushfires. In its portrayal of the struggle for existence through confrontation with the land, *The Tree of Man* deals with the quintessential Australian pioneer experience, endowed with a mythic and even epic quality. The last passage of the novel looks back to the first one, reaffirming the persistent presence of the trees: "In the end there are the trees" (TM, 479). But among the trees, we find a boy, Alan Parker's grandchild. As we watch him going back to the house where his grandfather has died, the continuity of the Parker genealogical line is affirmed, together with the enduring and engraved quality of human presence in this part of the Australian continent.

Magda, on the contrary, feels her presence and her life on the farm to be ephemeral and even phantasmagoric from a geographical point of view: they are "in the middle of nowhere," "on the road from no A to no B in the world, if such a fate is topologically possible."[27] And like Laura, she humbly acknowledges the impossibility of possession: "I am heir to a space of natal earth which my ancestors found good and fenced about. To the spur of desire we have only one response: to capture, to enclose, to hold. But how real is our possession? The flowers turn to dust, Hendrik uncouples and leaves, the land knows nothing of fences, the stones will be here when I have crumbled away" (IHC, 124). Stones — a reference that puts the emphasis again on the most purely geographical and even geological aspect of the surrounding context — with their enduring and resistant quality, contrast with the transient and evanescent quality of Magda's presence in the South African Karoo.

Alan Parker's physical relation with the surrounding natural world is endowed with a deeply spiritual and mysterious quality. As G. A. Wilkes has put it, he is "the mute visionary,"[28] and achieves his final illumination in the moment of his death, in which he becomes "mysteriously aware" (TM, 474) of a "large, triumphal scheme." "Grace descended on him" (TM, 475) and he understood that "One, and no other figure, is the answer of all sums" (TM, 477).

Grace and illumination, on the contrary, never arrive in the heart of the South African country, in which Magda's story is "a dull black blind stupid miserable story, ignorant of its meaning" (IHC, 5). Though she would like to turn his monologue into a dialogue by achieving communion/communication with the surrounding land and surrounding people — namely her servants, Hendrik and Klein-Anna — Magda fails in both attempts. The moment in which her yearning for Wordsworthian sympathy between self and landscape is most dramatically rendered takes place in passage 23, when she stands at the window, looking into the African night: "I stare out through a sheet of glass into a darkness that is complete, that lives in itself, bats, bushes, predators and all, that does not regard me, that is blind, that does not signify but merely is . . . There is no act I know of that will liberate me into the world. There is no act I know of that will bring the world into me" (IHC, 10). There is no dialogue whatsoever between Magda's interiority and the external world, to which she cannot attach any meaning. In

White Writing, Coetzee appeals again to geographical conditioning when he argues that European Romantic poets found contemplation and reflection mainly in bodies of still water, whose transparency made them "penetrable into [their] depth by the eye, the mind."[29] However, in the South African landscape, they found themselves facing a plateau with a near absence of surface water, so that the landscape appeared as "dead or sleeping or insentient — in Thoreau's figure, lacks an eye; . . . no dialogue can be carried on with it."[30] This is the kind of landscape faced by Magda, a landscape in which "the sky is merely clear, the earth merely dry, the rocks merely hard. What purgatory to live in this insentient universe where everything but me is merely itself!" (IHC, 73). It is a landscape of rocks and stones, of dryness and hardness, so that Magda cannot penetrate it, cannot "see into" it.

According to Bunn, "settler landscapes function as a sort of transitional symbolic space, enabling the establishment of a noncontradictory colonial presence" and "calling the ideologeme of domesticity into being."[31] This is certainly true of *The Tree of Man*, in which the domestic space created by Alan and Amy functions as the focal point of the whole novel. However, it is not the case in *In the Heart of the Country*, where the contradictions of colonial presence are never resolved, but rather accentuated, and where we find a most troubled and unusual domestic space, not only because the mother is absent and the father is killed, but also because the female protagonist is clearly posed against the conventional female character we would expect to find in an Afrikaner household, namely, "the good daughter humming the psalms as she bastes the Sunday roast in a Dutch kitchen" (IHC, 140). But what probably constitutes the most unsettling element in the domestic space is the presence of the African servants, Hendrik and Klein-Anna — first, through the affair of Magda's father with Anna, and then, through Magda's attempts to transform their relation of hierarchy into one of equality. And it is here that one of the main differences between Coetzee and White lies. Certainly, as Kerryn Goldsworthy has argued, in *The Tree of Man*, White uses "the trope of the innocent couple in an Antipodean Garden of Eden . . . at the expense of Australia's original inhabitants, virtually writing them out of the country's history."[32] On the other hand, in *In the Heart of the Country*, unequal power relations with the Hottentots are seen as a fundamental aspect of Afrikaner (anti)pastoral experience. At the end of *The Tree of Man*, the settler community is fully established, with no trace of the Aboriginal one. At the end of *In the Heart of the Country*, there is no community, but only Magda's solitary voice, lamenting that "the ghostly brown figures of the last people I knew crept away from me in the night" (IHC, 151).

Hence, if *In the Heart of the Country* is Coetzee's settler novel, it depicts a failing settler experience, or to put it another way, it deals with a most *un*settling settler experience. This relates to Coetzee's words in his 2003 interview with Attwell quoted above, in which he points to himself as "a late representative of the vast movement of European expansion that took place from the sixteenth century to the mid-twentieth century of the Christian era, a movement that more or less achieved its purpose of conquest and settlement in the Americas and Australasia, but failed totally in Asia and almost totally in Africa." This failure of

European settlement in Africa, with its "history of oppression behind it" — as Coetzee goes on to say — is related to a failure to "establish" itself in "this part of the world" and with "the people of that part of the world." This perception of European settlement in the African continent must be behind Coetzee's argument in *White Writing* about why the tradition of sublime landscape of Romantic Transcendentalism — in which landscape is "ingested," "absorbed and fixed by the expansive eye"[33] — has only emerged in a "tentative" and "stunted" way in South Africa. Given the link between landscape and nationalism, the American landscape was *seen*, by the Transcendentalists, as an expansive space where a personal and national destiny could triumphantly unfold, whereas a similar kind of nationalism did not "exist in South Africa before the 1930s, and then only as an adjunct of Afrikaner nationalism."[34]

Coetzee's narrative fully belongs to the tradition of the English-language South African novel, as characterized by Attwell. Attwell points out that whereas other settler-colonial literatures — first, the American; later, the Canadian and the Australian — embarked on a history of progressive independence from the metropolitan centre, both in terms of identity and language, in the case of English South African literature, this "regional settler- or postcolonial-white identity" has never been confidently affirmed, "since such constructions have been corrupted in South Africa by their proximity to, and possibly (at certain moments of history) reliance on, the project of apartheid."[35] Certainly, we do not find in the English South African novel — characterized by "provisionality" and "instability," as argued by Attwell — a celebration of settler-white identity similar to that we find in *The Tree of Man*. In fact, the novel usually considered as the founding South African literary text, Olive Schreiner's *The Story of an African Farm* (1883), actually inaugurates a white Southern African tradition in which, as analyzed by Stephen Gray, an "unyielding" landscape "dwarfs," "overwhelms" and "stunts" its inhabitants and "disallows them from achieving man's most sacred desire, the desire to take root in the land and belong."[36] It is interesting for our purposes that Schreiner brought, to South Africa and to her novel, her knowledge of Emerson's work. Her character, Waldo, a kind of "mute visionary" and spiritual seeker like Alan Parker, may even have been named after the American Transcendentalist, to whom he explicitly refers in the novel: "He heard the Transcendentalist's high answer."[37] The last scene of the novel shows him resting in the sunshine of the Karoo, precisely reflecting about the (im)possibility of *seeing into* nature: "There are only rare times when a man's soul can see Nature. So long as any passion holds its revel there, the eyes are holden that they should not see her."[38] Although he somehow anticipates the day in which "Nature will draw down her veil,"[39] full unveiling does not quite take place.

FLEAS, SPARROWS, BUTTERFLIES

The originality and value of Coetzee's literary production lies in his transformation of the sense of provisionality described in the previous section into a consciously chosen ethical position. And as it is the case of Magda, this provisionality is not only of a linguistic and narrative kind, but also consists of a geographical provisionality on the part of the South African person of European descent. If, as Coetzee seems to believe, European settlement has almost failed in South Africa, this implies that settlers are not actually *settlers*, since they have never fully settled. In the Introduction to *White Writing*, Coetzee points out that the poet of European ancestry "is seeking a dialogue with Africa, a reciprocity with Africa, that will allow him an identity better than that of visitor, stranger, transient."[40] But what Coetzee's novels actually ask is, what if we remain visitors? What if settlers do not regard themselves as settlers — with the associated connotations of rootedness, ownership and property — but as transients, as temporary guests?

Paradoxically, this *un*settling and transient identity goes hand in hand with a close attachment to the land, with what we could call a deep love toward the South African land. Again, it is Magda that best exemplifies this paradox. She is only "a ghost or a vapour floating at the intersection of a certain latitude and a certain longitude" (IHC, 19), but she is "corrupted to the bone with the beauty of this forsaken world" (IHC, 151). Her passionate passages about her deep love toward the Karoo and the farm will be echoed in *Boyhood* and *Summertime*. The boy of Coetzee's first memoir, though generally cold and detached, does not hesitate to use the word "love" to describe his feeling toward the familial farm, Voëlfontein: "there is no place on earth he loves more or can imagine loving more."[41] But this love does not entail a sense of property or possession. On the contrary, "the farm is not his home; he will never be more than a guest, an uneasy guest."[42]

The boy of *Boyhood* resolves the paradox between a loving attachment to the land and a "non-proprietorial consciousness" by carefully specifying that though he belongs to the farm, "the farm will never belong to him, he will never be more than a visitor: he accepts that . . . *I belong to the farm:* that is the furthest he is prepared to go."[43] On the contrary, Freek, a hired worker on the farm, "*belongs* here more securely than the Coetzees do — if not to Voëlfontein, then to the Karoo. The Karoo is Freek's country, his home; the Coetzees, drinking tea and gossiping on the farmhouse stoep, are like swallows, seasonal, here today, gone tomorrow, or even like sparrows, chirping, light-footed, short-lived."[44] Again, the same sense of transience and provisionality is attached to European presence in the Karoo, whereas as regards Hottentots, "not only do they come with the land, the land comes with them, is theirs, has always been."[45]

It is interesting that Elizabeth Costello uses a similar image of evanescence in order to characterize her presence in the Australian continent: "we are only fleas on Australia's backside, we late settlers."[46] Though Costello relates her assertion to the vastness of the Australian continent, the accent is certainly put on the insignificant and ephemeral nature of European (late) settlement in Australia. This is probably one reason why we do not find in *Elizabeth Costello* a true examination of Australian identity or of the relation between the self and the Australian land, and why the Australian land is patently absent. Most of the action either takes place in other countries, such as the United States, Holland or even South Africa; in the global, anonymous arena of airports, lecture halls and cruise ships; or even in a fully undetermined, dream-like, allegorical setting, such as that of the last lesson, "At the Gate."

In *Slow Man*, there is a stronger sense of place, especially as regards the city of Adelaide. However, what this novel is really about is the immigrant experience, shared by both Paul Rayment and Marijana, so that in its approach to the relation between the self and place, the emphasis falls not so much on the Australian context as on the ambivalent, multiple location occupied by the immigrant. Rayment, born in France, came to Australia, went back to Europe, only to return to Australia again: "*Is this where I belong?* I asked with each move. *Is this my true home?*"[47] As Costello tells him, "there are those whom I call the chthonic, the ones who stand with their feet planted in their native earth; and then there are the butterflies, creatures of light and air, temporary residents, alighting here, alighting there."[48] Like in *Boyhood*, an animal simile is used to convey a sense of light-footedness, evanescence and ephemerality, and though Costello seems to be applying this description to Rayment, it is to her that it truly applies, as "she has lighted on him, as a bee might alight on a flower or a wasp on a worm."[49] She is literally a "temporary resident," a guest in Rayment's home, and the novel hints at the possibility that she probably has no home but that of the characters she visits. When at the end of the novel, Rayment definitely closes the door of his home to her, she complains, "but what am I going to do without you?"[50] The question implicit in her complaint is, "but where am I going now?" As this novel depicts it, the writer has no geographical attachments apart from those derived from her literary activity.

Finally, in *Diary of a Bad Year*, there are hardly any glimpses of the world outside Sydenham Towers, where JC lives, and of the surrounding city of Sydney. Though one important theme of the book is the position of the writer in the contemporary world, and in spite of some specific references to the Australian nation, there is not at any moment an attempt to engage with the Australian context at a particular, geographically determined level. In *Diary*, the writer's geographical attachments are mostly limited to his private sphere. In these three novels, then, for different reasons and in different ways, the writer's relation to the surrounding national and geographical context tends to be rather neutral and unemotional, and at the far end from any engraved, enrooted position.[51]

And then came *Summertime*, in which, from the very first line, the question is John's inability to distance himself from the South African land and his full exposure to the atrocities being committed there: "So this is what he has come back to! Yet where in the world can one hide where one will not feel soiled? Would he feel any cleaner in the snows of Sweden, reading at a distance about his people and their latest pranks?"[52] And the relation between John and the South African soil is certainly going to be depicted as oscillating between the two poles already discussed: on the one hand, a feeling of deep attachment and love toward the land — again, the familial farm and the Karoo — and on the other hand, a sense of geographical provisionality, and even illegitimacy. It is the first feeling that accounts for the special relationship he and her cousin Margot share: "a love of this farm, this *kontrei*, this karoo."[53] They "feel blessed," as "to him and to her it was granted to spend their childhood summers in a sacred place."[54] It is the second "attitude toward South Africa" that he has in common with his supposed colleague at the University of Cape Town, Martin: "our presence there was legal but illegitimate . . . Our presence was grounded in a crime, namely colonial conquest, perpetuated by apartheid. Whatever the opposite of native or rooted, that was what we felt ourselves to. We thought of ourselves as sojourners, temporary residents."[55]

Hence, in the light of the evolution of his fiction, a statement Coetzee made in a 1984 interview has proved to be quite valid: "I do believe that people can only be in love with one landscape in their lifetime. One can appreciate and enjoy many geographies, but there is only one that one feels in one's bones. And I certainly know from experience that I don't respond to Europe or the United States in the same way as I do to South Africa."[56] Certainly, after moving to Australia, this was his answer — in an interview made to Random House — when asked about the possibility of him writing about the Australian landscape: "I moved there too late in life to have an understanding of that landscape."[57] His immediately previous statement had been that he had no lingering desire to write about the South African landscape, but perhaps his situation is similar to that of his fictional persona, John, in *Summertime*: no matter how far he goes, the South African soil will come to him. We may still wait for J. M. Coetzee to fully engage with the Australian land. However, as he has said, perhaps it is already "too late."

NOTES

This essay is part of a research project funded by the Spanish Ministry of Science and Innovation (ref. FFI2009-13244), whose support is gratefully acknowledged.

1 J. M. Coetzee, *White Writing: On the Culture of Letters in South Africa* (New Haven: Yale University Press, 1988), 10.
2 Sarah Nuttall, "Flatness and Fantasy: Representations of the land in two recent South African novels," in *Text, Theory, Space: Land, Literature and History in South Africa and Australia*, eds. Kate Darian-Smith, Liz Gunner and Sarah Nuttall (London: Routledge, 1996), 219.
3 Darian-Smith, Gunner and Nuttall, *Text, Theory, Space*, 1.
4 Glenn Hooper, ed., *Landscape and Empire, 1720–2000* (Farnham, Surrey: Ashgate, 2005), 1, 4.
5 J. M. Coetzee, "The Great South African Novel," *Leadership SA* 4 (1983): 79.
6 J. M. Coetzee, "Homage," *Threepenny Review* 53 (Spring 1993): 7, my emphasis.
7 White refers to the early conception of *Voss* in these terms in "The Prodigal Son" (1958).
8 Patrick White, *Voss* (London: Vintage, 1994; 1957), 35. Hereafter abbreviated as V.
9 Mark Williams, *Patrick White* (London: Macmillan, 1993), 69.
10 From a different perspective, Sue Rowley makes an interesting analysis of the role of imagination and creativity in the formation of Australian national identity through the myth of the journeying bushman: "Imagination, Madness and Nation in Australian Bush Mythology," in *Text, Theory, Space*, 131–44.

11 The epigraphs of other novels by White, *Riders in the Chariot* (1961) and *The Vivisector* (1970), are taken from William Blake. As Michael Griffith has argued, White's "work as a whole is suffused with references to Blake": "William Blake and the Post-colonial Imagination in Australia," in *Literary Canons and Religions Identity*, eds. Erik Borgman, Bart Philipsen and Lea Verstricht (Farnham: Ashgate, 2004), 129.
12 Northrop Frye, *Fearful Symmetry: A Study of William Blake* (Princeton: Princeton University Press, 1969; 1947), 21.
13 Coetzee, *White Writing*, 165, 167.
14 Coetzee, *White Writing*, 168.
15 Northrop Frye, *The Bush Garden: Essays on the Canadian Imagination* (Concord: Anansi, 1995; 1971), 224, 225.
16 Coetzee, *White Writing*, 172.
17 David Bunn, "'Our Wattled Cot': Mercantile and Domestic Space in Thomas Pringle's African Landcapes," in *Landscape and Power*, ed. W. J. T. Mitchell (2nd ed. Chicago: University of Chicago Press, 2002), 140.
18 Ralph Waldo Emerson, *Nature* (Boston: Beacon Press, 1985; 1836), 13.
19 Emerson, *Nature*, 11, my emphasis.
20 J. M. Coetzee and David Attwell, "An Exclusive Interview with J. M. Coetzee," *Dagens Nyeter* (8 December 2003), www.dn.se/kultur-noje/an-exclusive-interview-with-j-m-coetzee-1.227254 (accessed 13 October 2009).
21 Coetzee, *White Writing*, 172.
22 J. M. Coetzee, "Remembering Texas," in *Doubling the Point: Essays and Interviews*, ed. David Attwell (Cambridge: Harvard University Press, 1992), 52.
23 Patrick White, "The Prodigal Son" (1958), http://arts.abc.net.au/white/titles/other/whitespeaks.html (accessed 3 November 2008).
24 J. M. Coetzee, *Dusklands* (London: Vintage, 2004; 1974), 81, 78. Hereafter abbreviated as D.
25 David Michael Levin, ed., *Modernity and the Hegemony of Vision* (Berkeley: University of California Press, 1993), 2.
26 Patrick White, *The Tree of Man* (London: Vintage, 1994; 1955), 9. Hereafter abbreviated as TM.
27 J. M. Coetzee, *In the Heart of the Country* (London: Vintage, 2004; 1977), 150, 21. Hereafter abbreviated as IHC.
28 G. A. Wilkes, "Patrick White's *The Tree of Man*," in *Ten Essays on Patrick White*, ed. G. A. Wilkes (Sydney: Angus & Robertson, 1970), 27.
29 Coetzee, *White Writing*, 44.
30 Coetzee, *White Writing*, 44.
31 Bunn, "'Our Wattled Cot': Mercantile and Domestic Space in Thomas Pringle's African Landcapes," 143.
32 Kerryn Goldsworthy, "Fiction from 1900 to 1970," in *The Cambridge Companion to Australian Literature*, ed. Elizabeth Webby (Cambridge: Cambridge University Press, 2000), 111.
33 Coetzee, *White Writing*, 59, 60.
34 Coetzee, *White Writing*, 61.
35 David Attwell, "South African Literature in English," in *The Cambridge History of African and Caribbean Literature*, eds. F. Abiola Irele and Simon Gikandi, Vol. 2 (Cambridge: Cambridge University Press, 2004), 509.
36 Stephen Gray, *Southern African Literature: An Introduction* (New York: Barnes & Noble, 1979), 150, 151.
37 Olive Schreiner, *The Story of an African Farm* (Oxford: Oxford University Press, 1998; 1883), 258.
38 Schreiner, *The Story of an African Farm*, 267.
39 Schreiner, *The Story of an African Farm*, 268.
40 Coetzee, *White Writing*, 8.
41 J. M. Coetzee, *Boyhood: Scenes from Provincial Life* (London: Vintage, 1998; 1997), 79.
42 Coetzee, *Boyhood*, 79.
43 Coetzee, *Boyhood*, 96.

44 Coetzee, *Boyhood*, 87.
45 Coetzee, *Boyhood*, 62.
46 J. M. Coetzee, *Elizabeth Costello: Eight Lessons* (London: Secker & Warburg, 2003), 29.
47 J. M. Coetzee, *Slow Man* (London: Secker & Warburg, 2005), 192.
48 Coetzee, *Slow Man*, 198.
49 Coetzee, *Slow Man*, 238.
50 Coetzee, *Slow Man*, 263.
51 Costello's passionate speech, to the bench of judges, about the frogs of her childhood on the Dulgannon (*Elizabeth Costello*, 217–18) is the most notable exception to this.
52 J. M. Coetzee, *Summertime: Scenes from Provincial Life* (London: Harvill Secker, 2009), 4.
53 Coetzee, *Summertime*, 134.
54 Coetzee, *Summertime*, 132, 134.
55 Coetzee, *Summertime*, 209, 209–10.
56 J. M. Coetzee, "J. M. Coetzee: Interview, by Folke Rhedin," *Kunapipi* 6.1 (1984): 10.
57 J. M. Coetzee, "Author Interview," www.randomhouse.co.uk/readersgroup/readingguide.htm?command=Search&db=/catalog/main.txt&eqisbndata=0099526832#interview (accessed 22 October 2009).

PART TWO

FORM

CHAPTER 4

Coetzee's Opinions

Paul Patton

> *Final opinion about opinions.* — One should either conceal one's opinions or conceal oneself behind one's opinions. He who does otherwise does not know the ways of the world or belongs to the order of holy foolhardiness.
>
> Nietzsche, *Human, All Too Human*, II, 338

Diary of a Bad Year is in many ways a paradoxical book, as well as a book containing many paradoxes and aporias. It is divided into two parts, the first of which is called "Strong Opinions," without reference to any diary, while the second is called "Second Diary," without reference to any opinions. In fact there is both diary and opinion throughout the novel, if indeed it is a novel. As well as the strong opinions in Part One, Part Two contains what their author refers to as gentler or soft opinions. This immediately raises the question of the difference between these two kinds of opinion, if indeed they are different kinds. I propose to take this question as my guiding thread in reading *Diary* as a reflection upon the nature of opinions and our relationship to them. As implied by the citation above of opinion from *Human, All Too Human*, I take Nietzsche to be a guide to Coetzee's own final opinion about opinions.

Although the two series of strong and weak opinions make up the larger part of the text, *Diary* is not only a book of opinions. From the outset, the strong opinions are accompanied by another segment of continuous text on the bottom of the page, which has the form of a diary written by the author of the opinions on the page above. This text recounts the story of the author's encounter and subsequent relationship with a young woman, Anya, who lives in the same apartment building and whom he employs to transcribe and type the strong opinions being prepared for a German publisher. Then, from the beginning of Opinion 6 on page 25, this authorial voice is joined by that of Anya, who speaks in a third segment of continuous text on the page below the other two. She offers her own opinions about the author's strong opinions, while also recounting her relationship with the author and with her own partner, Alan. The story of the increasing entanglement of these three lives unfolds within the two narrative lines that accompany the strong and weak opinions until the end of the book.

One of the many uncertainties created by this structure is what kind of book this is and what is the relationship between the (two) successive series of opinions on top of the page and the (two) parallel narrative voices at the bottom. This is a first aporia at the heart of the book. On the one hand, we could read it as a novel in which the written opinions of the central character play a major role. However, this approach does not really do justice to the content of the opinions themselves or to the amount of space devoted to them. Alternatively, we could read it as a collection of miscellaneous opinions accompanied by a story which recounts the affective and interpersonal context of their composition. However, this approach does not do justice to the considerable amount of interplay between the content of the opinions and the content of the narrative that unfolds below. It is, after all, in response to a rupture in his developing relationship with Anya that the author resolves to begin writing "a second, gentler set of opinions."[1] Some of these take up topics suggested by Anya, such as birds or reminiscences of his erotic life. Others respond to comments she has made, such as the suggestion that English is not his "mother tongue" (DBY, 51). All of them are more intimate, less aimed at the world outside the self than the strong opinions which make up the first series. Even when they involve politics, as do many of the strong opinions in the first part of the book, it is from the more personal perspective of the emotional impact on the author. It does seem that these gentler opinions are in some way more real, more authentic than the strong opinions of the first part and, as such, opinions of a different kind.

Perhaps they are, although this partly depends on whose opinions we take them to be. This is a second aporia. Are they the opinions of the author of *Diary of a Bad Year*, J. M. Coetzee, or are they "merely" the opinions of the central character in a novel by Coetzee? This character was also a novelist and signs a letter to Anya with the initials "JC" (DBY, 123). From what we learn about him, both from his opinions and from the narrative, his life closely resembles that of Coetzee. He grew up and lived in South Africa before moving to Australia. He lived for periods of his life in France. He is a successful author, interested in music and mathematics. He is an admirer of Dostoevsky, and so on. At one point, the author of one of the second, gentler kind of opinions coincides with the author of the novel when he refers to "my novel *Waiting for the Barbarians*" (DBY, 171). This suggests that these are indeed all opinions of John Coetzee. However, there are other equally strong reasons to doubt that the author of the opinions in *Diary* is Coetzee. He is older, having been born in 1934, whereas Coetzee was born in 1940. He lives in Sydney rather than Adelaide. He says at one point that he hasn't written a novel in years, although the real Coetzee had published *Slow Man* just two years before.[2] It is true that taking this claim as evidence does beg the very question raised by *Diary* of what exactly constitutes a novel.

Just as the identity of the author of the hard and soft opinions is an irresolvable puzzle, so it seems that the choice between the two ways of reading *Diary* is genuinely undecidable. The answer to the question "is this a book of opinions or a novel?" can only be that it is neither one nor the other but both at once. Moreover, the tension between these two genres is part of the novelty and the charm of this generically ambiguous book. Coetzee's love of paradoxes and aporias is evident throughout *Diary*, from his discussion of Zeno's paradoxes to the paradox involved in quoting Kierkegaard's injunction "*Learn to speak without authority*" (DBY, 151, original emphasis), thereby turning him into an authority. There is also the textual aporia involved in recounting a dream that he wrote down, about which the author writes "What I did not record is the question that occurred to me in the act of writing: *Is she the one*?" (DBY, 59). However, all of these puzzles seem to be less important than the conflict of opinions, the presentation of the different kinds of opinions and the interplay between them.

The question of the relationship between opinions and those who hold them is raised quite early in the narrative. The author, whom Anya refers to as "Señor C," explains that he is engaged in writing his views on a range of topics, to be published in German along with similar views from five other eminent writers, in a book entitled (in English) *Strong Opinions*. He confesses to himself rather than to Anya that he accepted this commission willingly because it gave him "an opportunity to grumble in public, an opportunity to take magic revenge on the world for declining to conform to my fantasies" (DBY, 23). The role of fantasy in personal and interpersonal life is central to the narrative threads, from the author's account of his shame at the specificity of his sexual fantasy on seeing Anya (DBY, 8), to the argument between Anya and her partner Alan about the role of fantasy and opinions in economic life (DBY, 80). Opinions are also implicitly contrasted with dreams, as Señor C recounts a dream that he had about a young woman (Anya?) who will guide him to the gateway of death (DBY, 59). He later writes an opinion about a similar dream that then becomes an idea for a story (DBY, 157).

As well as being located alongside other products of the mind such as fantasies and dreams, opinions are classified into different kinds, as we have already seen with the contrast between strong and weak opinions. At one point, Señor C describes what he is writing as a set or a miscellany of "day by day opinions" (DBY, 54). These are contrasted with the more settled "passions and prejudices" out of which they grew (DBY, 125). This contrast is reflected in the choice that must be made between the two words in German that translate *opinion* in English: *Meinungen*, which are opinions subject to fluctuations of mood, and *Ansichten*, which are firmer and more reflective: "The *Meinungen* I held yesterday are not necessarily the *Meinungen* I hold today" (DBY, 129). Whereas Señor C prefers *Ansichten*, so that "Strong Opinions" in German becomes *Feste Ansichten*, the German editor is inclined to use *Meinungen* on the grounds that we cannot be sure "how firmly wedded each writer is to his opinions" (DBY, 131). This discussion of the appropriate German translation appears in the midst of Señor C's recounting the letter he wrote in an attempt to overcome the rupture in his relationship with Anya and to entice her to resume her secretarial work. He reflects on the way that his exchanges with her have begun to change, not so much his opinions as his opinion of those opinions (DBY, 136). It is at this point that he resolves to "put together a second, gentler set of opinions" (DBY, 145).

APHORISMS AND THE OUTSIDE

The uncertainty created by the structure of *Diary* affects not only the identity of the author of the opinions but also the very nature of the opinions presented: are these "real" or merely fictional opinions? Suppose for the moment that these are real opinions, in other words that they are truly the opinions of the author of *Diary*. As such, we could imagine them published without the narrative lines on the page below, in a book that would have the form of a series of opinions of varying lengths. Both the structure of such a book and the range of topics discussed — politics and political culture, universities; assorted moral phenomena such as shame, curse, apology and compassion; the body and its vicissitudes such as the erotic life and aging; the slaughter of animals; mathematics; language; music; famous individuals such as Tony Blair, Harold Pinter, J. S. Bach and Dostoevsky; writing; the afterlife, and so on — would closely resemble one of Friedrich Nietzsche's middle-period works, often described as works written in aphoristic style. *Human, All Too Human*, for example, included passages of varying lengths grouped under headings such as "The Religious Life," "From the Souls of Artists and Writers," "Tokens of Higher and Lower Culture," "A Glance at the State" and "Man Alone With Himself." Confronted with such a collection of aphorisms or opinions, the reader typically alternates between approbation and disapprobation, agreement and disagreement, depending on how these opinions stand in relation to his or her own opinions.

In a talk delivered at a conference on Nietzsche during the heyday of French anti-humanism, anti-authoritarianism and anti-authorialism, when the death of the subject and the death of the author were very much *à l'ordre du jour*, Gilles Deleuze sought to defend Nietzsche's aphoristic style as the appropriate vehicle for a new kind of thinking. He argued that it embodied a new kind of philosophy that did not rely on any kind of interiority, whether it be the consciousness of the author or the conceptual interiority of the book or system of thought. The essential feature of Nietzsche's aphorisms, he suggested, lay in their immediate relation with an outside, with forces outside the text. It is the always contingent and contextual relationship with this outside that determines the meaning of a given aphorism: "An aphorism is a play of forces, a state of forces which are always exterior to one another."[3]

This immediate relation to the outside is both a liberating feature but also a danger of this kind of nomadic thought. It liberates because it draws attention to the fact that the aphorism exists in an open-ended field of interpretative possibilities: to know what a given aphorism means becomes a matter of connecting it with a given force and, since the available forces will vary from one context to the next, the same aphorism may come to mean quite different things. The immediate relation of the aphorism to the outside is a danger because we cannot prevent it becoming connected with forces that are anathema to us or to our political sensibilities, passions or prejudices (fascism or anti-Semitism in Nietzsche's case). The danger arises because we have no control over the forces that might seize hold of a given opinion and give it a meaning. Coetzee or the author of the strong opinions points to this danger at the outset, when he admits that his preferred political philosophy, which he later describes as a kind of anti-political and pessimistic anarchism, "has acquired a bad name because all too often its roots lie in a reluctance to pay taxes" (DBY, 11). In other words, anti-political anarchism has been co-opted by an individualist libertarianism that defends the rights of property and the exploitation of one's fellow citizens but not the rights of all to a decent share in the wealth that is collectively produced.

There is also a converse danger, namely that the opinion in question might be so closely tied to particular historical forces or to a particular historical moment that its meaning fades as those forces and that moment pass into history. This is arguably the case with several of the strong opinions in *Diary* that are reflections on political events that took place in Australia and elsewhere between 12 September 2005 and 31 May 2006. For example, the suggestion that public prosecutors learned to see Al Qaida behind the most amateurish so-called terrorist groups as a result of being taught about the masters of suspicion in literature classes during the 1980s and 1990s seems very much the product of a particular moment of critical backlash against "theory" in American culture (DBY, 33). Similarly, with the passage of time, the question whether political action, rather than armed resistance or suicide, will suffice to save the honour of the American people from the events in Iraq and Guantanamo Bay seems like an overreaction (DBY, 40). Decisions of the US Supreme Court about the proposed military trials and the election of Barack Obama in 2007 suggest that the potential for a more measured political response to these events is not yet fully exhausted.

However, it is not clear that we should take these opinions at face value as the opinions of the author John Coetzee: *Diary* is not just a collection of aphorisms and opinions are not confined to the passages at the top of the page. Opinions are also expressed and recounted by the two narrative voices below: opinions of the putative author of the strong and weak opinions, but also the opinions of Anya and her partner, Alan, who is in many ways the antithesis of Señor C. He works in finance and makes a great deal of money. He reads the *Wall Street Journal* and *The Economist*, but also subscribes to magazines such as *The National Interest* and *Quadrant* (DBY, 84). He has opposing opinions on many of the things that Señor C writes about: paedophilia, the role of the state, politics and even mathematics. In between these two men is Anya, who also has opinions about some of Señor C's concerns, as well as her own opinions about the kinds of things that he chooses to write about, including politics, the erotic life, dishonour and honourable behaviour.

An important difference between *Diary* and a book of aphorisms is that the opinions expressed here are provided with a context internal to the book itself. The narratives on the page below serve to locate the explicit opinions in place and time and to re-insert them into the larger social field of conflicting opinions that make up a society at a given moment. As such, these opinions represent more than just the personal opinions of the characters that express them. They represent certain types. It belongs to the nature of opinions to gather us into groups according to what we believe or how we feel about something or other. It is no doubt that it is for this reason that, in *What is Philosophy?*, Deleuze describes opinions as functions linking particular perceptions of things to affections, and both of these to classes of subjects: "<faithfulness of dogs, detest: dog-haters >; <foul smell of cheese, love it: bon vivants>" etc.[4] Opinions follow this pattern whether they are banal everyday opinions or the more settled opinions in politics, philosophy, science and art that define certain tendencies: "<figurative painting, detest: modernists>; <literary genres, ironically admire: postmodernists>" etc. Deleuze is a philosophical critic of opinion. He regards it as the enemy of true thought and an obstacle to creativity in all its forms. For this reason, his conception of philosophy is defined in part by its struggle against opinion. Opinions serve to identify and reinforce existing types, whereas philosophy as the creation of concepts calls for new types or people yet to come.

Coetzee is also critical of opinions and their role in everyday life, although not for the same reasons as Deleuze. Having already confessed that the attraction of the German publisher's proposal lay in the opportunity it provided to vent his *ressentiment*, Señor C later questions his entitlement to express opinions on things about which he knows very little. In one of his gentler opinions entitled "On Having Thoughts," he asks himself whether he really qualifies as a thinker at all, "someone who has what can properly be called thoughts, about politics or about anything else" (DBY, 203). He goes on to equate thought with abstract thinking and, on this basis, offers the one original instance of such thinking that he can recall from "a lifetime's mental activity" (DBY, 204). This is the idea that the mathematical concept of a partially ordered set, in which not all the elements can be arranged in sequence on a given scale, might be a more useful way to think about moral phenomena than the kind of ordered-set thinking that underpins our everyday utilitarian intuitions. How does the death of one man atone for the Holocaust? What does it mean to say that six million deaths are worse than one death? "It is the question itself that is at fault" (DBY, 206). In other words, these are not phenomena that can be located on a fully ordered scale of moral significance.

It is Alan who offers the harshest assessment of Señor C's opinions, suggesting that these are, in the first instance, no more than a kind of devious courtship of Anya. In a sense they are, or at least they are the occasion of such a courtship. In the second instance, Alan suggests they are an attempt to attain guru status in Europe, where, in contrast to the plain English-speaking world, there is still a market for sages with white beards. This diagnosis of motives echoes Señor C's own admission that the will to power is in play in these opinions ("magic revenge"), even though they are the opinions of someone who distrusts politics in its entirety because it is an activity infected with "the drive to power" (DBY, 203). This admission refers to another paradox canvassed at the end of the very first strong opinion about politics and the origin of the state: "Why is it so hard to say anything about politics from outside politics? Why can there be no discourse about politics that is not itself political?" (DBY, 9).[5]

CONCEALMENT AND LIFE

All the concepts mentioned above, including ressentiment, magic revenge and the drive to power, are drawn from the philosophy of Nietzsche, which appears a number of times in *Diary*: Nietzsche is explicitly mentioned in the series of written opinions, such as the soft opinion "On Boredom," as well as in exchange of opinions between the characters lower down on the page. It is not unreasonable to think that he provides a clue to Coetzee's attitude towards opinions as this is expressed in *Diary* as a whole. This clue is implied in Nietzsche's "Final opinion about opinions," cited at the outset above: "One should either conceal one's opinions or conceal oneself behind one's opinions." This remark comes from paragraph 338 in volume 2 of *Human, All Too Human*, the title of which is *Assorted Opinions and Maxims* [*Vermischte Meinungen und Sprüche*]. Another of Nietzsche's *Meinungen* gives further detail as to why one should either conceal one's opinions or conceal oneself behind one's opinions:

> *Opinions.* — Most people are nothing and count for nothing until they have clad themselves in general convictions and public opinions — in accordance with the tailor's philosophy: clothes make the man. In regard to exceptional men, however, the saying should read: *only the wearer creates the costume* — here opinions cease from being public and become something other than masks, finery and camouflage.[6]

Concealment behind opinions is a recurrent theme in *Diary*. The relationship between Anya and Alan begins to fall apart because of their different responses to Señor C and his opinions. It breaks down completely once she becomes aware of Alan's plans to divert funds from his accounts. But the tensions in the relationship between Anya and Señor C also emerge through their different opinions of each other. He warns Anya against assuming that he is strongly attached to the opinions she is typing: she should realize that "the opinions that [she] happens to be typing do not necessarily come from my inmost depths" (DBY, 91). In turn, his own presumptions about her opinions, in particular about her own inmost feelings in relation to the rape she and a friend suffered at the hands of three American boys, are what lead to the rupture in their relationship that he resolves to repair by writing a second, gentler set of opinions. We might suppose that this second series of opinions is therefore more authentic, more genuine, than the first, but only if we take them to be the opinions of the fictional character Señor C and not Coetzee himself. As well as the reasons given earlier for distinguishing the two, it is clear that these opinions are neither original nor unique. The author's views about his relation to language, for example, which are a direct response to Anya's suggestion that English is not his mother tongue, echo Derrida's remarks about his own relation to the French language in *Monolingualism of the Other*.[7] The real parallels between Derrida's relation to French, which was his only language but nevertheless not his mother tongue since he is the child of an Algerian Jewish family brought up under colonial rule, and Coetzee's relation to English as the child of an Afrikaans-speaking family, are not the issue here. It is rather the sentiment that Señor C has of not being fully at home in English, the feeling that it is not really he who speaks even when he has said what he wanted to say. Derrida too makes this point in terms that are simultaneously particular and general: "My language, the only one I hear myself speak and agree to speak, is the language of the other."[8] So it is with all of us when we speak: we may indeed have only one language (if we are monolingual) but it is not our own. We are possessed by language as much as we possess it.

Perhaps the same is true of the opinions that make us who we are. Without these, as Nietzsche says, we are nothing, but at the same time they are not our own, at least not unless we belong to that exceptional class of individuals who really are the authors of their own opinions. When he was a younger man, Señor C aspired to be the kind of artist who stood apart from the masses and their opinions. But now he has come to the view that such a person could only produce art that lacks generosity and love and that fails to celebrate life (DBY, 170). Perhaps that is why, for all their limitations, their contradictions, their weaknesses and their dangers, Coetzee does not reject the opinions of Señor C, Anya or even Alan. The play of opinions is what makes each of them in their own way human, all too human; and in the end, *Diary* is a celebration of this life. It is, of course, a paradoxical celebration since it ends with Anya's promise to be the young woman of his dream who accompanies him at the moment of death, holds his hand and kisses him and whispers in his ear "sweet dreams, and flights of angels, and all the rest" (DBY, 227).[9] Her generosity towards the aging writer, his opinions and his anxiety about dying, like his own willingness to entertain kinder, gentler opinions in response to her dislike of his strong opinions, is in the end an affirmation of everyday life, the life that we share with animals but that is also expressed in our opinions, thoughts, fantasies and dreams.

NOTES

1 J. M. Coetzee, *Diary of a Bad Year* (London: Harvill Secker, 2007), 145. Hereafter abbreviated as DBY.

2 J. M. Coetzee, *Slow Man* (London: Secker &Warburg, 2005).

3 Gilles Deleuze, *Desert Islands and Other Texts (1953–1974)*, ed. David Lapoujade, trans. Michael Taormina (New York: Semiotext(e), 2004), 256.

4 Gilles Deleuze and Félix Guattari, *What is Philosophy?*, trans. Hugh Tomlinson and Graham Burchell (New York: Columbia University Press, 1994), 145.

5 I am grateful to Johan Geertsema for this point and for other helpful comments on an earlier version of this essay.

6 Friedrich Nietzsche, *Human, All Too Human: A Book for Free Spirits*, trans. R. J. Hollingdale (Cambridge: Cambridge University Press, 1986), 288.
7 Jacques Derrida, *Monolingualism of the Other, or, The Prosthesis of Origin*, trans. Patrick Mensah (Stanford, California: Stanford University Press, 1998).
8 Derrida, *Monolingualism of the Other*, 25.
9 Coetzee implicitly invokes Horatio in act 5, scene 2 of Shakespeare's *Hamlet, Prince of Denmark*: "Now cracks a noble heart. Good-night, sweet prince, / And flights of angels sing thee to thy rest" (5.2.338–9).

CHAPTER 5

Diary of a Bad Year

Parrhesia, Opinion and Novelistic Form

Julian Murphet

NOVEL, OPINION, TRUTH

> What I am in the process of putting together is strictly speaking not a book, I said, but a contribution to a book. The book itself is the brainchild of a publisher in Germany. Its title will be *Strong Opinions*. The plan is for six contributors from various countries to say their say on any subjects they choose, the more contentious the better. Six eminent writers pronounce on what is wrong with today's world.[1]

So speaks the narrator and chief actor of what is not strictly speaking a novel, but which hereby (and with the title of its opening section "Strong Opinions") highlights a reflexive relationship between its own modus operandi and the realm of published "opinions." Opinions will occupy the main stage of this "novel" — they will stand, numbered and titled, at the top of every page, and occupy at least one-third of each page — but they will not *name* it as they do the (strictly speaking non-) book for which they are being written. Rather, the book we hold is called a *diary*, and there will be not one but two diaries (of what we are led to believe is a bad year) vying for space at the bottom of most pages: the first (our narrator's) running consecutively from page 3 to page 124, and then resuming from page 137 to page 178; the second (belonging to his neighbour and amanuensis Anya) running from page 23 to page 124, and pages 129 through 178. The five-page break both diaries share allows a single opinion ("On the Afterlife") to stand alone as a culmination of the commissioned suite for the German publisher, before the "Second Diary" (something of a misnomer, since the first section was not called a diary at all) closes out the volume with a coda of softer and more personal notations.

Clearly, *Diary of a Bad Year* proposes a formal tension between its ostensible *raison d'être* (an "opportunity to grumble in public . . . to take magic revenge on the world for declining to conform to my fantasies," DBY, 22) and its formal mandate as a work of literary art. In order *not* to be what its narrator is officially writing — a series of pronouncements on "what is wrong with today's world," or a non-fictional *J'accuse* in the venerable tradition of Zola, Grelling and Greene — and to leaven its ponderous grumblings with the spirit of fiction, the "novel" runs an open interference with the polished articulation of its self-important opinions, an interference that takes the form of dual journals, written in ignorance of one another, but bound by the logic of an encounter to which each author (JC and Anya) remains more or less steadfast and faithful. This dualism is indicative. Opinions, immaculate and unbroken, enjoy a spatial hegemony here; but fictional journals, written in parallel and linked by a law of desire, run skirmishes in the underbrush and find ways of modifying the oracular tone of the opinions, if not their content as such.

And so it ever is, I want to argue now, with the novel as a form: working virtually exclusively with established opinions as its raw material, the novel has always had to find ways to "jam" this material from below, open it up via formal guerilla raids on the self-satisfied and complacent air of common sense, and expose it to the negative. Its art is the deformation of opinion, in the name of an elusive formal truth; but this vexed relationship has yet to be properly understood. For rather than recognize the novel's chief historical ingredient as "opinion," as I now advocate that we do, literary criticism has preferred either to generalize its condition into that far more indeterminate concept of "ideology," or defuse the philosophically spurious nature of the content into that productive but politically neutral concept of "discourse" — neither of which really grasps the dilemma in its acutest form.

Helpfully in this context, contemporary philosophy has returned to the old-fashioned distinction between philosophical truth and run-of-the-mill opinion. The distinction (which we recognize from Aristotle to Deleuze) is given particular emphasis by Alain Badiou, for whom truths (obscure, singular events of the highest significance in the domains of art, science, politics and love) are what shatter and render inoperable the edifice of opinion. Opinions, writes Badiou, are the "cement of sociality" — they are "the primary material of all *communication*," and in a vicious circle, communication is the medium of exchange of nothing other than opinions. "Opinions *without an ounce of truth* — or, indeed, of falsehood. Opinion is beneath the true and the false, precisely because its sole office is to be communicable. What arises from a truth-process, by contrast, cannot be communicated. Communication is suited only to opinions."[2] Truths enter the world in order to exact a costly fidelity from those rare subjects who recognize them as such; whereas opinions simply bind the social order of things together with an uncritical glue of communicability. The "ethic of a truth is absolutely opposed to opinion, and to ethics in general, which is itself nothing but a schema of opinion."[3] What happens when a truth enters to disturb the complacency of opinion is that it renders them dumb. A "truth transforms the codes of communication and changes the regime of opinions," writes Badiou. "Not that these opinions become 'true' (or false). They are not capable of truth, and a truth, in its eternal multiple-being, remains indifferent to opinions. But they become other. This means that formerly obvious judgments are no longer defensible, that others become necessary, that the means of communication change, and so on."[4]

One of the privileged regimes of thought through which truths may enter the world is that of art. Badiou has proposed, in his "inaesthetics," an entirely distinctive relationship between art and truth, a relationship at once singular and immanent: art is "rigorously coextensive with the truths that it generates," and these truths "are given nowhere else than in art . . . What art educates us for is therefore nothing apart from its own existence."[5] The truths that art makes possible call into doubt the very existence of art as such, given that "art," subject to the routine circulation of accepted conceptions, is constantly being colonized by opinions. Irreducible to any single work, a truth of art is an "(infinite) generic multiple of works" in which some artistic event is sworn fealty to through a series of "subject points" that press forward its procedure, and clear away the undergrowth of opinion that denies or repudiates these subject points as "not art."[6] Picasso's *Les demoiselles d'Avignon*, for instance, or some of Schoenberg's early twelve-tone piano pieces — these events are at first "indiscernible" since they have broken so radically from the dominant modes of comportment within their artistic traditions that they fail to appear as art at all, until a certain number of adherents and disciples begin to act as though, not only are these works of art, but they open up new continents for an infinite practice of subsequent fidelity. Each such event implies this: here is now a new truth, a truth *of this art*, an "art-truth"[7] that is irreducible to any other truth in any other domain (political, scientific, amorous), but which convokes a trans-historical network of subjects impelled to elaborate an entire aesthetic configuration out of its implications.

One such configuration, brought into being by the inaugural events of Rabelais and Cervantes, and continuing at least until Joyce and Beckett, is that of the novel ("a configuration for prose"[8]) — an infinite arc of variegated faithful subject points, each of them a node through which the configuration *thinks itself* as a condition of truth. But it must be said that, of all the "configurations" specific to art, the novel is that about which Badiou remains least convincing and least attuned, despite various protestations to the contrary, and significant attention to at least one prose writer (Beckett, who often enough modulates into a dramatist). Badiou approaches the literary field of artistic truth almost exclusively from the vantage point of "the Poem," and this entails some very particular stipulations with regard to what a truth-procedure might look like in literary art. The "evental" Poem is to be understood as "a truth of sensible presence lodged in rhythm and image but without the corporeal captation of rhythm and image."[9] And what this "sensible presence" is charged with doing is nothing less than deploying "literary resources" to present "the unpresentable void in language."[10]

When it comes to the novel, however, Badiou remains on sketchy ground to say the least, and there is perhaps a good reason for this. The novel is a unique art form, after all, precisely in its formal proximity to *opinion* as such; if truth is what "opposes" opinion, how might it do so here, when "opinion" more or less entirely constitutes the raw material of a novel's formal discipline? In the better materialist histories of the form, the "realist novel is understood to have offered a formula for shuttling between the literary and opinion or the news."[11] It would be possible to go further and maintain that the novel is the genre in which the literary emerges as such *only* as a formal shuttling between opinions or varieties of the news. Artistic prose is that which, whenever it attains to truth, deposes opinion without disposing of it as other than what it is; its relationship with opinion is genetic, and the "ethic" of its truth as a form consists in taking "what is communicable" (opinion as such) to its interior limit. Unlike "the Poem," which forcefully renames the world from the void of the say-able, the novel is trapped wholly within the names of the world; but it uses that prison-house as a vantage point for an immanent break with the world itself. Two indispensable theories of the form have argued just this, in altered terminological frameworks.

The Bakhtin circle's work on the novel, and on metalinguistics more generally, pioneered the thesis that all national languages are heteroglotic (composed of a rich variety of accented idiolects, jargons and phylogenetically diverse linguistic materials) and that the novel was the privileged social institution in which that heteroglossia was tested and pressed into service as a mechanism for thinking social relations immanently. For Bakhtin, the novel absorbs the linguistic diversity of a national language in order to expose its ideological fault-lines and antagonisms — not at the level of content, but very precisely as a matter of formal elaboration, as a novel modulates between opinionated idiolects and is radically sensitized to the retroactive pressure of "other tongues" on its narrative discourse. The most radical of the interventions of the Althusser group, on the other hand, was Pierre Macherey's insistence that the hermeneutic pursuit of positive cognitive material in the novel was doomed to failure, and that the only way to access what novels truly have to teach us is to attend to the surface of the text, to the clash and interplay of discourses in their frayed ideological vestments, and to what remains "unsaid" in the mutual friction of that heteroclite substance. "The necessity of the work is founded on the multiplicity of its meanings; to explain the work is to recognize and *differentiate* the principle of this diversity."[12] In place of a suppositious depth, we attend to the actual play of differences on the surface of the text: "rather than an ideal and illusory plenitude [a proper investigation] takes as its object that hollow speech which the work utters so discreetly; it measures the *distance* which separates the *various* meanings."[13]

The idea in both of these accounts is that novels teach *negatively*, not through what they explicitly say, but through their manner of saying other people's words, as a dynamic mashing of irreconcilable language games. What gives the novel its distinctive cognitive yield in modernity? For Macherey, it is the gaps and fissures in the novelistic substance, where the hand of the author has failed organically to suture these diverse ideological materials (opinions) into a coherent whole. For Bakhtin, it is the dialogic interpenetration of these materials themselves, constantly adjusting each to the pressures of the others. The form thinks, then, not by finding a fitting integument for a preconceived thesis, but by exposing linguistic and ideological antagonisms to the trials of attempted syntheses, that invariably fail: novels use opinions against themselves. Their unique artistic truth concerns, precisely, the deposition of opinions as incapable of truth; but that truth can only be felt negatively, in the minute intervals between opinions, and not in the positive form of some privileged discursive "truth" or "lesson" intruded into the play of novelistic language. A great novel is one whose form is so powerful that, without "saying" anything at all, it nevertheless dissolves the suture binding together an enclosed situation, and a social horizon, by dissociating that situation's network of opinions from itself.

PARRHESIA AND FORM

The underlying problem in all of this is that some authorial ideologies find it hard to resist the lure of opinions: not, to be sure, the "ordinary" opinions immanent to a state of affairs, but higher-order opinions, a currency of the Absolute that is not *true* in Badiou's sense of an event-to-come, but in the sense of a revealed wisdom, a doctrine or creed. In the usage of Michel Foucault, what this amounts to is a novelist's performance of *parrhesia*. It is interesting to note that Foucault derives his systematic treatment of the varieties of *parrhesia* in the ancient Greek city state (Athens) from a reading of Euripides' drama *Ion* — itself neither, of course, a novel nor one of the great tragedian's better dramas; arguably, indeed, a dramatic failure. This is important, since Foucault entirely bypasses the question of aesthetic truth (the truth embodied in the play's form) in order to concentrate exclusively on the presentation of truth-telling internal to the tragedy; i.e., as a matter of *content*. There he demonstrates that, in the dramatization of the internal requirements of democracy, Euripides explores three versions of *parrhesia*, one explicitly, and the others implicitly: "on the one hand, the explicitly named notion of political *parrhesia* [a way of exercising power by what is said and by truth-telling], and then, on the other, two schemas, two dotted outlines, if you like, of practices of truth which will later be called *parrhesia*: judicial *parrhesia* [the cry of the powerless against someone who misuses his own strength] and moral *parrhesia* [confessing the offense which weighs on one's conscience]."[14] Furthermore, Foucault goes on to argue that political *parrhesia*, the most important in the play and as an internal condition of democracy itself, concerns a certain superiority of character, which is "shared with others, but shared in the form of competition, rivalry, conflict, and duel. It is an agonistic structure. Even if it implies a status, I think *parrhesia* is connected much less to status than to a dynamic and a combat, a conflict."[15] Foucault then concludes that "What I think is associated with the game of *parrhesia* is speaking the truth in order to direct the city, in a position of superiority in which one is perpetually jousting with others."[16] This is what distinguishes *parrhesia* from Polybius's second fundamental characteristic of democracy, *isegoria*, according to which "everyone has the right to give his opinion," an equal right before the law, "constitutive of citizenship."[17] There can be no *parrhesia* without this basic right, but once again Foucault insists that it is not reducible to it. "It is not just the constitutional right to speak. It is an element which, within this necessary framework . . . allows a certain ascendancy of some over others. It is what allows some individuals to be among the foremost, and, addressing themselves to the others, to tell them . . . what they think is true . . . and thereby, by telling the truth, to persuade the people with good advice, and thus direct the city and take charge of it." It is "the free and, consequently, courageous activity of some who come forward, speak, and try to persuade and direct the others, with all the attendant risks."[18] Or as Coetzee's narrator caustically puts it, "Six eminent writers pronounce on what is wrong with today's world" (DBY, 20). The eminence is the point: "*éminences grises* who have clawed our way up the highest peak" (DBY, 21); and it is *parrhesia* which allows these "first among equals" to attain their eminence.

Foucault does not allow himself to think the meaning of this constitutive democratic tension between *isegoria* and *parrhesia* within the aesthetic dimension of the text he is scrutinizing; as so often with philosophical uses of literary texts, Foucault plunders *Ion* for its dramatically articulated notional contents. And indeed, in the context of our own argument, it appears that on this precise issue (the tension between opinions and truths) we stumble upon a sometimes poorly sutured fissure in the aesthetic substance of literary works, a fissure that modulates between a text's literary and extra-literary dimensions. Consider the paradoxes and contradictions at stake when a novelist, whose art (we have seen) consists in shaping current opinions into a form that punctures a hole in their complacent circulation, feels the need directly to intervene in the mindless mill of *isegoric* reproduction, and "courageously" "persuade the people with good advice." On the one hand, the literary text is obliged on these occasions of *parrhesic* outspokenness to divest itself of its very literariness and stand naked, exposed, as an attempt to "direct the city" — ceasing to be fiction, it modulates suddenly into truth-speaking. On the other hand, it is the very logic of novelistic discourse to surround all of its interpolated idiolects and voices in the invisible quotation marks of an irreducible irony, to "double-voice" its ideological materials, such that no one element can stand unmolested by the "dialogical imagination" of the form. The novel is constitutively resistant to the *parrhesic* impulse; it has an irresistible tendency to undermine the unmediated deposition of any authorial statement, by virtue of its compulsive relativization of all discourse. There are, accordingly, two ways for a novelist to embrace *parrhesia*. Either she speaks outside her art, in the public square (as Elizabeth Costello is presented as doing in her eponymous novel, and as JC tries to do in *Diary of a Bad Year*), or she puts what she has to say into her art. The first is a risky strategy for a writer of fictions, as JC reflects in his entry "On Harold Pinter" (who has just won the Nobel Prize for literature in the narrative): "When one speaks in one's own person — that is, not through one's art — to denounce some politician or other, using the rhetoric of the agora, one embarks on a contest which one is likely to lose because it takes place on ground where one's opponent is far more practised and adept" (DBY, 107). This kind of exposure, however, is less risky still than the alternative option, in which the "rhetoric of the agora" is modified and adapted to the novelistic context, and rendered immanent to a work of literary art.

The very type of this second option is of course Tolstoy. "During his later years," JC tells us, "Tolstoy was treated not only as a great author but as a authority on life, a wise man, a sage. His contemporary Walt Whitman endured a similar fate. But neither had much wisdom to offer: wisdom was not what they dealt in. They were poets above all; otherwise they were ordinary men with ordinary, fallible opinions" (DBY, 122). But Tolstoy decided, despite this evident fallibility and the ordinariness of his own opinions, to introduce them directly into his later work, dissolving in the event the very apparatus of realism he had earlier perfected. JC, in a later "gentle opinion," reflects particularly on this fact:

> The classic case is that of Tolstoy. No one is more alive to the real world than the young Leo Tolstoy, the Tolstoy of *War and Peace*. After *War and Peace*, if we follow the standard account, Tolstoy entered upon a long decline into didacticism that culminated in the aridity of the late fiction. Yet to the older Tolstoy the evolution must have seemed quite different. Far from declining, he must have felt, he was ridding himself of the shackles that had enslaved him to appearances, enabling him to face directly the one question that truly engaged his soul: how to live.
>
> (DBY, 155)

There are some crucial ambivalences here, whose history within Coetzee's thoughts on the matter we will soon explore: the accent on following "the standard account" implies a critical distancing from that accepted wisdom about a "long decline into didacticism"; while the psychological turn to what Tolstoy himself "must have felt" in the shift to outright "didacticism" in his fiction entails a sympathetic understanding of motivations ("he was ridding himself of the shackles that had enslaved him") that is really only available to the kind of narrator that Tolstoy himself tended to favour — but implies a not-so-subtle endorsement, if not on the part of Coetzee himself, then at least that of his avatar here.[19] That is, just where we may have expected a novelist of the stature of JC (author, we are told, of *Waiting for the Barbarians*, and cautious enough to be writing his own series of opinions for publication in a non-fiction collection) to counsel against the unchecked didactic impulse in a work of art, there is instead an omniscient narratorial rehabilitation of the *parrhesic* drive in fiction. And this rehabilitation has both an historical dimension and a contextual function that can be developed into an argument for the *Diary*'s unique status as a formal act in its own right; an act in need of proper evaluation.

COETZEE AND TOLSTOY

The historical dimension of the rehabilitation of the later Tolstoy's didacticism is easily addressed. I want to examine Coetzee's 1985 reading of Tolstoy's *The*

Kreutzer Sonata, in order to deduce from it an acute self-consciousness, in this author's theory of the novel, with regard to the unmediated intrusion of "authorial ideology" into the frame of a novelistic discourse. It is at one and the same time an inadmissible aesthetic lapse, according to the notoriously fussy and ascetic strictures of this late modernist; and a perfectly defensible gesture, in the hands of a "late stylist" such as Tolstoy, in whom Coetzee recognizes the hard-earned right to "cut to the chase" and simply get on with the task of teaching the revealed truth, more or less directly. This apparent contradiction, I want to suggest, has in fact driven the later fictions of Coetzee himself — the recent phase especially, from *Elizabeth Costello* through *Diary of a Bad Year* — whose increasingly strange formal devices strive to accommodate this very impatience with the usual mechanics of fictional "truth-telling" and accept a certain Tolstoyan *diktat* about revealed truth itself: that it is better, more urgent than artistic truth, and can and must be forced into the aesthetic domain, not via a Trojan horse or the sugar-coated pill of the Fancy, but immediately and without ambivalence. What Macherey calls "the Tolstoyan ideology, that foreign body in their midst"[20] is now driven explicitly into the van of his works without any need for subterfuge or circumlocution; it stands revealed like a burning bush of discourse consuming all the other elements around it.

Let us reprise, briefly, how Coetzee reproaches the later Tolstoy in his long 1985 essay, "Confession and Double Thoughts." He recounts for us the narrative situation of *The Kreutzer Sonata* (1889), in which one Pozdnyshev tells for some fellow travelers on a train journey the story of how he came to murder his wife. Coetzee reminds us that the character of Pozdnyshev is an "odd" one, with "his air of agitation, the funny little sounds he makes . . . his strange ideas about sex, and the history of violence behind him": so odd, indeed, that we expect ourselves to be reading "one of those books in which the speaker believes himself to be telling one truth while to us it slowly emerges that somehow another truth is being told."[21] But such, it would seem, is not the case. Although Coetzee finds it perfectly simple to deduce such a reading from the story (the Freudian story "of a man who sees the phallus everywhere," who "feels the anguish of the Oedipal child,"[22] and so on), this is to be categorically rejected, since Tolstoy himself spelled out very precisely what it was he meant by his puzzling story in an "Afterword" — namely, just exactly what Pozdnyshev had hectored his auditors about. "It is wrong for unmarried people to indulge in sexual intercourse. People should learn to live naturally and eat moderately . . . Contraception and the practice of intercourse during lactation should cease. Chastity is a state preferable to marriage."[23] Strong opinions indeed! As far as Coetzee is concerned, we know these are Tolstoy's opinions, not just because of the Afterword, but because "when one looks to the narrator for signs of a questioning attitude, one finds only silence."[24] Indeed, unlike Tolstoy's earlier excursions into the fraught terrain of fictionalized confessional ambivalence, "what one finds . . . in *The Kreutzer Sonata* is a lack of interest in the potential of the confessional form in favor of another, dogmatic notion of what it means to tell the truth."[25] There is, governing the story, an "authoritarian position," uncontested by the curiously silent intradiegetic narrator, according to which "whatever the will behind the confession may be . . . the truth transcends the will behind it."

> In other words, the position taken up in *The Kreutzer Sonata*, both in the framework of interpretation with which Tolstoy surrounds it and in its own lack of armament against other, unauthorized readings, other truths — a lack of armament that one must finally read as contemptuous, disregarding — is one of short-circuiting self-doubt and self-scrutiny in the name of an autonomous truth.[26]

Coetzee seems not to want to dwell on the operative irony whereby Tolstoy, by putting his "strong opinions" in the mouth of a convicted and rather disarrayed wife-murderer, clearly marks a *gap* between some putative oracular pronouncement of "the truth," and its mediation in this instance — the vessel of truth's disambiguation here, while it may not be harried by all the usual heroic "willingness to confront the worst in himself," nevertheless is given to the reader (and narrator for that matter) in such a way as to undermine its *parrhesia* from within. (We ought to ask ourselves here: what would be the status of Tolstoy's "Afterword" if its author had indicted it after killing the Countess Tolstoy?; and to remind ourselves of the fate of Althusser's later philosophy, following his murder of Hélène Legotien.) That is to say, the Afterword can by no means overcome the disjunction within the story between the "truth" and its characterological mediation; rather, it adds yet another dimension of irony to a text already steeped in it. Why cannot Coetzee appreciate this very obvious point? Why is it necessary for him, having toyed with his own Freudian "second reading," to reject its solicitations toward the dominion of irony, and insist instead upon the text's alleged "dogmatic notion of what it means to tell the truth," its "impatience with the novelistic motions that must be gone through before truth may emerge?"[27]

Much rests here on the concept of *confession* on which Coetzee's argument is turning: if the protagonist is not to be found wrestling in the coils of a confessional dialectic, the story goes, then his or her *parrhesia* is perforce univocal and direct — a simple conduit for the authorial ideology. But why should this be the case? Authors who indulge the dangerous frolic of giving themselves intradiegetic mouthpieces almost always do so, not by embroiling these figures in the confessional logic of Augustine and Rousseau, but by framing them within the plausible deniability of irony: Faulkner's Gavin Stevens, Roth's Zuckerman, and so on — these (who tend to speak in the accents and to affirm the ideological schemas of their authors) are figures not of confession, but of ironic authorial self-dramatization. Coetzee, as we shall see, has his reasons for wanting to foreclose this possibility; what is striking is that such a blind spot should emerge in an essay that turns on the distinctive approaches of Tolstoy and Dostoevsky toward the confessional knot. For it is within this comparative frame that Tolstoy must be reduced to the figure of anti-irony, allowing Dostoevsky fully to occupy the vacated terrain.

Diary of a Bad Year, which contains three sections that involve reflection on

Tolstoy, concludes with a section simply entitled "Dostoevsky," whose life story has of course served as the material for one of Coetzee's better novels; and for whom he evidently feels the greatest regard as a practicing novelist. But this regard can only be properly felt as long as it is held immediately against its counterpart and (one would think) antagonist. "And one is thankful to Mother Russia too," writes JC, "for setting before us with such indisputable certainty the standards toward which any serious novelist must toil, even if without the faintest chance of getting there: the standard of the master Tolstoy on the one hand and the standard of the master Dostoevsky on the other" (DBY, 177). The watchword Tolstoy, in the context both of our argument so far, and of the novel in which it is used here, contains within itself that testy "late style" in which (supposedly) an impatience with the usual mechanics of novelistic truth-disclosure "short-circuit[s] self-doubt and self-scrutiny in the name of an autonomous truth." Recall how, even as JC distances himself from the received wisdom of the "standard accounts" of Tolstoy's late style (which dismiss it as "grossly imperfect," and "obsessively unintelligent"[28]) he nonetheless endorses the main thrust of their charge against Tolstoy (as Coetzee himself had done, in 1985): that he subordinates the frivolity of aesthetic play to the seriousness of ethical didacticism *at the expense* of artistic truth. JC, we would be willing to speculate in this context, is a relative incarnation of play and aesthetic frivolity as against the heavy-handed manner in which Pozdnyshev embodies his own author's moral didactics. Or is he?

For now we come to the highest irony of all, which is the fact that *Diary of a Bad Year* makes use of just the sort of "mouthpiece" character who undergoes no particularly severe trial by crisis and confession, and whom the Coetzee of 1985 had seen fit to criticize rather fiercely in the later Tolstoy. JC himself joins the ranks of the Zuckermans and Stevenses and Pozdnyshevs whose job it is, here particularly obviously, to profess the "ordinary, fallible opinions" (DBY, 122) of their all-too "ordinary" authors. And in this case, when not acquitting himself of that time-worn function, JC is also to be caught enacting the very exasperation and impatience with fictional technique that a younger Coetzee had spotlighted in the older Tolstoy. "Days could be spent," he tells us about his first encounter with Anya, in the separate narrative track reserved for that material, "in devising felicitous coincidences to allow the brief exchange in the laundry room to be picked up elsewhere. But life is too short for plotting. So let me simply say that the second intersection of our paths took place in a public park . . ." (DBY, 11–12). Here, what begins by looking as though it is merely a psychological description of subjective fantasizing, quickly resolves itself into a flippant statement about technique, much like the exhausted narrative tone near the outset of *Elizabeth Costello*: "I cannot be bothered with complex bridging operations. Life is too short." This reluctance to go through with the charade chimes exactly with Tolstoy's supposed "disillusionment, [his] boredom with this particular mill for cranking truth out of lies."[29] So, on the one hand, JC is a Pozdnyshev figure whose apparent function it is to administer "the revealed truth," the world according to J. M. Coetzee without any of the earned authority of the tortured confessant, while on the other, as a narrator rather than an opinionator, he is precisely the kind of Tolstoyan "late stylist" for whom "the novelistic motions" that typify his chosen art form are crankily dismissed, belittled, in order that the bare "truth" of his strong opinions stand revealed, unimpeded by mere narrative conceit. Even as JC reads the "waning of creative power" in the later Tolstoy against the grain as "a liberation, a clearing of the mind to take on more important tasks" (DBY, 155), he is being not-so-subtly deflated by his very literal identification with the Tolstoyan "late stylistic" process whereby the "texture of their [older writers'] prose becomes thinner, their treatment of character and action more schematic" (DBY, 155). The question is: To what extent is this substantive flirtation with "the master Tolstoy" corrected or contested by a contrary pull in the direction of the other "master Dostoevsky"?

THE TWO MASTERS

Intriguingly, Tolstoy and Dostoevsky stand as the negative and positive poles respectively of Bakhtin's remarkable "polyphonic" theory of the novel developed in his landmark *Problems of Dostoevsky's Poetics* (1929), a work to which Coetzee refers approvingly in his "Confession" essay.[30] As distinct from the extraordinary richness and polyphony of Dostoevsky's dialogical art form, Tolstoy's stands high and aloof. "Tolstoy's world is monolithically monologic . . . Tolstoy's discourse and his monologically naïve point of view permeate everywhere, into all corners of the world and the soul, subjugating everything to its unity."[31] One late story "contains only *one cognitive subject*, all else being merely *objects* of its cognition."[32] Tolstoy, that is to say, is the literary artist par excellence in the late nineteenth century who persevered within the idiom of what Bakhtin called the "direct authorial word," the epic monoglossia of a finished and imperturbable worldview. "Whatever discourse types are introduced by the author-monologist, whatever their compositional distribution, the author's intentions and evaluations must dominate over all the others and must form a compact and unambiguous whole."[33] As for Dostoevsky:

> Dostoevsky's works astound us first of all by their extraordinary diversity of types and varieties of discourse . . . Clearly predominant is vari-directional double-voiced discourse, in particular internally dialogized discourse and the reflected discourse of another: hidden polemic, polemically colored confession, hidden dialogue. In Dostoevsky almost no word is without its intense sideward glance at another's word.[34]

The "strong opinions" of JC and the contents of Elizabeth Costello's lectures and lessons are the closest Coetzee has yet come to the importation of what Bakhtin calls "direct authorial discourse," "single-voiced discourse" of the monologic type into his novels; and, I would argue, are meant to be sensed and recognized as such. And yet they are *objectified*. Not only placed in the hands of characters and narrators about whom we come to learn disagreeable or at least alienating things

— self-deprecatory, intolerant and inhospitable characters in many ways — these "strong opinions" are also patently stylized as excessively "literary" by the standards of Coetzee's own typical style — degree-zero severe minimalism — and his utter distaste for flourish and colour. By these standards, this "direct authorial discourse" is already deformed, ever so slightly, from within, made minimally foreign, since it beats at a higher frequency and is red-shifted further along the stylistic colour band than what we have taken to be Coetzee's characteristic style.

These delicate matters of discrimination are of great importance in learning how to parse works such as these in which, as I want to suggest, the author wants to have his cake and eat it, wants to enact his Tolstoyan will to *parrhesia*, and yet partially retract it via the Dostoevskian compositional devices available to his elected form: dialogical decentrement and ironization. These blocks of prose, that we are virtually forced to take at first pass for the opinions of J. M. Coetzee, are dissociated almost imperceptibly from themselves, in order to attain to a barely recognizable second-order evaluation within the novelistic prose. They become what Bakhtin calls minimally "double-voiced," since they are obliquely dissonant, unequal to themselves, made "someone else's." We begin to understand that, in being set down in such a way, these opinions congeal into something else whilst remaining precisely what they are: eloquent and persuasive arguments, viable and often valid opinions — but for all that, flat and uninspired and non-artistic — *untrue*. Here, for instance, is a sample of the opinionated prose of JC:

> A few days ago I heard a performance of the Sibelius fifth symphony. As the closing bars approached, I experienced exactly the large, swelling emotion that the music was written to elicit. What would it have been like, I wondered, to be a Finn in the audience at the first performance of the symphony in Helsinki nearly a century ago, and feel that swell overtake one? The answer: one would have felt proud, proud that *one of us* could put together such sounds, proud that out of nothing we human beings can make such stuff. Contrast with that one's feelings of shame that *we, our people*, have made Guantanamo. Musical creation on the one hand, a machine for inflicting pain and humiliation on the other: the best and the worst that human beings are capable of.
> (DBY, 40, original emphasis)

Here are some familiar rhetorical features that run throughout the various opinions: the rhetorical question, rapidly (and redundantly) answered; banal anecdotal occasion; a loosely conscriptive subjunctive mood; repetition; brusque contrast, *a contrario*; the flight to polar extremes as a form of hyperbole. These features do little, in fact, to locate the opinion within a recognizably subjective dimension, and this despite the openly first-person pitch of the anecdote itself. Indeed, perhaps the first thing we need to say is that, precisely in their having been set down so firmly, these opinions begin to seem immanently *objective* — just precisely where they should seem subjective. The opinions give of the voices of "others" — *das Man*, in Heidegger's sense[35] — because, indeed, they are nothing but powerfully expressed common or garden-variety verities, with no clear markers of authorial "sincerity."

Nor are they capable of anything like an artistic truth. As Badiou says of opinions in general, this kind of expression is the glue of a social body, sentences that scarcely raise themselves above the level of an editorial, let alone to the sublime heights of Adorno's *Minima Moralia*. Or, as Paul Patton paraphrases Nietzsche elsewhere in this volume, "Without [opinions], as Nietzsche says, we are nothing, but at the same time they are not our own, at least not unless we belong to that exceptional class of individuals who really are the authors of their own opinions." The language of the "strong opinions" strives towards the status of that "exceptional class," but the subjective mood modulates imperceptibly into the objective, "*Dasein*" into "*das Man*." What looks as though it ought to be the occasion for a flight of political *parrhesia* has keeled over into the rudimentary form of *isegoria*: the freedom of all to speak their own opinions, provided nothing changes. The novel allows for this double reversal to take place, this immanent torsion between the subjective and the objective, not through anything as cogent as parody (the opinions are not parodied), but through a much more subtle and elusive stylistic mechanism in which we detect the shading of a "personal" conviction into a chattering of other people's words, a burbling liberal anonymity of the world's "left" opinion pages. There is an ideological antagonism at stake here, but it is a very curious antagonism in which the "authorial" word has no positive position as such to pit against the dimension of chattering generality it has discerned in its own midst; rather, it simply wishes, with great discretion, to locate that dimension and to ironize it gently, without jettisoning the "baby in the bathwater" that is the opinion itself.

But of course, this is not how the *Diary of a Bad Year* finally decides to subject its "strong opinions" to the Dostoevskian textual operations whereby "almost no word is without its intense sideward glance at another's word." For as every reader knows, it is not left to subtle and immanent stylistic nuances to deflect these opinions against themselves, but to the parallel tracks of (first) JC's own diaristic account of his flirtation with, employment of and eventual friendship with Anya; and (second) Anya's diaristic account of the same, including her often acerbic opinions on the portentous opinions she is employed to type up ("What he says about politics sends me to sleep," DBY, 31). It is thanks to the often quite elaborate, but always unsubtle, relationships between these three tracks of textual material (according to which, for instance, a word inscribed monologically in the "opinions" is taken up by Anya, critically or quizzically, and then re-appropriated by JC in his own diaristic sniping at Anya's appalling grasp of the language; and according to which, too, the entire "second, gentler set of opinions" at the end of the book is conceived and written as an appeasement of Anya's outrage at JC's insensitivity to her rape narrative, and explicitly takes up themes and hints offered by Anya throughout their relationship) that no single opinion of the Coetzee mouthpiece character is allowed to congeal into Tolstoyan monologism. That is to say, if, as Coetzee suggests, Pozdnyshev had not encountered sufficient resistance from his auditor-narrator adequately to destabilize his own will-to-truth, and if that *parrhesia* was as a result readily interpretable as Tolstoy's own *parrhesia*, then here Anya's wholesale resistance to JC's will-to-truth, expressed both in her own and in JC's narrative texts, prevents any such *parrhesic* impulse from rising out of the ashes of mere opinion.

> What has begun to change since I moved into the orbit of Anya is not my opinions themselves so much as my opinion of my opinions. As I read through what mere hours before she translated from a record of my speaking voice into 14-point type, there are flickering moments when I can see these hard opinions of mine through her eyes — see how alien and antiquated they may seem to a thoroughly modern Millie, like the bones of some extinct creature, half bird, half reptile, on the point of turning into stone. (DBY, 107–8)

What Dostoevsky is deployed to teach Tolstoy, then, is not so much the error of his opinions (although this is a temptation: "I should thoroughly revise my opinions, that is what I should do," DBY, 115), as the trick of discerning them as though they belonged to somebody else, to some *thing* else. By routing the opinions through the mill of novelistic deformation — a radical encounter with the word of the other — what happens is not that they lose their conviction, but that their authority is dismantled. After all, "the passions and prejudices out of which my opinions grew were laid down long before I first set eyes on Anya, and were now so strong — that is to say, so settled, so rigid — that aside from the odd word here and there there was no chance that refraction through her gaze could alter their angle" (DBY, 100–1); and yet if "what the great authors are masters of is authority" (DBY, 123), then there is no question that the refraction of JC's opinions in Anya's eyes has invalidated that vain ambition at least; with the consequence that JC is no Tolstoy, no "great author."

ALLEGORY

The whole elaborate but brittle formal apparatus of the novel stands as a working allegory of how the *parrhesic*, Tolstoyan impulse is to be outflanked by a Dostevskian polyglossia and irony today — not immanently, but extrinsically. That is to say, the polyglossic dimension is indeed immanent in a style that (as we have seen) too readily betrays its innermost constitution by the opinionated prattle of *das Man*, but it is as if Coetzee can no longer trust his reader to make this kind of fine-grained distinction. Instead, that whole operation is held in check, ironized by an adjacent pair of segregated narrative tracks, in which not *parrhesia* but the *erotic encounter* orchestrates the shadow of an event. But it is perfectly just to complain that it does not, in that sense, amount to a "form" at all, since, as it stands, this allegory cannot not itself be the solution it "stands (in) for." It is offered as a rather too convenient hypothetical schema in which, for instance, the opinions of a quietist anarchist might come before the eyes of the very enemy those opinions want so reticently to name — a free-marketeer merchant banker, Allen, god-child of Thatcher, Reagan and Howard. The mediations that allow for this unlikely traversal of a profound schism in the social (from intellectual dissident to ruling-class lackey) are, principally, that of the foreign-born woman's body, irradiated by both men's desire, and secondarily the network of media through which JC's opinions are distributed in his clumsy courtship of that woman through the old-fashioned agency of the word. As his opinions leave his mouth to be imprinted as electromagnetic signals on his tape recorder, and thence under Anya's hand to be tapped out onto the keyboard where the data will be coded by software in Allen's computer, remediated as print on his monitor, and then printed as inked letters on his printer, JC's "words" are thoroughly dissociated from the "Enlightenment" discourse network under whose lingering ideological shadow they are conceived (remember that the publisher of the edited collection of *Strong Opinions* is a German firm). What the erotic encounter between Anya and JC enables is a *formal* transcendence of the discourse network in which his opinions, as a firm set of repeatable contents, are hopelessly ensnared. The encounter jolts his opinions out of the superannuated protocols of twentieth-century book publication (at least initially), and re-disposes them in such a way that they traverse the "Other" they most want to engage: the erotic neighbour, and, with her, the enemy neighbour. It is of course a sheer fantasy of form, a fantasy as transparent and futile in its Utopian aspirations as the medieval romances out of which the novel first heroically strove for emancipation, which is one reason why the form so crudely devolves into a tripartite schema of discrete layers.

In its "transcendence" of the old discourse network of the book, and of literature, this allegorical operation signals an abandonment of the old-style close reading, according to which the "opinions" might already be read for their novelistic self-distanciations. In its place is put a very obvious, and spatially distributed, parallel tracking of a *new* discourse network that is no less dialogical than the old one. The three textual bands are literally materialized as such, in a stratified page-view that emanates clear allegorical signals: overweening opinionated universalism conceived on "the ground floor" at the top of the page, and the seedy machinations of a penthouse-dweller at the bottom, while in between, the very stuff of desire and the erotic event is squeezed. Thus, ideas are apparently "free-floating" and detached, while narrative itself is fractured and internally differentiated into two strands: masculine and feminine, proving that sexual difference is ineluctable and intractable (multiple ironies proliferate in the interval between bands two and three). As we read, we note that there is a feedback mechanism from the narrative (of desire) and Anya's journal from below, and into the ideas proper. The Dostoevskian impulse infects the Tolstoyan *idées fixes*, breeds interference and temperance, and precipitates the "gentler opinions" that finish the book. This is the novelist's nod to the power of form over the fixity of ideas; but it is nevertheless felt as artificial and forced, and is not even remotely "novelistic," in the way it separates out into parallel dimensions what ought (by the strictures of a Bakhtinian or a Machereyan prescription) to be imperfectly amalgamated on the *same* textual plane. In this sequestered textual space, laundering the inflexible "opinions" in the eye of the Other merely "softens" them, deflects them from the abiding political urgency that impels the first suite of *parrhesic* outcries, and yet leaves those outcries ironically in place. In this new discourse network of computerized relays and the threat of an implanted "spyware," the novel breaks down into a set of discrete signals, orchestrated by a Dostoevskian hand, but incapable of surmounting the polyglossia it conjures on its own terms. In that sense precisely, it could be argued that *Diary of a Bad Year* does not amount to an artistic truth, as Badiou would have it; instead, it invokes an *erotic* truth procedure (the encounter of JC and Anya), and abandons the irreconcilable opinions of its "content" to that extrinsic truth procedure, rather than use those opinions *against themselves*. It is not, in that sense, a novel as such, but a working hypothesis for what will follow the novel: a rhetorical form in which an earned *parrhesia* makes room for the routine circulation of *isegoria*, and for the "democratic" potential of that common-touch corrective to the pretentions of those who would "direct the state." As such, it is not yet, and perhaps cannot be, an art form capable of its own, aesthetic truth.

A character in the fictionalized biography *Summertime* puts the case I am making very bluntly, as if to say that Coetzee knows exactly what is taking place in his most recent phase of post-novelistic thinking. It is an angry accusation that poses the aesthetic stakes in their least palatable form:

> After *Disgrace* I lost interest. In general I would say that his work lacks ambition. The control of the elements is too tight. Nowhere do you get a feeling of a writer deforming his medium in order to say what has never been said before, which is to me the mark of great writing. Too cool, too neat, I would say. Too easy.[36]

What is lacking in *Diary of a Bad Year*, for all its superficial deformation of the novelistic page, is a truly dialogical deformation of the discourses of which it is constituted. Its allegory is too neat, and it lacks the mark of great writing, even as it lacks the authority for which JC continues to venerate Tolstoy. Perhaps one could simply say that it is a work without truth, *parrhesic* or artistic. It is, arguably, a dead end, less than the sum of the opinions that give it form.

Another possibility suggests itself, however. And that is that, today, in what is, according to the formal proposition of the book itself, a post-novelistic horizon, the pretense of persevering within the novel form is itself the grossest kind of deception on a public for whom the routine consumption of "novels" is indistinguishable from the routine consumption of opinions themselves. There is an implacable logic about a series of books, like that running from *Elizabeth Costello* to *Diary of a Bad Year*, which fail very precisely to be novels, and which elevate that failure into their *raison d'etre* as texts in the first place. That logic has to do with a resolute fidelity to the novel as a form historically capable of truth, even if it means that, here and now, the greatest task is to dismantle that capacity from within: to disarm the novel of its history of truth, to subtract its truth-procedure from its post-mortem enactments. The novel, having fallen under the wheels of opinion to the point where its truth has all but bled its last into the digital matrix, is perhaps awaiting its rebirth in the new media; until then, Coetzee's recent anti-novels attest to a bitter negation all the more disturbing for being mistakable as capitulations to the power of opinions as such.

NOTES

1 J. M. Coetzee, *Diary of a Bad Year* (Melbourne: Text, 2008), 20. Hereafter abbreviated as DBY.
2 Alain Badiou, *Ethics: An Essay on the Understanding of Evil*, trans. Peter Hallward (London and New York: Verso, 2001), 50.
3 Badiou, *Ethics*, 52.
4 Badiou, *Ethics*, 80.
5 Alain Badiou, *Handbook of Inaesthetics*, trans. Alberto Toscano (Stanford, California: Stanford University Press, 2005), 9.
6 Badiou, *Handbook of Inaesthetics*, 12.
7 Badiou, *Handbook of Inaesthetics*, 13.
8 Badiou, *Handbook of Inaesthetics*, 13.
9 Alain Badiou, *Conditions*, trans. Steven Cocoran (London and New York: Continuum, 2008), 44.
10 Badiou, *Conditions*, 45.
11 The phrasing is Patricia Ticineto Clough's, in her "The Case of Sociology: Governmentality and Methodology," *Critical Inquiry* (Summer 2010) 36.4: 634. But she is drawing of course on Michael McKeon's *The Origins of the English Novel: 1600–1740* (Baltimore: Johns Hopkins University Press, 1987).
12 Pierre Macherey, *A Theory of Literary Production*, trans. Geoffrey Wall (London and New York: Routledge Kegan Paul, 1985), 78.
13 Macherey, *A Theory of Literary Production*, 78–9.
14 Michel Foucault, *The Government of Self and Others: Lectures at the Collège de France 1982–1983*, ed. Frédéric Gros, trans. Graham Burchell (Houndmills: Palgrave Macmillan, 2010), 154.
15 Foucault, *The Government of Self and Others*, 156.
16 Foucault, *The Government of Self and Others*, 157.
17 Foucault, *The Government of Self and Others*, 157.
18 Foucault, *The Government of Self and Others*, 157–8.
19 It is worth pointing out that, far from being perceived as a dismissible quirk by the mass of his contemporary readers, this drift into didacticism was if anything understood as a direct embrace of the masses who read him. Lenin himself wrote of "an epoch that could give rise to Tolstoy's teachings and in which they were inevitable, not as something individual, not as a caprice or a fad, but as the ideology of the conditions of life under which millions and millions actually found themselves for a certain period of time" (Macherey, *A Theory of Literary Production*, 115). Needless to say, Coetzee does not register this unique status of Tolstoy's teachings, but prefers with most critics to dismiss them as merely a personal hobby-horse.
20 Macherey, *A Theory of Literary Production*, 124.
21 J. M. Coetzee, "Confession and Double Thoughts," in *Doubling the Point: Essays and Interviews*, ed. David Attwell (Cambridge: Harvard University Press, 1992), 253–4.
22 Coetzee, "Confession and Double Thoughts," 257.
23 Coetzee, "Confession and Double Thoughts," 255.
24 Coetzee, "Confession and Double Thoughts," 258.
25 Coetzee, "Confession and Double Thoughts," 262.
26 Coetzee, "Confession and Double Thoughts," 263.
27 Coetzee, "Confession and Double Thoughts," 293.
28 Coetzee, "Confession and Double Thoughts," 258.

29 Coetzee, "Confession and Double Thoughts," 293.
30 Coetzee, "Confession and Double Thoughts," 422, n. 40.
31 Mikhail Bakhtin, *Problems of Dostoevsky's Poetics*, trans. Caryl Emerson (Minneapolis: University of Minnesota Press, 1984), 56.
32 Bakhtin, *Problems of Doestoevsky's Poetics*, 71.
33 Bakhtin, *Problems of Doestoevsky's Poetics*, 203.
34 Bakhtin, *Problems of Doestoevsky's Poetics*, 203.
35 "Everyone is the other, and no one is himself. The 'they,' which supplies the answer to the question of the 'who' of everyday Dasein, is the 'nobody' to whom every Dasein has already surrendered itself in Being-among-one-other." Martin Heidegger, *Being and Time*, I, IV, 27: H128, trans. John Macquarie and Edward Robinson (Oxford: Basil Blackwell, 1962), 165–6.
36 J. M. Coetzee, *Summertime* (London: Harvill Secker, 2009), 242.

CHAPTER 6

Realism and Intertextuality in Coetzee's *Foe*

Anthony Uhlmann

Much critical attention has been paid to the relationship between the works, in particular the early works, of J. M. Coetzee, and the mode of allegory. Indeed, this has been such an important tendency in studies of Coetzee's aesthetic method that Derek Attridge has recently developed a strong argument against this approach.[1] While it is clear that works such as *Dusklands, The Life and Times of Michael K, Waiting for the Barbarians* and others in Coetzee's oeuvre, have apparently allegorical overtones, it is equally true that Coetzee has taken a strong interest in "realism" and the potentials of this mode, and that this interest has informed much of his work. If Coetzee makes use of both "allegorical" and "realist" modes to create meaning in his works, a third approach which both informs and deforms the other modes is intertextuality. That is, for example, in works such as *Foe* (where he situates his own work in relation to Daniel Defoe) and *The Master of Petersburg* (where he refers to Dostoevsky), Coetzee interacts in fundamental ways with the works of other writers. A similar, though much more elliptical relation might be seen in *Diary of a Bad Year,* where the Section title "Strong Opinions" seems to ask us to consider Coetzee's practice as being in some way related to that of Vladimir Nabokov, who famously uses this title for a somewhat stage-managed book of interviews. These references in turn enter into dialogue with Coetzee's methods, and ask us to consider how the notions of artistic practice which surround the works of these writers might be usefully related to his own methods. Indeed, the effect of this relation is to interrogate and explore the nature of the other modes and the limits and potentials of literary form for both producing and questioning meaning.

Here I will argue that a number of literary practices: allegory, realism, symbolism, negative theology and intertextuality are isomorphic in structure, as each involve the generation of meaning through the staged reflection of one surface with another: what I will call below the interaction of a Sign A and a Sign B. I will begin by outlining the manner in which, following Paul de Man, allegory and symbolism might be understood to operate, and link this to an understanding of negative theology, before turning to Coetzee's use of realism and intertextuality.

ALLEGORY, SYMBOLISM, AND NEGATIVE THEOLOGY: MEANING THROUGH REFLECTION

While literature builds upon the function of the relation between signs that generates all meaning, it also develops processes that allow for the deepening of this sense of meaning. It does this by amplifying the various relations between signs, on the one hand, and, paradoxically, by making the manner in which they interact unstable. Yet it further tends to emphasize how one point of relation (a Sign A) carries meaning which is modified or rendered unstable by its associations with a second point of relation (a Sign B). This is apparent, for example, in the use of the symbol (the heart, A, as a symbol of love, B, for example), or allegory (The Faerie Queen, A, as Queen Elizabeth I, B, in Spenser's poem) or metaphor (a broken heart, A, and an emotional state, B) or intertextuality (where one text, A, is modified by its relations to another text, B, whose meanings it also qualifies). This process of relation between and/or within signs has underwritten much of the literary and cultural criticism of the twentieth century, and the importance of "doubling" to the process of generating meaning has often being noted. So too, an understanding of the importance of "mirroring" to the production of sense or meaning itself has come to be recognized as a crucial element within understandings of consciousness in cognitive science.

In his highly influential essay "The Rhetoric of Temporality" Paul de Man develops a reading of the significance of the distinction drawn, in the Romantic era, between the use of symbols and the mode of allegory.[2] Both the German and English Romantic traditions came to validate the use of symbols in part by differentiating this usage from the mode of allegory. While both forms of expression generate powerful feelings of meaningfulness by drawing the general, abstract, or "ideal" into relationship with the particular, concrete, or represented "real," they do so in different ways.[3] Goethe states that:

> There is a great difference, whether the poet seeks the particular for the general or sees the general in the particular. From the first procedure arises allegory, where the particular serves only as an example of the general; the second procedure, however, is really the nature of poetry: it expresses something particular, without thinking of the general or pointing to it.[4]

The distinction between the two forms is usefully clarified by Samuel Taylor Coleridge, who argues that the symbol works through synecdoche: that is, that the symbol draws its power from the fact that it is a part that expresses a whole. For example, a "sail" is not only a symbol for a ship, it is also a part of the ship itself. That is, for Coleridge, the nature of the connection between the symbol and the ideal realm it conjures forth is not arbitrary. Rather, the symbol is directly connected with this ideal realm, which is the realm of meaning itself, the realm, that is, of stable meaning.[5] The ideal realm presupposed here resembles Plato's: forms exist in this ideal realm, and the forms and meanings of actual existing things are drawn from this ideal realm. For example, a triangle in nature can be understood because we already understand the idea of the triangle that exists as an ideal form.

It is important to stress this function, which connects the ideal with meaning, because this function remains in place whether one considers the nature of allegory or the nature of the symbol. Allegory, for Coleridge and the other European Romantics de Man considers, differs from and is inferior to the symbol, because it works through an arbitrary relation between two orders of sign: the idealist or deep meaning, and a surface or "realist" meaning. While there is no direct connection between the two levels of meaning in the allegorical mode (the connection is arbitrary and conventional) the symbol is conceived of as offering a bridge that directly connects these two levels within a literary text.[6]

De Man argues, then, that the symbol attempts to affirm an immediate connection between the ideal meaning it makes manifest and the *real* (that is, the real outside and surrounding the literary text). To put this another way, the symbol affirms that there is a direct connection between the representation and the thing represented. From this point of view, then, the symbol is that part of the ideal which erupts into or penetrates the real.

De Man then sets out to redefine allegory in a positive light. For de Man it is a strength of the allegorical mode that it *does not* involve direct connections. That is, to use terms which are not adopted by de Man, Sign A is put into relation with Sign B, but there is a gap between them which enables unstable meanings to emerge: A relates to B, but A does not necessarily equal B. De Man describes this relationship as "temporal" because it always involves a Sign (B) referring back to a previous Sign (A). Meaning is generated in this process of referring back. The structure of the ideal in relation to the real, the general in relation to the particular, which has been set out above, is maintained, however. The prior sign is the ideal and represents an existence that is maintained over time. The time of the particular subject that is represented through allegory (as Sign B) is drawn together or given meaning by being connected to the indefinite time of this ideal (Sign A).[7] He offers an image from Wordsworth to underline this point: the forest (as idea) is maintained even while particular trees grow and die within it.[8]

A third mode, that which operates in negative theology, offers an important variation on this model. We have seen how Paul de Man connects allegory to the notion of temporality as it presupposes a Sign A (the ideal), which is prior to a Sign B (the represented real). Yet Buning shows us how in the *via negativa* of negative theology the second sign, the surface sign (Sign B) reveals the absence of the first sign, the profound sign (Sign A).[9] It is something like a negative image: you see the outlines of the presence of Sign A in its absence. That is, its absence is revealed in Sign B. The structure is clearly somewhat different to that described by de Man, then. Here Sign A exists *through* Sign B, or the absences apparent in it, rather than in and of itself. One might wonder whether this might not also be the case with allegory more generally. Is it possible that allegory too can work by constructing a Sign A through the Sign B? Surely we come to the surface before we encounter the depth. Why should Sign A, in this sense, be considered prior? For the moment, however, to avoid confusion, we will continue to label the surface as Sign B and the depth, that element which defines or encapsulates meaning, as Sign A.

COETZEE AND THE REAL

A standard definition of "realism" suggests that it too approaches the universal through the particular: in being made to feel the reality of the particular, the world behind that particular thing opens up, and we are made to believe in that reality.

So here the effect described above is reversed: rather than the profound Sign A underwriting the meaning of the surface Sign B, it is the plausibility of the surface Sign B which establishes the truth of any profound Sign A. That is, in realism, just as with de Man's "modern" allegory, and negative theology, what is involved is not a one-to-one relation; rather, Sign A is only hinted at by Sign B.

Yet when we consider this more closely it is apparent that "realism" differs in other ways from the models of allegory or negative theology. As we have seen above, Coleridge relates the symbol to synecdoche. This relation, however, stresses the importance of ideas: the symbol ("the sail") is an idea which is part of a greater idea ("the ship"), an ideal which affirms the truth or meaning. While de Man underlines how this relation is in turn associated with the "real," this is because the ideal itself underwrites or gives meaning to the real within symbolic systems. In realism, however, the particular Sign B announces itself as being a part of a greater whole, a Sign A, that is material rather than ideal. That is, "Sign A," that which gives value or meaning, is the world itself, the material real itself.

This point might be underlined by considering Virginia Woolf's reading of Daniel Defoe. For Virginia Woolf the description of the particular — the particular "fact" of a given moment's existence (however fabricated, however imagined) — is what gives Defoe's realist fiction its power:

> Defoe, by reiterating that notion that a plain earthenware pot stands in the foreground, persuades us to see remote islands and the solitudes of the human soul. By believing fixedly in the solidity of the pot and its earthiness, he has subdued every other element to his design; he has roped the whole universe into harmony.[10]

This idea is echoed by Susan Barton, the fictional narrator of J. M. Coetzee's novel *Foe*. While she must, of course, have thought this long before a Woolf or a Nabokov had been born, Coetzee, who guides her hand, was quite probably thinking of Virginia Woolf, whom he mentions elsewhere in a critical essay on Defoe, in *Stranger Shores*:

> For page after page — for the first time in the history of fiction — we see minute, ordered description of how things are done. It is a matter of pure writerly attentiveness, pure submission to the exigencies of a world which, through being submitted to in a state so close to spiritual absorption, becomes transfigured, real. Defoe is a great writer, one of the purest writers we have. This, I think, Poe recognised, and Virginia Woolf, and others among Defoe's large and unlikely seeming band of admirers.[11]

In *Foe*, Coetzee develops these ideas of the relation between the detail and the real still further. Susan Barton tells Cruso that he needs to attend to details in telling his story:

> "The truth that makes your story yours alone, that sets you apart from the old mariner by the fireside spinning yarns of sea-monsters and mermaids, resides in a thousand touches which today may seem of no importance, such as: When you made your needle (the needle you store in your belt), by what means did you pierce the eye? When you sewed your hat, what did you use for thread? Touches like these will one day persuade your countrymen that it is all true, every word, there was indeed once an island in the middle of the ocean where the wind blew and the gulls cried from the cliffs and a man named Cruso paced about in his apeskin clothes, scanning the horizon for a sail."[12]

What is involved, then, is not a logic of ideas (as the symbolic idea is part of a greater ideal), but a logic of *things* which affirms that the world itself has meaning. There are still other differences, however.

While allegory, negative theology and symbolism generate much of their meaning through the primary relation between Sign B and Sign A, with realism meaning is not available in, or generated through, the relation between Sign B (the particular) and Sign A (the world, or universe, or nature). That is, while the particular ropes "the whole universe into harmony," the universe itself is not a meaning. Rather, in realism this relation only serves to guarantee that such meaning is possible. It is the world, or universe or nature, after all, that one is constantly seeking to understand. It is the world too, that allows us to understand (as our understandings are products of natural relations). Realism, then, in the first instance, does not offer us a meaning; rather, it offers us a sense of meaning, a powerful feeling or intuition that there is meaning ("that it is all true"). As such it might be argued that realism often serves as an underlying or overlaid form, which works with other forms and modes (such as symbolism, or allegory, or intertextual dialogue) to underwrite or guarantee the meanings that these other forms generate. That is, realism sets the stage for meaning, authorizes it, or renders it plausible. Once such an authorization of the real has been established, meaning can populate the work through the integration of other forms. It has, as we will see, however, the potential for a second, double role. As well as being that which assures us of the truth (that is, that makes us feel a sense of meaning), it can at the same time render the nature of that truth unstable.

In "The Rhetoric of Temporality" de Man argues that Daniel Defoe's *Robinson Crusoe* should be read as an allegory rather than as a realist novel.[13] Yet far from being mutually exclusive, realism has always been open to interaction with other forms. Before turning to a reading of Coetzee's use of intertextual dialogue as a means of both generating and questioning meaning, it is worth pausing to consider in more detail some of the implications of the differences I have attempted to outline here, so that the value of generating a sense of meaning which is guaranteed by the existence of a material reality might be better understood.

"SYMPATHY" OR INTUITIVE UNDERSTANDING[14]

In *Elizabeth Costello*, J. M. Coetzee has the eponymous character state that there is a faculty — sympathy — which "allows us to share at times the being of another"[15] (Coetzee, 79) and she goes on to claim that literature has the capacity to develop this faculty to an extremely high level: "If I can think my way into the existence of a being who has never existed, then I can think my way into the existence of a bat or a chimpanzee or an oyster, any being with whom I share the substrate of life."[16]

Elizabeth Costello takes issue and enters into dialogue with the philosopher Thomas Nagel, who argues that it is not possible for us to understand what it is to be a bat, because our minds are inadequate to the task.[17] She disagrees, arguing that we can enter into relation with the bat, share, in a sense, something of its existence, through the faculty of sympathy:

> "The heart is the seat of a faculty, *sympathy*, that allows us to share at times the being of another . . . there is no limit to the extent to which we can think ourselves into the being of another. There are no bounds to the sympathetic imagination."[18]

Elizabeth Costello is a follower of literary modernism: the work that makes her famous enters into dialogue with James Joyce's *Ulysses* in developing the story of Molly Bloom. Her understanding of sympathy, then, enters into relation with modernist understandings of the term, which were strongly influenced by the work of Henri Bergson.[19]

In *Creative Evolution* Bergson considers three means through which life has developed its capacities to interact within the world, both responding to and creating the environment of which it forms a part: torpor, instinct and intelligence. Torpor largely concerns Bergson's understanding of plant life. Of most interest to us here is the interaction between instinct and intelligence, which allows us to understand how a relation to the material real both differs from and relies upon a relation to ideal forms.

The terms intuition and intelligence are not held in opposition: rather, they are complementary, and can and do coexist. Yet instinct is most highly developed in certain parts of the animal kingdom. Indeed, it is, for Bergson, the dominant means through which animals, from the simplest to the most complex, interact within their environment.

It is only more highly developed animals which make use of "intelligence," and the animal which makes most use of intelligence is the human. For Bergson all life must answer the question of how it can act on the material world. For animals, he argues, nature has developed two responses (though these are interconnected); two ways in which tools might be used to have an effect on the environment. Both of these might be understood to involve some kind of "thought," but they are different in nature. Both involve a response to the world. A useful way of understanding them is the example of the use of tools.

Instinct involves an organism using those tools which are a part of its body to effect a task: a butterfly uses its proboscis, for example, to suck nectar from flowers. It has, for Bergson, been organized, or, if you prefer, it has evolved, in order to perform this task among other tasks. It makes use of instinct in performing this task. Instinct, then, is a kind of organized thought. Intelligence, on the other hand, is that capacity which allows certain animals to find or invent tools within their environment with which they might act on that environment. If instinct is thought which has already been organized and is coextensive with the organism it inhabits and comprises, then intelligence is organizing thought: thought which allows for the development of instruments that will serve to affect the environment in a certain way.[20]

There is another way of looking at the difference. Instinct involves acting on material things: seeing the world in terms of those actual particular things upon which we might act. Intelligence, on the other hand, concerns itself with the abstract forms we use to organize our understanding of things in a general way.

Intelligence, then, is a knowledge of forms or ideals, whereas instinct is a knowledge of matter. When one starts to think in terms of knowledge and knowing our place in the world, however, there is a paradox for Bergson:

> There are things that intelligence alone is able to seek, but which, by itself, it will never find. These things instinct alone could find; but it will never seek them.[21]

This is because instinct excels in fitting itself to reality: reality for Bergson is movement.[22] Intelligence, on the other hand, works by fixing things in place, rendering them artificially static, or abstracting them from movement. That is, intelligence conceives of the living as if it were lifeless.[23] Intelligence alone, then, is incapable of fully comprehending reality. Instinct fully comprehends the movement of reality, but it simply acts, it does not reflect. For Bergson, then, "The intellect is characterised by a natural inability to comprehend life."[24]

How, then, is it that we feel that we can comprehend life, at least intuitively, at least instinctively? This is because we, like those organisms which act through instinct, have a sympathy with the world, with our environment. Bergson compares life to a musical theme: there is an original theme which has been played into an immense range of variations in life on earth. How can we grasp the original theme?

> As for the original theme, it is everywhere and nowhere. It is in vain that we try and express it in terms of any idea: it must have been, originally, *felt* rather than *thought*.[25]

A few pages on, Bergson concludes that the concrete explanation of the "original theme" is no longer scientific or purely concerned with intelligence: rather, "it must be sought . . . not in the direction of intelligence, but in that of sympathy."[26] This kind of thinking is then explicitly linked not only with a philosophical project, which Bergson calls metaphysics, but with certain artistic practices:

> Intelligence and instinct are turned in opposite directions, the former towards inert matter, the latter towards life . . . But it is to the very inwardness of life that *intuition* leads us — by intuition I mean instinct that has become disinterested, self-conscious, capable of reflecting upon its object and of enlarging it indefinitely.[27]

He continues:

> That an effort of this kind is not impossible, is proved by the existence in man of an aesthetic faculty along with normal perception. Our eye perceives the features of the living being, merely as assembled, not as mutually organized. The intention of life, the simple movement that runs through the lines, that binds them together and gives them significance, escapes it. This intention is just what the artist tries to regain, in placing himself back within the object by a kind of sympathy, in breaking down, by an effort of intuition, the barrier that space puts up between him and his model.[28]

The powerful connection, sympathy, which Coetzee appeals to through Elizabeth Costello, involves a natural affinity between ourselves and our environment; an environment understood as being comprised of those relations themselves.

The form of realism seems at first glance, then, to be adapted to the generation of sympathy and intuition which, like intuition, sees the meaning of things without seeking to fix them in place, it concerns itself with the material. Allegory, symbolism and negative theology, on the other hand, seem to work with forms of understanding or ideals, and involve the kind of conceptual categorizations developed through the intelligence. It is not quite this simple, however. Coetzee interrogates these problems still more forcefully through the use of intertextuality, which involves not just putting any Sign A into relation with any Sign B, but in reflecting one complex literary text with another, thereby extending the relationship of signs indefinitely.

FOE AND INTERTEXTUALITY

We have seen how a doubling works in symbolism, allegory, negative theology and to different purpose in realism. An equally familiar form of doubling as a means of generating meaning is intertextuality. J. M. Coetzee often works with intertextuality. In *Foe* Coetzee chooses to work in relation to *Robinson Crusoe*. He does a similar thing, of course, with Dostoevsky in *The Master of Petersburg* and other works.

I will not attempt to define intertextuality here. I am, rather, more interested in a particular relation: the doubling or co-reflection of signs that generates thinking in literature. Here it is "intertextual," a general term, but the manner in which it works is particular. A particular set of relations is built between *Foe* and *Robinson Crusoe* with the meaning of Sign B (Coetzee's *Foe*) being underwritten by the often absent, occluded or distorted Sign A (which is both the novel *Robinson Crusoe* and the life and other works of its author Daniel Defoe).[29]

As we relate Coetzee's novel *Foe*, then, to *Robinson Crusoe* and to Defoe's life, we trace points of connection, but we also notice points of rupture, confusion or discontinuity. So the doubling might not just involve two signs: there may well be, as in this case, further signs behind these two (just as Defoe's life underwrites the meaning of certain interpretations of *Robinson Crusoe*). Coetzee's "Foe" is, in some senses, like the Daniel Foe of history who changes his name, through vanity perhaps, to Daniel Defoe,[30] but does not resemble him in other ways: there is a confusion, for example, of chronology. Coetzee's character Foe is working, for an extended, even indefinite time, on Susan Barton's story, and seems already to have imagined or published other works such as *Memoirs of a Cavalier*, *Captain Singleton*, even *An Essay on the History and Reality of Apparitions*, works which we know were written, even in the latter case, long after *Robinson Crusoe* appeared in 1719.[31]

Unlike Defoe, whose wife stoically suffered his absence for many years while raising their children alone,[32] Foe's wife, we are told, is dead (though Susan Barton may simply have been misled on this point). Indeed, there are many other points of non-relation, in particular with regard to the story of the island and Cruso and Friday, in Defoe's work, and Susan Barton's story.

We might account for some of these by accepting the word of the anonymous writer of the blurb on the cover of the Penguin edition of *Foe*, who informs us that Defoe stole and changed Susan's story, but nothing in the story itself confirms this: the story itself ends (the first time it ends, with Susan's narrative) with both Foe and Susan searching for a way of filling or crossing a gap in the story: the black hole of Friday's lost tongue. That is, they are searching for a mirroring ideal: as in negative theology and modern allegory a Sign A is apparent in what is absent in the surface Sign B we read: the missing ideal meaning of Friday's tongue which itself is the instrument for generating meanings.

This novel, then, not only generates a sense of meaning through realism and through the interaction of Sign A and Sign B through intertextuality, it also draws attention to the problem of making connections which promise meaning: that is, it encourages us to draw incomplete, unsustainable, conclusions. Further, it draws attention to the instability which resides, and long has lived, at the core of literary logic: the lack, or the apparent instability of a meaningful Sign A. In this way it challenges us to think. Proust claimed that the way to truth was through art, through the truth of particular perceptions. So too, as we have seen, for Coetzee's Susan Barton the true and real are linked through the material body and the images which impress themselves on the body.[33] For the ancient Stoics bodies were real, the only real things, and other things which affected us, such as the meaning of words, the interpretation of the meaning of events, for example, were incorporeal.[34] Yet if we are supposed to be given access to the truth through this kind of writing, through the construction, for readers, of the "reality" of particular things, isn't this kind of art, "realism," at its very core, based on deception, on conjuring, on making substantial things emerge from the incorporeal meaning which is attributed to words? The problem is, paradoxically, not understood through reference to an "ideal" by Coetzee, but through reference to what has been made to pass for "the real": the *real life* on which any work is based. Coetzee indeed shows us how the real itself is everywhere both generated through and undermined by stories. We are left, then, with a ground that has become groundless (as Samuel Beckett and others had understood before him): the "material" which underwrites the truth of realism can only be accessed through what is said about it.

DECEPTION IN *FOE* AND DEFOE

Defoe, who wrote what has come to be considered the first realist novel in English, *Robinson Crusoe*, was himself a master of deception, a "master of fictions" as his biographer Maximillian Novak has it. Critics, such as Novak and Richetti, have argued that role-playing: the serious shifting of positions and adoption of personas both in person and in his writings would have helped him, perversely, to develop into a successful writer of fiction. That is, he was already able to put himself into someone else's shoes. For example, he worked as a spy for the English Government against the Scottish and in other capacities, and in performing his duties for the government he often wrote political pamphlets making use of personas, such as a "Quaker gentleman": he would also disguise his handwriting because handwriting could be used as evidence to establish authorship. He was also able, though this is something he was reviled for, to argue different sides of an argument under different pseudonyms, anonymously of course in pamphlets he was asked to write by his patrons the Chief Ministers of the English Parliament, Harley or Godolphin, and even to promote that side of the argument which he seemed to believe in least in order to foster a given set of political interests.[35]

It is well known, of course, that art and poetry had been criticized for telling lies long before Defoe came along. In the English context Sir Philip Sidney defended poetry from this charge in the sixteenth century by suggesting poetry didn't lie because it did not affirm anything within its domain to be true.[36] Yet Defoe, unlike Sidney, was noted for using the deceitful methods of art for pragmatic purposes *in life*.

In Defoe's own defence he argued that this is what was needed at this time and place. It was the best means of both surviving and making a useful difference. "An age of Mysteries and Paradoxes" he called it on one occasion, on another in a private letter he stated: "This, Sir, is an Age of Plot and Deceit, of Contradiction and Paradox. It is very hard, under all these Masks, to see the true Countenance of any Man."[37]

The most interesting defence Defoe makes of himself, perhaps, comes in a letter to Harley:

> Tho' this Part of conduct is Call'd Dissumulation, I am Content it shall be Call'd what They will, But as Lye Does Not Consist in the Indirect Positioning of words, but in the Design by False Speaking, to Deciev and Injure my Neighbour, So dissembling does Not Consist in putting a Different Face Upon Our Actions, but in the further Applying That Concealment to the Prejudice of the Person; for Example, I Come into a persons Chamber, who on a Surprise is Apt to Fall into Dangerous Convulsions. I Come in Smileing, and Pleasant, and ask the person to Rise and Go abroad, or any Other Such question, and Press him to it Till I Prevail, whereas the Truth is I have Discovred the house to be On Fire, and I Act thus for fear of frighting him. Will any man Tax me with Hypocrisye and Dissimulation.[38]

This argument, in life, would have to be drawn into line with events as they unfold. Yet does the analogy hold for literature? What possible good could we be led towards in being faced with deception in art, with the deceptions indeed that comprise art? In Coetzee's short introduction to *Robinson Crusoe* he asks how we are supposed to read the patent lie made in several prefaces by Defoe that Crusoe is a real person and the author of the tales. Coetzee concludes that what we see at certain moments is the castaway merging with author from whose head he emerges: we get a true glimpse of a real man, then, a particular man, through the false image of his double.[39]

In Nabokov's novel *Despair* Hermann Karlovich intends to lie to the insurance salesman Orlovious from whom he has purchased a life insurance policy. As part of his plan to kill his "double" Felix and thereby commit both a poetic crime and receive (or at least have his wife receive) the benefit of his life insurance, Hermann arranges a chance meeting with Orlovious and tells him that his (Hermann's) wife Lydia has been unfaithful so that Orlovious will not expect her to be too sympathetic at the funeral. As I mentioned, Hermann intends to lie, but when we read closely we realize he has in fact, and without himself ever realizing it, betrayed the truth, which, as Orlovious lets him know, had already been betrayed to Orlovious (as it had to the reader) through close observation.[40]

In *Despair* and elsewhere Nabokov uses the figure of the mirror, in indicating how the reflected mirror image corrects the original mirror image. The first mirror image shows us the world back to front: my reflection is left-handed while I am right-handed. The reflection of the reflection in this case, rather than degrading the image, makes it whole. We are able to see the "true" nature of Hermann's character in *Despair* through the various deceptions he propagates.

We can see two possible readings of the mirroring process of repeated and answering deceptions, then, a process which itself is mirrored in the production of works of fiction through the linking of a Sign B with an apparent or absent Sign A. The more common is the idea of infinite regress or *mise-en-abîme* highlighted through the 1960s by writers of the French new novel such as Alain Robbe-Grillet and Claude Simon: a groundlessness in which an infinitely repeated image extends into eternity. The second is that shown to us here by Nabokov, where the first lie corrects the second: "minus x minus = plus," as Hermann also tells us.[41] How, then, can you claim that anything is true in literature? Perhaps through a double deception, the falsity of the reflection can cancel the falsity of a prior reflection or self-perception.

Might it be that Coetzee, at least in *Foe*, like Nabokov in *Despair*, emphasizes the deceptions in the surface Sign B so as to ground or produce a truth in Sign A? In *Foe* there is a sense of the possibility of the "true" (which might be related to the ideal) and the "real" (which might be related to material things). These are seen not as things which are available, or in any sense readily achieved, but, rather, as that which it is necessary to pursue. One must pursue these things, even while they might remain out of reach.

This is most clearly apparent in the figure of the gap, which eventually comes to form a kind of centre to *Foe*, the gap which is Friday's absent tongue, a tongue which (differing in this, of course, from *Robinson Crusoe*) has been cut from Friday's mouth. Susan Barton, in *Foe*, claims there are different kinds of silence: on the one hand there is a chosen and purposeful silence, like that she herself keeps from Foe with regard to her time spent in Brazil prior to being shipwrecked and meeting Cruso and Friday; and on the other hand there is a helpless silence, which is the kind she attributes to Friday.

Yet clearly while Friday is unable to tell his story because of the absence of this tongue, it is shown to be equally possible, as the story proceeds, that he also may not wish to tell his story. Learning Friday's true story, however, becomes, both for Susan Barton, and Daniel Foe the key. Susan, who in writing letters to Foe urging him to tell her story has herself become a writer, tells Foe, whom she has at last tracked down, and whose lover she has become:

> "In the letters you did not read . . . I told you of my conviction that, if the story seems stupid, that is only because it so doggedly holds its silence. The shadow whose lack you feel is there: it is the loss of Friday's tongue."[42]

There is a gap, then, but rather than this being left as the final word, there is a suggestion, at least, that some response to the problem is possible. That is, through the kind of sympathy available through the imagination; through the kind of thinking possible in writing fiction.

The passage I have just cited continues as follows:

> Foe made no reply, and I went on. "The story of Friday's tongue is a story unable to be told, or unable to be told by me. That is to say, many stories can be told of Friday's tongue, but the true story is buried within Friday, who is mute. The true story will not be heard till by art we have found a means of giving voice to Friday."[43]

This process begins with Foe giving Friday the means to write. There is also a suggestion that some imaginative faculty might allow the means of leaping this gap, or, to put it another way, of generating an absent Sign A through a surface Sign B. The dialogue involves, of course, the gap between positions, a gap which is, deliberately, not closed for us. The use of the double and techniques of reflective doubling, like that made use of by Nabokov in *Despair*, is another example of how one might generate these kinds of gap.

In reading *Foe*, however, we are conscious of the awfulness of the feeling of suspension. Susan Barton experiences this through the silence of Foe himself. She eventually pursues him and tracks him down, however, insinuating her way into his house, the house of the writer, and seating herself at his desk, writing at his table. Later she finds Foe himself and the silence he had maintained is cancelled. Then there is the silence of Friday, which it seems impossible to overcome. A silence which leaves us in suspension because it means that we cannot know, that we therefore cannot find the true or the real that Susan seeks. Yet this too is overcome, though only via a direct invocation to the power of art, by a core element of that art: "sympathy." It is again important to underline how doubling includes both possibilities: the making whole of an image by correcting the false reflection with the reflection of that reflection, and of setting up a series of ungrounded reflections which extend to infinity.

Yet we see a different response to this, as the novel proceeds. By itself doubling the notion of double creation the final section of the novel offers a new narrative. The greater part of the novel is given to us between quotation marks and is attributed to Susan Barton who writes in the first person. The final section, which is no more than five pages in length, proceeds without these quotation marks, in an unidentified narrative voice, which is clearly not that of Susan or any other character who has appeared in the novel. This narrator, who, we feel, is the one who has quoted Susan's words for us, (re)enters the story where it had appeared to come to a halt.

This second narrative doubles and distorts the first, just as the novel as a whole doubles and distorts Daniel Defoe's *Robinson Crusoe*, just as, perhaps, that story doubled and distorted the stories of Alexander Selkirk, whose story Defoe was accused of plagiarizing, and even that of Defoe himself. One of Defoe's first and most ardent critics, Charles Gildon, accused Defoe of being himself a "Rambling, Inconsistent Creature" and projecting this "whimsical, inconsistent Being" on to

Crusoe.[44] Defoe responded to this criticism by hinting that "the truth of *Robinson Crusoe* is somehow related to the truth about Daniel Defoe."[45] The intertextual relations, then, move both outside and inside books and lives, much like the stream issuing from Friday's mouth, in the final paragraph of the novel.

> His mouth opens. From inside him comes a slow stream, without breath, without interruption. It flows up through his body and out upon me; it passes through the cabin, through the wreck; washing the cliffs and shores of the island, it runs northward and southward to the ends of the earth. Soft and cold, dark and unending, it beats against my eyelids, against the skin of my face.[46]

As stated above, two possible readings can be made of the doubt which occurs because one is confronted with a groundlessness (the absence of a Sign A which would generate meaning), as what we know seems built on an ever receding chain of lies, the deceptions of fiction which are an analogue of the little deceptions and self deceptions which make up much of the substance of our lives. One might turn to Samuel Beckett, an important point of reference for Coetzee, who exemplifies such images of groundlessness in works such as *The Unnamable*. On the other hand, as Coetzee seems to do here, one might turn back to art and its sympathy, which makes us feel, if not know, the real.

NOTES

1 See Derek Attridge, *J. M. Coetzee and the Ethics of Reading: Literature in the Event* (Chicago: University of Chicago Press, 2004).

2 This essay is part of a larger project and I consider elements of these ideas in relation to the work of Marius Buning elsewhere: see Anthony Uhlmann, "Negative Allegory: Buning on Allegory and the *Via Negativa*," in *Where Never Before: Beckett's Poetics of Elsewhere, "Samuel Beckett Today/ Aujourd'hui"*, ed. Sjef Houppermans et al. (Amsterdam: Rodopi, 2009).

3 See Paul de Man, "The Rhetoric of Temporality," in *Critical Theory Since 1965*, eds. Hazard Adams and Leroy Searle (Tallahassee, FL: University Press of Florida, 1986), 199–201.

4 Cited in Angus Fletcher, *Allegory: The Theory of the Symbolic Mode* (New York: Cornell University Press, 1964), 13.

5 On this point, see Fletcher, *Allegory*, 15–20; and de Man, "The Rhetoric of Temporality," 201–2.

6 See de Man, "The Rhetoric of Temporality," 202–3.

7 See de Man, "The Rhetoric of Temporality," 208–10.

8 de Man, "The Rhetoric of Temporality," 204.

9 See Marius Buning, "The 'Via Negativa' and its first stirrings in *Eleutheria*," in *Beckett and Religion/ Beckett/Aesthetics/Politics, "Samuel Beckett Today/Aujourd'hui"* 9, eds. Marius Buning, Matthijs Engelberts and Onno Kosters, with guest editors, Mary Bryden, Lance St John Butler, and Peter Boxall (Amsterdam: Rodopi, 2000), 44–6.

10 Virginia Woolf, "Robinson Crusoe," in Daniel Defoe, *Robinson Crusoe*, ed. Michael Shinagel (New York: Norton, 1994), 287.

11 J. M. Coetzee, *Stranger Shores: Essays 1986–1999* (London: Secker & Warburg, 2001), 24.

12 J. M. Coetzee, *Foe* (London: Penguin, 1987), 18.

13 de Man, "The Rhetoric of Temporality," 208.

14 I consider elements of these ideas in relation to Gilles Deleuze's understanding of the connections

between ethics, ethology and art elsewhere: see Anthony Uhlmann, "Deleuze, Ethics and Ethology," in *Deleuze and Ethics*, eds. Daniel W. Smith and Nathan Jun (Edinburgh: Edinburgh University Press, forthcoming 2011).

15 J. M. Coetzee, *Elizabeth Costello* (London: Vintage, 2004), 79.
16 Coetzee, *Elizabeth Costello*, 80.
17 Coetzee, *Elizabeth Costello*, 76.
18 Coetzee, *Elizabeth Costello*, 79–80.
19 On this influence, see Paul Douglas, *Bergson, Eliot, and American Literature* (Lexington: University of Kentucky Press, 1986); Hilary L. Fink, *Bergson and Russian Modernism 1900–1930* (Evanston, Illinois: Northwestern University Press, 1999); and Mary Ann Gillies, *Henri Bergson and British Modernism* (Montreal and Kingston: McGill–Queen's University Press, 1996).
20 Henri Bergson, *Creative Evolution*, trans. Arthur Mitchell (Mineola: Dover, 1998), 139–42.
21 Bergson, *Creative Evolution*, 151, original emphasis.
22 Bergson, *Creative Evolution*, 155.
23 Bergson, *Creative Evolution*, 161.
24 Bergson, *Creative Evolution*, 165, original emphasis.
25 Bergson, *Creative Evolution*, 172, original emphasis.
26 Bergson, *Creative Evolution*, 176.
27 Bergson, *Creative Evolution*, 176.
28 Bergson, *Creative Evolution*, 177.
29 I will leave aside the further sets of relations to colonial and post-colonial political practice, as a good deal of work has already been dedicated to considering these issues in relation to *Foe*.
30 Maximillian E. Novak, *Daniel Defoe: Master of Fictions* (Oxford: Oxford University Press, 2001), 116.
31 See Novak, *Daniel Defoe* for the publication details of these other texts.
32 See Novak, *Daniel Defoe*, 313.
33 Coetzee, *Foe*, 18.
34 See Émile Bréhier, ed., *La théorie des incorporels dans l'ancien stoïcisme* (Paris: Librairie philosophique J. Vrin, 1997; 1908).
35 See Novak, *Daniel Defoe*, 338–59, 464–82.
36 Sir Philip Sidney, *The Defence of Poesy*, ed. Lewis Soens (Lincoln, Nebraska and London: University of Nebraska Press, 1970), 35.
37 Novak, *Daniel Defoe*, 356.
38 Cited in Novak, *Daniel Defoe*, 235.
39 Coetzee, *Stranger Shores*, 21.
40 Vladimir Nabokov, *Despair* (London: Penguin, 2000), 112–14.
41 Nabokov, *Despair*, 102.
42 Coetzee, *Foe*, 117.
43 Coetzee, *Foe*, 118.
44 Charles Gildon, *The Life and Strange Surprising Adventures of Mr. D----- De F--, of London, Hosier, who has liv'd above fifty Years by himself, in the Kingdoms of* North *and* South Britain. *The various Shapes he has appear'd in, and the Discoveries he has made for the Benefit of his Country. In a Dialogue between* Him, Robinson Crusoe, *and his Man* Friday. *With Remarks Serious and Comical upon the Life of Crusoe* (London: Printed for J. Roberts in Warwick-Line, 1719), x, viii.
45 Everett Zimmerman, "Defoe and Crusoe," *ELH* 38.3 (1971): 378.
46 Coetzee, *Foe*, 157.

PART THREE

LIMITS

CHAPTER 7

The Trope of Following in J. M. Coetzee's *Slow Man*[1]

Mike Marais

During the apartheid period, Coetzee frequently articulated his reluctance to "follow" history by treating it as an a priori structure that a writer has no choice but to represent and so "supplement." While this stance is most apparent in articles such as "The Novel Today" and "Into the Dark Chamber," it also emerges in the repeated attempts of the protagonists of the fiction of the period to refuse predetermined positions in the political conflicts in their contexts and, instead, to locate a point outside history — usually catachrestically figured as a spectral and invisible underworld — from which history may be interrupted.

Has Coetzee's emigration to Australia led to a change in his view of the relationship between the aesthetic and history? If his writing has changed radically, it must surely evince a departure of some sort from the obsession with the limits of culture and history in the South African corpus. I find little evidence of such a shift in this writer's Australian fiction, though. For Coetzee, the novelist is still, in Elizabeth Costello's description, a "secretary of the invisible."[2] In this essay, I support this contention by tracing the metaphor of following in *Slow Man*. From my reading of this novel's self-reflexive articulation of its relationship to the invisible, it will hopefully become clear that Coetzee's preoccupation with the possibility of aesthetic autonomy is every bit as strong in his Australian fiction as it was in his South African writing of the apartheid period. His allegiance is still to that which history corrupts but which at the same time may interrupt history. My purpose, then, is to attempt to deduce what Coetzee himself seems to be saying about writing in one of his Australian novels. This is to say that I am about to embark on the kind of exercise in critical fundamentalism that the novel in question calls for but renders profoundly ironic.

Coetzee's preoccupation with following the invisible in *Slow Man* becomes apparent in Chapter 13, which introduces Elizabeth Costello. Upon entering the novel, this character recites its opening sentences, which deal with Paul Rayment's accident. Accordingly, the reader is required to reread this passage as an allegory of the accident of inspiration, of the writer's loss of control in the moment of writing. That is, the repetition of the passage makes the reader aware that when she reads of "something coming" to Paul Rayment, she is also reading of *him* happening to Elizabeth Costello. Indeed, the presence of the typewriter in this description indicates that Rayment's sense of his ontogenesis is his visitation of Costello, his unannounced arrival or "coming" to her: "Something is coming to him. A letter at a time, clack clack clack, a message is being typed on a rose-pink screen that trembles like water each time he blinks and is therefore quite likely his own inner eyelid."[3]

Importantly, Costello later describes having *heard* the opening words of the novel. Evidently, they "come" to her; she receives them, which is to say Paul Rayment, from an unknown source. As her reference to Marianna intimates, they are a command issued from a source that is wholly other: "SHE CAME TO me as you came to me," says Costello. "A woman of darkness, a woman in darkness. *Take up the story of such a one*: words in my sleeping ear, spoken by what in the old days we would have called an angel calling me out to a wrestling match" (SM, 115, original emphasis).

In this novel, the trope of sleep connotes the extreme passivity of the self in the moment of inspiration. The metaphor of the "sleeping ear," which implies a contrast with a wakeful and masterful eye, suggests a pre-reflective state of openness to an alterity that would be foreclosed upon by intentional consciousness. What is at stake here is a form of waiting without expectation or intention for the command of the other. Crucially, the time of such waiting is beyond the time of history. In being exposed to the other, the self encounters that which cannot be reduced to an object for intentional consciousness, and so rendered *present*. Being entirely non-phenomenological, the "instant" of this exposure to what is essentially invisible is what Emmanuel Levinas would call a "lapse of time,"[4] or discontinuity, that cannot form part of a retentional past or a present from which the future may be anticipated. Hence Levinas refers to "the diachrony of the instant."[5] The instant or *Augenblick* in question is an interruption of temporal experience. During the *Augenblick*, the eye "listens"[6] or, as John Llewelyn puts it, "opening one's eyes is called to make way for opening one's ears."[7]

Apart from elaborating on its temporality, Costello's description of it makes the point that inspiration is a process through which the writing subject is subordinated to an unknown authority. In the description, the reference to the "sleeping ear," to a passive form of hearing, emphasizes the obedience of the inspired self. Indeed, the very word *obey* is etymologically related to *audire*, "to hear."[8] To be inspired is to be mastered, to respond unquestioningly to an order received from a wholly unknown and unknowable source. In the passage, the alterity of this source is stressed through its association with the face of the Judaeo-Christian God. It is Jacob who wrestles with an angel, a messenger, and thereafter, relieved at having survived seeing God "face to face," names the place where the bout occurred Peniel, which means "face of God" (Gen. 32.30).[9]

Similarly to the earlier fiction, then, this novel depicts inspiration as a form of unconditional hospitality.[10] That which inspires cannot be invited. When it arrives, it does so unannounced by infiltrating the individual's consciousness and possessing him or her. The writer becomes host to an unknown and unknowable visitor. Nevertheless, the host is not sovereign in this relationship: he is invaded and taken hostage by the unannounced visitor and, in the process, dispossessed of self-possession. To respond obediently to inspiration in the way described by Costello is thus to *give* oneself up to that inspiration in an act of selfless generosity or love. It is to write, and therefore to act, while being acted upon by an unknown authority.

As in his earlier fiction, Coetzee, in *Slow Man*, uses the metaphor of following to convey the notion of the other's mastery of the writer through inspiration. In the later novel, though, this metaphor also foregrounds the deeply ambivalent, conflicted nature of the responsibility concomitant with the writer's inspiration by the invisible. In order to follow the invisible, the writer must follow the text — that is, he must respect the language, grammar and representational logic of the form of the novel. At the same time, though, he must ensure that the text *does* obey, which is to say follow, the invisible.

In terms of *Slow Man*'s self-reflexive illusion, Rayment depends on Costello's authorship for his being as a character. Oppressed by her authorial authority, he attempts to resist "her schemes," but fears that were he to look in a mirror, he would see "grinning over his shoulder, gripping his throat, the shape of a wild-haired, bare-breasted hag brandishing a whip" (SM, 164). Notwithstanding this image, which derives from the story of the old man of the river's persecution of Sinbad, the text makes it very clear that Costello is as dependent on Rayment as he is on her. She "follows" him throughout, a state of servitude that becomes apparent in her remarks that she "must wait upon" him (SM, 136), and that "his is the power of leading," and hers of "following" (SM, 233). Costello is mastered by Rayment because she is enthralled to the invisible by which she has been inspired to write. As she puts it when he wishes her to leave his apartment: "I am to accompany you" (SM, 84). She follows him because she has no choice in the matter: he is the "penance" that she is "sentenced to speak" (SM, 162).

Costello depends on Rayment because he is the means through which she must obey the command received in her "sleeping ear." That is to say, he is quite literally the "sentence," the medium and form through which she gives herself up to the alterior source of her inspiration. In terms of this novel's logic of transubstantiation, Rayment, namely the language and form of the novel, must embody Costello's gift of self and thereby instantiate her unconditional love. It is for this reason that she is depicted as being incorporeal, an insubstantial presence. On reflecting on her "blankness" (SM, 120), Rayment, for instance, "finds her so colourless, so featureless" (SM, 160). He — the medium and form of the novel — must invest her with substance.

Costello must therefore obey both the invisible *and* the text. To obey the former, she must obey the latter. The problem, of course, is that the text is resistant to following the invisible. Paul Rayment, the text-figure, is an amputee, a slow man. He is words, part of the language of what Levinas refers to as the same — that is, the order of intentional consciousness. Accordingly, he is antipathetic to otherness. As is so often the case in his writing, Coetzee's point here is that the invisible cannot be named and therefore grasped in language. Language cannot accommodate the writer's self-sacrificing generosity. For this reason, Costello complains as follows to Rayment about the text's lacklustre description of his discovery of her by the riverside, feeding ducks: "it is not good enough. It does not bring me to life. Bringing me to life may not be important to you, but it has the drawback of not bringing you to life either" (SM, 159). In his turn, Rayment reflects that the language he speaks "does not come from my core" (SM, 198). Instead of coming "from the heart" (SM, 231), which is earlier described as the seat, or indeed home, of love (SM, 149), his words come from the "word-box" that he carries around in place of a heart (SM, 230, 234). English, in Costello's description, is part of his "tortoiseshell armour" (SM, 230), a depiction that recalls Dostoevsky's suspicion that while he is called upon to be "a lyre-player," to raise the dead through the lyre's music of love, he is a purveyor of words and thus unable to do so: "And the truth? Stiff shoulders humped over the writing table, and the ache of a heart slow to move. A tortoise heart."[11]

The motif of slowness, in *Slow Man*, thus signifies language's resistance to unconditional hospitality. Although a product of love, the work, as its very title announces, may be the loss of that by which it has been inspired. To apply to it Foe's description of the story of the island, *Slow Man* is a "slow story,"[12] ill-equipped to follow the invisible. Like Dostoevsky in *The Master of Petersburg*, this novel is capable only of a "plodding chase . . . after the rumour of a ghost."[13]

Given Paul Rayment's inertia, it is hardly surprising that much of *Slow Man* consists of Costello's attempts to coax, cajole, even harry and harass, him into following the invisible. If she is to obey the order she has received, she must *make* him lead her. Her following must be more than simply a following: it must become a pursuit, and thereby a form of following that is a not-following. Exactly because the medium and form of the novel are hostile to love, the inspired writer must make them accommodate it; must open them out to that which they seek to exclude. Whether or not this is possible is quite simply beside the point. Under inspiration, the writer cannot but obey the command to do so. Despite herself, then, she must render language hospitable to that to which it is hostile. Despite itself, the medium of the novel must be made hospitable.

Hence Costello repeatedly accuses Rayment of "dithering" (SM, 159), complains that "nothing is happening" (SM, 141), urges him to "hurry up" (SM, 160) and berates him with these words: "I urge you: don't cut short these thought-trains of yours. Follow them through to their end. Your thoughts and your feelings. Follow them through and you will grow with them" (SM, 158). In fact, her following of him progressively becomes a persecution (a word whose etymology signifies a form of following), as emerges when she herself uses the Sinbad story as an analogue for her relationship with him: "As I keep telling myself, Have patience, Paul Rayment did not ask you to descend upon his shoulders" (SM, 160). Her following is *both* an act of obedience *and* a tyranny, pursuit or persecution.

The paradoxical nature of this form of following is articulated in yet another of Costello's invocations of the Sinbad story. After having promised to keep out of Rayment's way during her visit, she goes on to say: "Most of the time you won't notice I am here. Just a touch on the shoulder, now and then, left or right, to keep you on the path" (SM, 87).

Ultimately, then, what we find in *Slow Man* is an erosion of the apparent opposition between following and not-following. While the logic of this metaphor seems to suggest that the writer, to follow the invisible, must follow the text, it simultaneously indicates that she can only follow the text through interrupting the process of following. Not-following, it would appear, may enable following. Disobedience may enable obedience. In a discussion of the figures of the *acoluthon* ("follower," "acolyte") and *anacoluthon* ("without following"), Derrida clarifies exactly this paradox:

> There is no simple opposition between the acolyte, or the "acoluthon" and the "*an*acoluthon." That is a problem, because to accompany, or to follow in the most demanding and authentic way, implies the "*an*acol," the "not-following," the break in the following, in the company so to speak. So, if we agree on this, a number of consequences will follow: you cannot simply oppose the acolyte and the anacoluthon — logically they are opposed; but in fact, what appears as a necessity is that, in order to follow in a consistent way, to be true to what you follow, you have to interrupt the following.[14]

In this view, not-following is part of the process of following. By the same token, disobedience is a necessary part of obedience, and betrayal a part of fidelity.

Costello's following, through not following, of Paul Rayment accounts for the unresolved tension between love and betrayal in *Slow Man*'s ending, which stages the outcome of her pursuit of him. In the penultimate scene, she, having finally managed to persuade Rayment to leave his apartment-prison, accompanies him on an "UNANNOUNCED visit" to the Jokić family (SM, 239). Once they arrive, she enthuses at the animate nature of the text's descriptions: "So real! . . . Who would have thought it!" (SM, 242). Interestingly, Rayment notices that she "is leaning back, eyes shut, abstracted" (SM, 247). The implication is clear: she is writing under inspiration or, as Mrs Curren, in yet another invocation of the *Augenblick*, puts it, writing with eyes "shut."[15] Costello, in short, is trying to invest her gift of self with form and substance through language. On the final page of the novel, when Rayment "takes a good look at her," she is no longer "blank," "colourless" and "featureless": "In the clear late-afternoon light he can see every detail, every hair, every vein" (SM, 263). From this description, it would seem that her writing has indeed been able to accommodate her gift of self in the instant of inspiration. Nevertheless, this conclusion is immediately qualified by the fact that Rayment's scrutiny of Costello's physiognomy coincides with a disavowal of love in his response to her questions "Is this love, Paul? Have we found love at last?": "No . . . this is not love. This is something else. Something less" (SM, 263). Costello's reply to this response, "And is that your last word, do you think?" (SM, 263), suggests the necessarily inseparable nature of fidelity and betrayal.

Importantly, in this regard, Rayment's "last word" is a variant of the standard accusation in Coetzee's fiction of abandonment, of the parent's inability to love the child well enough. As much is connoted by the intersection of the metaphor of following with the trope of childbirth in this novel. Under inspiration, Costello bears Rayment in order for him to bear the invisible. She is both mother and midwife. Accordingly, her following, indeed persecution, of him sometimes takes the form of an adjuration to deliver an infant. We twice read that she "urges" him to "push," a word that he associates with "a woman in labour" (SM, 83, 204). Alternatively, she urges him to speak, to "*Say* something" (SM, 100, original emphasis). In this context, Paul Rayment's "final word" may be read as an accusation of abandonment: the text accuses the writer of having abandoned it. For most of the novel, as we have seen, it is Rayment, the text-figure, whom Costello accuses of inadequate love. The ending changes this: what is now at stake is the writer's betrayal of the text. What is at stake, that is, is Costello's betrayal of Rayment, her infidelity, her following through *not* following.

In order to divine the nature of Costello's not-following, one has to consider the relationship of which her relationship to Rayment is but a figure, namely that between J. M. Coetzee and the novel entitled *Slow Man*. In this novel, this writer constantly parodies the ability of language and narrative to invest with substance his gift of self and thereby thematize unconditional hospitality. So, for instance, the word "care," through deliberate overuse, becomes increasingly ambivalent and eventually signifies only the dissonance between itself and that which it claims to signify. Most obviously, though, this parody is apparent in the contrived nature of the novel's presentation of the narrative of Paul Rayment's *Bildung*. *Slow Man* does not present itself as Paul Rayment's growth to love, but as a *literary* representation of such a development. Through its sheer artificiality, contrivance and stylized nature, this narrative representation parodies itself and therefore Rayment's progression from "slow man" to "rocket man" (SM, 258), from emotional torpor to the point at which the child, Ljuba, whose name coyly and tritely signifies "love" (SM, 30), smiles on him for the first time in the novel (SM, 258). The tropes of the child and the follower thus suggest that Rayment, now capable of love, is able to follow the invisible, the child. Yet, even as they suggest this, their extravagant, indeed farcical, nature draws attention to their tropological status and, in the process, they come to parody their representational claims. In fact, farce announces itself as farce when Ljuba, after smiling at Rayment, incredulously observes: "You aren't Rocket Man, you're Slow Man!" (SM, 258). The novel's parody of its metaphors, of their inability to metaphorize that which they purport to metaphorize, continues when Costello suggests to Rayment, whom she has earlier described as her "knight with the doleful countenance" (SM, 256), that they tour around Australia in motorized bath chairs. Through this allusion to Don Quixote and Sancho Panza, the metaphor of following turns in on itself and indicates that the text cannot follow what it purports to follow.

By means of his use of parody, Coetzee therefore constantly foregrounds his novel's separation from that which it professes to "represent," to follow. As a representation, it is different from, separate to, that which it claims to present. It comes after, is the past of, that which it seeks to render present. In effect, Coetzee stages the aporia evident in the question that Maurice Blanchot asks of the writing process: "How can I recover it, how can I turn around and look at what exists *before*, if all my power consists of making it into what exists *after*?"[16] The novel always comes *after*. It follows. Indeed, as we have seen, the *Augenblick* or instant of exposure to alterity is diachronous, not "assemblable in a recollection of a representable representation."[17] Precisely this divorce is emphasized by the work's self-reflexive depiction of Costello's inspiration, which, even as it claims to present the moment of the text's coming into being, exposes its exile from that moment by revealing itself to be merely a representation thereof. The work lays bare the ineluctable pastness of the event of its inspiration by presenting Elizabeth Costello as a surrogate author, and thereby, in fact, distancing itself from its actual ontogenesis, that is, the moment of Coetzee's inspiration with Costello, the sentence *he* is sentenced to speak. *Slow Man* is belated, too late, too slow.

Through his use of parody, then, Coetzee, in the very process of following the text, breaks company with it. His parodic subversion of the novel's following of the invisible is, of course, a betrayal of sorts. It is for this reason that Rayment, the text-figure in *Slow Man*, questions the nature of the love that Costello, the writer-figure, feels has come into being in their relationship. It is also for this reason that, after Rayment's "last word," the novel concludes with his formal farewell to Costello, with their breaking of company.

The point I wish to emphasize, though, is that Coetzee's use of parody makes of his following of the text a pursuit and that this not-following is, in fact, necessary for him to follow the text *and* the invisible faithfully and authentically. His betrayal or abandonment of the work is therefore a form of fidelity. Tellingly, in this regard, this writer, in having his novel suggest that it may be the disabling condition for unconditional hospitality, opens it to exactly this experience. It should here again be noted that, rather than presenting Paul Rayment's growth to love, Coetzee presents his novel's failure to present this development. He makes the novel's narrative form signify not presence but a failure thereof and, in the process, indicate the limitlessness that its limits inevitably imply. While it may not have the ability to present love — may well be the very condition of impossibility thereof — the novel thus does have the ability to gesture beyond itself, to gesture to that which is not just different to but more than, indeed infinitely other than, its form and medium. Through investing it with this capacity to point beyond its "givenness"[18] and thereby, crucially, to distance itself from itself, Coetzee opens out the form of his novel to not its opposite but, as Derrida puts it in a discussion of language and hospitality, "an other than itself which is no longer *its* other."[19] In failing to name, invite, and so control, the invisible, the novel opens itself to the possibility of being visited, invaded, possessed and controlled by it. After all, its inability to master that which it seeks to present, precludes this novel from not only including this otherness in, but also excluding it from, its textual economy. If it is hospitable, then, the text is so despite itself. Despite itself, *Slow Man* holds itself open to that which is other than itself.

Although present in Coetzee's earlier novels, this argument is developed in *Slow Man* by the trope of following. In order to follow the invisible, Coetzee must both obey and break the rules of language and the novel. Simply to follow the text would be profoundly irresponsible. To enable *it* to break company with the invisible and thereby be possessed by it, the writer must abandon the text. The form of the abandonment in question, that is, Coetzee's use of parody, is therefore, paradoxically, an act of remaining true to not only the invisible, but also the work. Parody, as Coetzee well knows, pays homage to that which it attacks, betrays. Coetzee betrays the work to be true to it; he interrupts his following of the work in order to follow both it and the invisible. The betrayal at issue is an ineluctable part of this fidelity. What is new in *Slow Man*, then, is not Coetzee's departure from these weighty aesthetic and ethical issues but the explicit manner in which he has engaged with them.

I have thus far limited my discussion of the trope of following to the relationship between writer, text and the invisible. Quite obviously, though, this trope has a bearing on the reader's reading of the work. In responding to the command of the invisible, the writer writes and as soon as he does so a reader is implied by this relationship; from the first, that is, the reader is implicated in the writer's relationship to the invisible. Not only the writer, but also the reader follows the work that "plods" after the invisible. By the same token, the logic of following that informs the writer's relationship to the text also informs the reader's relationship to it. In effect, the novel leads the reader; it is the reader's guide, and a wholly unreliable one at that. Accordingly, the reader must distrust the work. In *Age of Iron*, where the analogy between Vercueil as messenger and text as messenger amplifies the metaphor of following to include the reader, the necessity for such distrust is directly articulated in Mrs Curren's injunction to her daughter:[20]

> I tell you the story of this morning mindful that the storyteller, from her office, claims the place of right. It is through my eyes that you see; the voice that speaks in your head is mine. Through me alone do you find yourself here on these desolate flats, smell the smoke in the air, see the bodies of the dead, hear the weeping, shiver in the rain. It is my thoughts that you think, my despair that you feel . . . To me your sympathies flow; your heart beats with mine.
>
> Now, my child, flesh of my flesh, my best self, I ask you to draw back. I tell you this story not so that you will feel for me but so that you will learn how things are. It would be easier for you, I know, if the story came from someone else, if it were a stranger's voice sounding in your ear. But the fact is, there is no one else. I am the only one. I am the one writing: I, I. So I ask you: attend to the writing, not to me. If lies and pleas and excuses weave among the words, listen for them. Do not pass them over, do not forgive them easily. Read all, even this adjuration, with a cold eye.[21]

If the reader is to follow the text faithfully, he must do so through not following, which is to say betraying, it.

In *Slow Man*, Coetzee's use of parody has much the same effect as Mrs Curren's injunction: it serves as a narrative strategy through which the work urges the reader to distrust and ultimately betray it. The irony is patent: in reading this novel, one follows the metaphor of following only to find that to follow the text responsibly one must not follow its metaphors. Or so it seems. On reflection, it becomes clear that the further irony is that if one simply obeys the text's injunction not to follow it, one, of course, follows it and is therefore still too credulous and trusting in one's relationship to the untrustworthy. As Mrs Curren's words indicate, one must disobey even the injunction to disobey. What is here at stake once more is the absence of a clear-cut opposition between the *acoluthon* and the *anacoluthon*. To disobey it, one must first obey the text. The point, then, is not *not* to follow the text, but not to follow it *in* following it: one must interrupt the logic that informs the text's economy.

Mrs Curren's argument is ultimately the same as Dostoevsky's when he, in *The Master of Petersburg*, tells Maximov, after having read Pavel's political parable about a revolutionary's killing of a landlord, that the reader of this narrative must be the arm, be the axe *and* be the skull that receives the blow.[22] The imperative, here, is therefore to read *against* the differential discourses inscribed by the text's worldliness. In other words, one's reading should resist following the story in its following of history. It should interrupt the narrative's following of history. To read like this is precisely *not* to follow the text *in* following it. Like Elizabeth Costello's following of Paul Rayment, the reader must pursue the text, that is, follow *and* guide it. To follow it faithfully, the reader must betray the text. To trust it, she must distrust it.

Should one manage to read in this way, one will have guided the work to a point at which it exposes one to that which it, through its failure to present (the very slowness, that is, which renders it an unreliable guide), has been unable to exclude from its economy. One will have encountered an otherness which the text hosts despite itself. Indeed, one will have been exposed to an alterity that haunts the text.

Ironically, then, the reader, in following the work as an *anacoluthon*, that is, by persecuting it, by guiding it in its pursuit of the invisible, may be inspired by the invisible. She may become a "secretary of the invisible," which is to say that she will no longer simply pursue but be pursued by the invisible beyond the bounds of the text that she thinks she has "finished" reading. Like Paul Rayment, who, "haunted by the idea of doing good" (SM, 155), eventually follows the Jokić family, the reader's relations in the present in the realm of conditional hospitality will be inspired by, and consequently inflected with, the ethic of absolute hospitality. In the terms of Levinas's argument about the social effect of the self's singular relation to the human other, they will be conducted "in the trace of transcendence, in illeity";[23] they will be interrupted by unconditional care's insistence on coming into being.

Interestingly, in a much earlier work, namely *Age of Iron*, just this desire to pursue and preside over the reader's worldly actions is projected in Coetzee's depiction of Mrs Curren's letter — itself an analogue for the literary text — as a Fury. In an allusion to the Fury's task of accusing and persecuting the violators of filial piety and respectful human relations by, to quote Robert Graves, pursuing them "relentlessly, without rest or pause, from city to city and from country to country,"[24] Mrs Curren first "accuses" her daughter, and letter-reader, of filial impiety and then anticipates her response to her letter: "*I do not need this* you say to yourself through gritted teeth: *this is what I came here to get away from, why does it have to follow me?*"[25] What is striking here, is that the text pursues or follows a follower of history. Very pointedly, Mrs Curren's daughter is depicted as being "like iron"[26] — a person who has been brutalised by the apartheid state's "message." Earlier in the novel, the deforming power of this "message" emerges in the following passage:

> Television. Why do I watch it? The parade of politicians every evening . . . What absorbs them is power and the stupor of power. Eating and talking, munching lives, belching. Slow, heavy-bellied talk. Sitting in a circle, debating ponderously, issuing decrees like hammer-blows: death, death, death. Untroubled by the stench. Heavy eyelids, piggish eyes, shrewd with the shrewdness of generations of peasants . . . And their message stupidly unchanging, stupidly forever the same. Their feat, after years of etymological meditation on the word, to have raised stupidity to a virtue. To stupefy: to deprive of feeling; to benumb, deaden; to stun with amazement. Stupor: insensibility, apathy, torpor of mind. Stupid: dulled in the faculties, indifferent, destitute of thought or feeling. From *stupere* to be stunned, astounded. A gradient from *stupid* to *stunned* to *astonished*, to be turned to stone. The message: that the message never changes. A message that turns people to stone.
>
> We watch as birds watch snakes, fascinated by what is about to devour us.[27]

In contrast to this deforming "message," which "fascinates" its receivers and makes of them followers of history, the novel seeks to interrupt its readers' following of history. As the self-representational device of the letter indicates, *Age of Iron* is able not only to follow but also to pursue and harass those who follow the state on being deformed by its "message." Like the Furies, this novel, in invading and possessing the reader, persecutes and maddens the children of iron. In fact, it cannot *not* do this: possessed as it is by the reader it has possessed, the novel both obediently follows *and* despotically persecutes him or her. It is mastered and burdened by what it masters and burdens. The image of the Furies, that is to say, points to the performative nature of Coetzee's text's engagement with apartheid history: its "rivalling" of the state's message is grounded in the event of possession which makes of it, and indeed the reader, a protector of that which the forms of history deform.[28]

Although set and written in apartheid South Africa, *Age of Iron*'s conception of the literary text's pursuit of its reader is thus remarkably similar to that implicit in *Slow Man*. Indeed, in the later, Australian novel, Paul Rayment, and so the work itself, is portrayed as aspiring to be a guardian angel that "hovers" over and protects others (see, for example, SM, 224). Even more striking, however, is the implicit analogy between the text's pursuit of the reader and that of Sinbad by the old man of the river. In burdening the reader with responsibility for the invisible, for "something that has not yet emerged,"[29] the novel "descends" on his or her shoulders. It pursues *and* guides the reader in his or her social interactions. Costello's aforementioned words to Rayment apply equally to the text's relationship to its reader: "Most of the time you won't notice I am here. Just a touch on the shoulder, now and then, left or right, to keep you on the path" (SM, 87). The novel as *acoluthon* and *anacoluthon* seeks to interrupt, mediate, even justify, the reader's relations in the realm of conditional hospitality.

What is at stake in *Slow Man*'s bid to affect the reader is an attempt to extend the scope of ethical concern to everyone irrespective of identity. Should the reader be moved to responsibility in the course of his engagement with the novel, he will no longer be in a position to choose freely and autonomously his other commitments, to decide independently and rationally to what or whom he will extend care and concern. His relationships will no longer be determined solely by the calculus of invitation and, accordingly, the kind of differential exclusion that engenders ethical indifference. If the novel's ethic of hospitality is to work, the pre-reflective experience of reading must affect the reader's conscious and reflective life. The moment of reading must be an *Augenblick*, a blink of the eye, in which the reader's intentional consciousness is interrupted not only by what it fails to include but also by what it fails to exclude. In other words, Susan Barton's sexual experience with Cruso on the island in *Foe* is exactly the effect that *Slow Man* wishes to have on its reader: "We yield to a stranger's embrace or give ourselves to the waves; for the blink of an eyelid our vigilance relaxes; we are asleep; and when we awake, we have lost the direction of our lives."[30]

Elsewhere, Barton reflects on the way in which such ecstatic experiences remain with one as an "after-memory"[31] or, in Blanchot's description of ecstasy, an "extratemporal memory or remembrance of a past which has never been lived in the present (and thus a stranger to all *Erlebnis*)."[32] It is because she can "summon back nothing distinct" that the "aftermemory" remains with her and ceaselessly insists on being remembered.[33] In aspiring to make of the reading experience an *Augenblick*, *SlowMan* seeks to remain with and in the reader as an insubstantial "aftermemory" which cannot be, and so incessantly demands to be, "summoned" back. Like the Furies, who in their pursuit and persecution of them, drove mad those who had perverted respectful human relations, *Slow Man* thus seeks to drive the reader mad. Should this novel follow and so remain with the reader, and constantly demand that she render possible an impossibility, it will have precisely this effect on her. In requiring her to make of the same a home for the other, to be infinitely responsible despite being a finite being, it will drive him or her mad. It will do so by ensuring that she is always unequal to her infinite responsibility, and so never able to love well enough, always necessarily guilty of betrayal, of irresponsibility. Burdened with a form of responsibility that exacts irresponsibility, the reader will find herself in a double bind and, as Derrida argues, "When you want to make someone mad, you put him or her under a double bind, insisting on it, not just for a minute but *constantly*. If the double bind is the condition for responsibility, or ethics, then ethics are mad."[34]

Ultimately, then, the *Bildung* that is really at issue in this novel is that of not Paul Rayment but of an equally slow man or woman — the reader. In this regard, at least, there is little difference between Coetzee's South African and Australian fiction. In fact, even the element of parody in the later novel's depiction of itself as too "slow" to follow the invisible is already implicit in *Age of Iron* where the novel, in likening itself to a moth,[35] mocks its grandiose ambition to be a Fury. Tellingly, in this connection, Mrs Curren, who turns on one of the police "in a fury"[36] in her attempt to protect John, is only able to follow this child of iron in her imagination. While she protectively "hovers" over him in his final moments, he is already dead.[37] She is too late, too slow.

NOTES

1 Versions of this essay previously appeared in "Coming into Being: J. M. Coetzee's *Slow Man* and the Aesthetic of Hospitality," *Contemporary Literature* 50.2 (2009): 27–98, and *Secretary of the Invisible: The Idea of Hospitality in the Fiction of J. M. Coetzee* (Amsterdam and New York: Rodopi, 2009).

2 J. M. Coetzee, *Elizabeth Costello: Eight Lessons* (London: Secker & Warburg, 2003), 199.

3 J. M. Coetzee, *Slow Man* (London: Secker & Warburg, 2005), 3. Hereafter cited as SM.

4 Emmanuel Levinas, *Otherwise than Being or Beyond Essence*, trans. Alphonso Lingis (The Hague: Martinus Nijhoff, 1981; 1974), 38.

5 Levinas, *Otherwise than Being*, 49; see also 38, 50.

6 Levinas, *Otherwise than Being*, 30, 37–8.

7 John Llewelyn, *Emmanuel Levinas: The Genealogy of Ethics* (London: Routledge, 1995), 55.

8 *Oxford English Dictionary*, 2nd ed., s.v. "Obey."

9 *The Holy Bible*, King James Version (New York: Thomas Nelson Publishers, 1984).

10 Jacques Derrida distinguishes between conditional and unconditional hospitality. At stake here are the ethical implications of the ways in which the subject constructs itself in relation to other identities. The distinction is between a form of subjectivity constituted through a hostile process of inclusion and exclusion and one that comes into being in the self's pre-reflective and traumatic exposure, without inhibition, to otherness. In Derrida's argument, conditional hospitality involves extending an invitation to a guest who is thus named and identified in advance (*Of Hospitality: Anne Dufourmantelle Invites Jacques Derrida to Respond*, trans. Rachel Bowlby (Stanford, California: Stanford University Press, 2000), 25ff.). This form of hospitality, which emanates from the sets of expectations attendant on the self's location in a cultural domain, consequently precludes the possibility of being surprised by the strangeness of a visitor. Instead, the host engages in an exclusionary process of self-affirmation that not only shields him from the strangeness of others but also, through placing them at a distance, enables ethical indifference. Conversely, unconditional hospitality is distinguished by responsiveness to otherness. In Derrida's account, it denotes a receiving of difference "before any determination, before any anticipation, before any *identification*" (*Of Hospitality*, 77). Since the arrival of the stranger or other is unannounced and wholly unexpected, he cannot be known in advance from within a previously formed system of linguistic conceptuality.

11 J. M. Coetzee, *The Master of Petersburg* (London: Secker & Warburg, 1994), 152–3.

12 J. M. Coetzee, *Foe* (Johannesburg: Ravan, 1986), 114.

13 Coetzee, *The Master of Petersburg*, 53.
14 "Following Theory: Jacques Derrida" in Michael Payne and John Schad, eds., *life. after. theory.* (London: Continuum, 2003), 7.
15 J. M. Coetzee, *Age of Iron* (London: Secker & Warburg, 1990), 159.
16 Maurice Blanchot, "Literature and the Right to Death," in *The Work of Fire*, trans. Charlotte Mandell (Stanford, California: Stanford University Press, 1995; 1949), 327.
17 Levinas, *Otherwise than Being*, 51.
18 Theodor W. Adorno, *Aesthetic Theory*, trans. C. Lenhardt, eds. Gretel Adorno and Rolf Tiedemann (London: Routledge and Kegan Paul, 1984; 1970), 67, 386.
19 Jacques Derrida and Anne Dufourmantelle, *Acts of Religion*, ed. Gil Anidjar (New York: Routledge, 2002), 362, original emphasis.
20 Cf. Geertsema's discussion of this passage: "'We Embrace To Be Embraced': Irony in an Age of Iron," *English in Africa* 24.1 (1997): 96–7; "Irony and Otherness: A Study of Some Recent South African Narrative Fiction" (Doctoral thesis, University of Cape Town, 1999), 255.
21 Coetzee, *Age of Iron*, 95–6.
22 Coetzee, *The Master of Petersburg*, 40–1.
23 Levinas, *Otherwise than Being*, 158.
24 Robert Graves, *The Greek Myths*, Vol. 1, 2nd ed. (Harmondsworth: Penguin, 1960), 122, see also 37–8.
25 Coetzee, *Age of Iron*, 127, 178, original emphasis.
26 Coetzee, *Age of Iron*, 68.
27 Coetzee, *Age of Iron*, 25–6, original emphasis.
28 See J. M. Coetzee, "The Novel Today," *Upstream* 6.1 (1988): 2–5.
29 J. M. Coetzee, *Doubling the Point: Essays and Interviews*, ed. David Attwell (Cambridge, Massachusetts: Harvard University Press, 1992), 246.
30 Coetzee, *Foe*, 30.
31 Coetzee, *Foe*, 104.
32 Maurice Blanchot, *The Unavowable Community*, trans. Pierre Joris (Barrytown, New York: Station Hill, 1988; 1983), 19.
33 Coetzee, *Foe*, 104.
34 Payne and Schad, *life. after. theory.*, 36.
35 Coetzee, *Age of Iron*, 118–19.
36 Coetzee, *Age of Iron*, 139.
37 Coetzee, *Age of Iron*, 159–60. See Thangam Ravindranathan, "*Amor Matris*: Language and Loss in J. M. Coetzee's *Age of Iron*," in *Safundi: The Journal of South African and American Studies* 8.4 (2007): 399; and Ian Duncan, "Narrative Authority in J. M. Coetzee's *Age of Iron*," in *Tydskrif vir Letterkunde* 43.2 (2006): 180.

CHAPTER 8

Literary Migration

Shifting Borders in Coetzee's Australian Novels

Sue Kossew

> I am not the we of anyone.
>
> Paul Rayment in *Slow Man*, 193

> I can pass among Australians [as an Australian] . . . That, as far as I am concerned, is all there is to it, to the national-identity business.
>
> Paul Rayment in *Slow Man*, 197

> That is the root of your guy's problem: Africa. That is where he came from, that is where he is stuck, mentally. In his mind he can't get away from Africa.
>
> Alan in *Diary of a Bad Year*, 78

These three quotations from Coetzee's two "Australian novels" (those with an Australian setting) provide me with a useful way of focusing on the topic of this paper: Coetzee's personal and literary migration from South Africa to Australia in 2002 and the implications of this relocation for his fiction. The first two of these quotations, from *Slow Man*, reflect on the constructed nature of national identity and the refusal of the character, Paul Rayment, to "join" this "national-identity business." While Rayment is clearly a fictional character and should not therefore be elided with Coetzee the author, Coetzee has himself commented on his similar reluctance to join with the crowd or to be "the we of anyone." Looking back at his student self, and still identifying with it in an interview with David Attwell, Coetzee comments: "Masses of people wake in him something close to panic. He cannot or will not, cannot and will not, join, shout, sing: his throat tenses up, he revolts."[1] Despite this clearly sceptical approach to national identity and a reluctance to embrace a sense of belonging, Coetzee has become an Australian citizen. Indeed, on taking on citizenship in March 2006 at a special ceremony held during Adelaide Writers' Week, Coetzee made a speech that is now featured on the Australian Government's website, including the following tribute to his new country:

> I was attracted by the free and generous spirit of the people, by the beauty of the land itself and — when I first saw Adelaide — by the grace of the city that I now have the honor to call my home. In becoming a citizen one undertakes certain duties and responsibilities. One of the more intangible of those duties and responsibilities is no matter what one's birth and background, to accept the historical past of the new country as one's own.[2]

Senator Amanda Vanstone, then Immigration Minister for the Coalition Government under John Howard's leadership, regarded Coetzee's commitment to Australia as a "tremendous compliment" paid to a country in which, she said, "we value basic rights — democracy and equality under law and equality of treatment and opportunity."

Certainly, Australia has begun to embrace Coetzee as an "Australian writer" with his essays regularly appearing in the annual collections of *Best Australian Essays* and the Nobel prize for literature ensuring his being claimed as Australia's *second* literary Laureate. Australia has obviously begun to appear as a physical location in his two most recent novels, both set in Australian cities: Adelaide and its streets provide the physical setting of *Slow Man* and an apartment block in Sydney's Darling Harbour that of *Diary of a Bad* Year. But, as Elleke Boehmer has pointed out, Coetzee's Australia is more often than not an "Australia of the mind," a metaphorical setting, rather than a realistic one. Taking up this metaphorical focus, this chapter will examine the ways in which Coetzee deploys the trope of the border or threshold (both physical and ideological) to explore the condition of migrancy itself and the notion of nationhood in these two novels. I will argue that, by *textualizing* the concept of the border, Coetzee explores the paradoxes and contradictions of national belonging as well as questioning the authority of the text itself.

The idea of the power of the State and its control over its citizens is one that is imbedded in *Diary of a Bad Year* as its opening pages and the title of its first "strong opinion," "On the Origins of the State," declare. What does it mean to take on Australian citizenship? How does the modern state control its borders and the access it affords to citizenship? These are ethical questions that both these texts, *Slow Man* and *Diary of a Bad Year*, pose on numerous levels in ways that are familiar to obsessive Coetzee readers: questions of freedom and entrapment for characters and readers; questions of authorship and authority, of who writes and who controls narrative; and questions of choice (whether free or predetermined) that govern political and personal decisions. The principle of equality referred to by Senator Vanstone, while clearly a fundamental aspect of Australian identity, was sorely tested while restrictive laws on migration and freedom of speech were introduced by the Howard Government at the height of the "war on terror." It is during this time that Coetzee's *Diary of a Bad Year* is set. Thus the trope of the border that is deployed in both novels, operating as it does so obviously as a disruption to familiar practices of reading, and related as it is (particularly in the Opinions in *Diary of a Bad Year*) to ideas of state control of national borders, seems to me to warrant special attention.

Jacques Derrida has suggested that writing itself is always at the "running border" or on the edge of "what used to be called a text" and that this instability is a productive one that infinitely defers signification and subverts the dividing lines between "a fiction and a reality," thereby "overrun[ning] all the limits assigned to it."[3] The work of J. M. Coetzee has always engaged with the problematics of borders and thresholds, not just by means of the meta-textual relationship between text and reader referred to by Derrida, and by Coetzee's constant allusions to his own authorship and to the nature of authorship itself, but particularly through his exploration of how borders relate to binaries; binaries of here and there, self and other, body and soul, human and animal, life and afterlife, inside and outside. Where binaries and boundaries mark out difference and separate one entity from another with the certainty of conviction, *unsettling* these certainties by drawing attention to the constructedness of these divisions creates ambivalence, a "neither yes nor no," a "both/and" rather than an "either/or," an ambiguity that is characteristic of all of Coetzee's works.[4]

I suggest that Coetzee's literary use of the border as a trope draws on both these approaches: that is, it engages with the productive instability of the imagined borders of text and reader and also subverts and questions the discourses of certainty that set up material and state borders. As Coetzee states in an interview in *Doubling the Point*, "my difficulty is precisely with the project of stating positions, taking positions."[5] In his essay, "Reflections on Exile," Edward Said has, like Derrida, used the trope of the border to underline epistemological uncertainties associated not just with the idea of home but also with institutionalized constructions of nationhood:

> The exile knows that in a secular and contingent world, homes are always provisional. Borders and barriers, which enclose us within the safety of familiar territory, can also become prisons, and are often defended beyond reason or necessity. Exiles cross borders, break barriers of thought and experience.[6]

While this border-crossing is linked here with exilic identity, Said also called for the wider cultural practice of "a paradoxical mode of thought"[7] that entails "thinking against identity," which, is, as Gougouris suggests, a "call to subvert any *orthodox* tendencies, no matter what their purpose or justification."[8] Such thinking works against the "prisons" of fixed and restrictive national identities. The ultimate fragility of national boundaries is also articulated by post-colonial theorist Bill Ashcroft who has drawn attention to the notion of the colonial boundary as "crucial to the organization of surveillance" instituted by colonialism, yet always "subject to slippage and provisionality."[9]

In relation to this borderline exilic subjectivity articulated by Said, it is important to note that his concept of "late style" (which he develops from Adorno's theory of lateness) *links* a sense of mortality with the state of exile, identifying as one of its fundamental qualities the idea of a "radical discontinuity" and the evading of categorization. Said characterizes a tension inherent in late style that "insists on [its] increasing sense of apartness and exile and anachronism."[10] For Said, one of the marks of late style is its "power to render disenchantment and pleasure without resolving the contradictions between them." In his discussion of Constantine Cavafy,[11] he continues:

> What holds them [these contradictions] in tension, as equal forces straining in different directions, is the artist's mature subjectivity, stripped of hubris and pomposity, unashamed either of its fallibility or of the modest assurance it has gained as a result of age and exile.[12]

Coetzee's two Australian novels are certainly works of "mature subjectivity," both in terms of his own "late style" as he approaches the age of seventy and in their thematic preoccupations. As David Attwell has pointed out, *Slow Man* "deals with bodily frailty and fears of senescence and obsolescence";[13] and *Diary of a Bad Year* has a writer-figure who describes himself as an "old man" who, in the company of five other distinguished writers, has been asked to contribute his "strong opinions" for a German publication. Reflecting on what wisdom such age and eminence may have conferred, the writer figure suggests the following:

> We [six writers] find that we are too old and infirm to enjoy the proper fruits of our triumph. *Is this all?* we say to ourselves, surveying the world of delights we cannot have. *Was it worth all that sweat?*[14]

It is this bodily frailty in the form of deteriorating eyesight and a loss of motor control that gives the writer a reason to employ his young and attractive amanuensis, Anya, who transposes the writer's tape-recorded words onto computer files and whose own commentaries on his opinions provide one of the "running borders" of the text. But it is the text's enactment of unresolved contradictions and of the paradoxical provisionality of borders that most productively engages with Said's linking of "lateness" and exile.

Let me start with the most obvious border in the texts: that of the Australian state itself. For readers of Coetzee, the question of what he would write about once he had left South Africa and taken up residency in Australia was a central one. Would he continue to be "stuck, mentally" in Africa (as Alan accuses the writer-figure, John, of being, in my epigraph from *Diary of a Bad Year*)? In what I can only imagine must have been a somewhat frustrating interview, rather ironically entitled "J. M. Coetzee in conversation with Jane Poyner," she asks Coetzee: "Has your move to Australia opened up new possibilities for writing?" His monosyllabic reply, "Yes," is, of course characteristically, all that he will venture.[15] But his acknowledgement that Australia *has* opened up new possibilities for his writing is an important one, obvious to anyone who has read his two "Australian novels."

What Zoë Wicomb has identified as "the problem . . . of writing about home that has for some time not been home"[16] has been avoided by Coetzee in these last two novels by his foregrounding the very condition of migrancy or border-crossing itself. The new citizen or the migrant is a restless figure; one who is neither at home nor completely displaced; a borderline figure who has intimations of another culture while also inserting him/herself in a host culture. The proliferation of migrant metaphors (to use Elleke Boehmer's term) in these texts not only underscores the ambivalence, plurality and shifting identities of the condition of migrancy itself[17] but also draws attention to the ultimately unstable nature of all fixed identities, ideological discourses and essentialist notions of nationhood despite the modern state's often paranoid policing of these. Perhaps the idea that Australia is often regarded as a land of migrants (apart from — or from another perspective even including — its indigenous peoples) merely emphasizes the ironic positionality of the migrant as well as Australia's historical attempts to police and control its national borders. Nationalist discourses were, of course, at a high pitch during the Howard years, when Coetzee migrated to Australia. With his finely tuned ear for humbug, he clearly picked up the paradoxes of belonging and exclusion that came to a climax during this conservative political regime; ironically, of course, this was also the government under which his citizenship was granted, in the person of Minister Amanda Vanstone herself. The clear contradiction between Minister Vanstone's assertion quoted earlier that Australia values "basic rights . . . and equality of treatment and opportunity" and the Australian government's treatment of would-be asylum seekers at the same time in history would not have escaped him.

As indigenous commentator Aileen Moreton-Robinson has put it:

> Who calls Australia home is inextricably connected to who has possession, and possession is jealously guarded by white Australians . . . the current Australian government, under the leadership of Prime Minister John Howard, ran its 2001 election campaign along race lines . . . It asserted its right to choose who enters Australia — that is, who will be granted the status of migrant and who will be deemed "illegal" trespasser . . . This occurred despite its avowed policies of "multiculturalism" and the ostensible breakdown of hegemonic whiteness.[18]

What is clear in both his "Australian" novels is that Coetzee has — on a number of levels — *taken on* his Australian citizenship. That is, he has become an Australian citizen and that has entitled him to critique that very notion. For Coetzee has always been sceptical of the idea of belonging and, like many ex-South Africans, deeply suspicious of nationalism. So it is not surprising that both novels question and unsettle ideas of Australian-ness, thereby performing what Edward Said suggested should be the role of the public intellectual — that is to disrupt "dominant norms . . . so intimately connected . . . to the nation, which is always triumphalist, always in a position of authority, always exacting loyalty and subservience."[19]

It is significant that a number of the characters in *Slow Man*, for example, do not identify themselves as Australian. As I have already intimated, Paul Rayment himself, we are told, migrated to Australia from France as a child, but has never felt himself at home in Australia — "I can pass among Australians. I cannot pass among the French . . . That is all there is to it, to the national-identity business,"[20] as he says to Elizabeth. In other words, national identity is not embodied or essential but merely performative: "passing" for Australian is "all there is to . . . the national-identity business." Such scepticism about the essentialist nature of national identity spills over into *Diary of a Bad Year*, too. The writer figure says of Anya (in the middle band of text) that she "likes to present herself as a Filipina, a little Filipina guestworker. In fact she has never lived in the Philippines. Her father was an Australian diplomat who married a woman he met at a cocktail party in Manila . . ." (DBY, 59). Similarly, the national origins of the writer figure are muddled: Anya continues to call him Señor C and Juan, even after she is made aware that Mrs Saunders, who "says he is from Columbia" (DBY, 41), is wrong, and that he is not from South America but from South Africa. Such "cavalier" attitudes towards national identity clearly push against the drawing of clear boundaries that is so essential to nationalist discourses.

In both novels, too, a crucial aspect of the migrant perspective is at the level of language. Paul Carter, in his *Living in a New Country: History, Travelling and Language* (1991) writes of the migrant's "ontological angst" relating to the "fragile nature of communication in a new country."[21] For Carter, as for Coetzee, this linguistic alienation is not a measure of the migrant's loss of "expressive power" but rather a way of revealing "the rhetorical and contextual conventions governing *all* expression."[22]

For example, in *Slow Man*, Paul's lack of belonging or being at home in Australia is not simply a matter of nationality, even though he was born in France (he calls himself "the boy from Lourdes" (SM, 52)). He admits to Elizabeth that he speaks English like a foreigner because he is a "foreigner by *nature*" (SM, 231, my emphasis) and has been a foreigner all his life. There is an interesting link here with Coetzee's own musings, in an interview with David Attwell in *Doubling the Point*, about his own sense of being an outsider. Here he is describing his lack of homesickness for South Africa when he was in Britain or the United States, characteristically referring to himself in the third person, as he does in both his "memoirs," *Boyhood* and *Youth*:

> A sense of being alien goes far back in his memories . . . by the age of twelve he has a well-developed sense of social marginality . . . All this confirms his (quite accurate) sense of being outside a culture that at this moment in history is confidently setting about enforcing itself as the core culture of the land.[23]

While he is talking about his alienation from Afrikaner nationalism within South Africa in this extract, there is clearly in the character of Paul and even more clearly in the character of JC in *Diary of a Bad Year*, a parallel sense of alienation from the exclusionary discourses of nationalism generally. While Paul in *Slow Man* recognizes that this outsider status is how he marks out his own sense of individuality, he relates this border zone to that policed by the nation state — "If there were no foreigners there would be no natives" (SM, 231). For Paul, Australian history itself is a history from which he feels excluded — "foreigners keep out," "an affair for the English and the Irish" (SM, 52). In this way, the authority of the nation and the dominance of its norms referred to by Said control and mark out its physical and psychological borders.

Linked to this awareness of not quite belonging is the sense in which language operates as a marker of national identity. While the first-generation Jokić family retain their Slavic version of Australian English that marks them as migrants, Paul (a "native speaker") is nevertheless also distanced from the English language in which he asserts he has never felt at home but speaks rather like "a kind of ventriloquist's dummy . . . it is the language that is spoken through me" (SM, 198).

The writer figure in *Diary of a Bad Year* asserts a similar linguistic homelessness to that articulated by Paul Rayment. He poses the question:

> Does each of us have a mother tongue? . . . Perhaps — is this possible? — I have no mother tongue . . .
>
> Are these words, printed out on paper, truly what I wanted to say? . . . Perhaps it is so that all languages are, finally, foreign languages, alien to our *animal* being. But in a way that is, precisely, inarticulate, inarticulable, English does not feel to me like a resting place, a home. It just happens to be a language over whose resources I have achieved some mastery.
>
> (DBY, 156–7, my emphasis)

Thus what could be seen as the "joke" (much earlier in the text) of Anya's crediting him with speaking "very good English . . . considering English isn't . . . [his] mother tongue" (DBY, 44–5) — promulgating the fiction of his being South American rather than South African — takes on a somewhat different dimension. For, as Carter asserts in his *Living in a New Country*, the "ghostly aspect that words assume in migrant discourse"[24] simply reveals the constructedness of *all* expression, all language. The condition of migrancy, in other words, is not limited to migrants: it is the condition of humanity itself (or, in Coetzee's words, "all languages are . . . alien to our *animal* being"). By emphasizing migrant restlessness — the lack of a home, a resting place, a mother tongue — as transcending national identity and suggesting that perhaps "all languages are . . . finally foreign languages," JC is ironically articulating the alien and fragile nature of subjectivity itself.

By drawing attention to the constructedness of national borders (both physical and linguistic), Coetzee's Australian texts underline the paradoxical limitations of both nation and text. The tropes of the cage and of surveillance — whilst providing a contemporary political reference point to Guantanamo Bay and the internment of David Hicks there and to the Baxter Detention Centre, closer to home in South Australia — are also deployed in *Diary of a Bad Year* to explore more *abstract* ideas of freedom and entrapment. Whereas in *Slow Man*, Paul is trapped within his own textual representation — "All the time he thought he was his own master he has been in cage like a rat . . . with the infernal woman [Elizabeth Costello] standing over him, observing, listening, taking notes, recording his progress" (SM, 122) — for the writer in *Diary of a Bad Year*, the cages are self-imposed or perhaps imposed by being human. The resonant description of the relationship between the writer figure and the "magpie-in-chief" whereby they reach a mutual compromise about ownership of the public park provides an example:

> . . . he [the magpie] is prepared to entertain the possibility of a compromise: a compromise, for example, in which I beat a retreat into one of the protective cages that we human animals have erected on the far side of the street, while he retains this space as his own; or a compromise in which I agree to come out of my cage only during specified hours, between three and five in the afternoon, say, when he likes to take a snooze.
>
> (DBY, 163)

What this paragraph does is to expose the flimsiness of the borders we have set up between animals and humans ("we human animals," "protective cages") and consequently to expose the limitations of our own sense of freedom and power. It is only through "compromise" that the relationship here, figured also as a flipped kind of host and visitor one, can proceed; paradoxically, of course, it is the bird "of the air" who has the upper hand (as it were) in this transaction of belonging, this agreement of settlement. The competing territorial instincts of human and animal are humorously evoked with reference to this most territorial of Australian suburban birds.

Similarly, a cockatoo that visits the park holds out a plum kernel to the writer as if to offer him a bite:

> I want to say: "This is a public garden. You are as much a visitor as I, it is not up to you to offer me food." But public, private, it is no more than a puff of air to him. "It's a free world," he says.
>
> (DBY, 165)

The contrast between the human notion of boundaries (public, private, visitor, owner) and the birds' borderless world provides another perspective on the power of the state to control entry. The world of the birds does not recognize borders, does not seek entry or exit permits, and thereby *undoes* human attempts to control national borders, both psychologically and physically.

The very real consequences of crossing the political borderline and the contrast between this "free world" of the birds and that of Howard's Australia are starkly drawn by the writer-figure in his "opinion" entitled "On Asylum in

Australia" where he posits the similarities between Baxter Detention Centre and Guantanamo Bay and poses the question:

> How can a decent, generous, easygoing people close their eyes while strangers who arrive on their shores pretty much helpless and penniless are treated with such heartlessness, such grim callousness? I suppose . . . they have to close their eyes and ears.
>
> What they have created . . . is a system of deterrences, and indeed a spectacle of deterrence.
>
> *Behold: this is what happens to those who cross the line we have drawn. Be warned.*
>
> (DBY, 93–4, original emphasis)

It is, of course, significant that the "line" or threshold of the nation state is described as one "we" have drawn, emphasizing the complicity of all those who participate in such exclusionary discourses and practices. The state's system of control over those allowed to enter its borders, then, is, according to the writer figure, comparable to past transportation to the Antipodes: in a more typically Coetzeean phrase, "Today's refugees find themselves in much the same boat as yesterday's transported" (DBY, 94). Why, JC implies, do white Australians, with their own history of past injustices, not empathize with these refugees? This "heartlessness" and "callousness" and the closing of "eyes and ears" amounts, according to JC, to a national shame, which is in turn related to a legacy of settler shame. Like the generations of white South Africans "to which I belong" who are "bowed under the shame of the crimes committed in their name" (DBY, 39–40). JC suggests that Australians, too, are complicit in their government's support of America's "war on terror" and its consequent establishment of a "laager mentality" to keep out potential "terrorists." It is useful to note that Coetzee himself, echoing JC's opinion, was reported as having compared Howard's anti-terrorism laws to "apartheid-era human rights abuses in his native South Africa" during a public reading at the National Library in Canberra in 2005.[25]

The text's suggestion, then, of an equivalent shame shared by South Africa and Australia in their restrictions of human rights at this time during the "war on terror" draws explicit parallels with the apartheid state. The word "crimes" here is a key one in linking the two settler colonies, referring both to the convicts transported to Australia and also to the "crime" of apartheid.[26] In this context, the line drawn, the borderline that separates one set of people from another, takes on further significance as a "threshold of tolerance" (to quote French President Mitterand) to immigration itself.[27] As in apartheid South Africa, crossing this line or border has serious implications, separating "host" from "foreigner" or even "intruder." Derrida's teasing out of the differences between conditional and unconditional hospitality draws attention to the innate hostility in a nation's taking on the role of "host" — what he terms "hostipitality."[28] Perhaps Coetzee's comparison of settler shame between his ex-homeland South Africa and Australia also forms part of his rather more subversive way of "accept[ing] the historical past of the new country as one's own," in the words spoken at his citizenship ceremony and quoted earlier.

But political borders are only one aspect of the text. There are personal and textual borders, too — as Anya makes a daily journey down from her penthouse apartment to deliver her typing to Señor C's apartment and collect the next tape, so too the borderlines between the textual voices start to affect/infect one another, travelling across time and space. She mistypes his words, which he then has to retype; he incorporates her suggestions and changes the text so that, for example, "Talk Radio" (more of an American than Australian phrase) becomes Australianized to "Talkback Radio." Her comments on his work make the reader flip backwards and forwards, checking and rereading, rewriting the text, as do his comments on her responses. Thus the most obvious borderline of the linear narrative (the page) is disrupted and undermined, its fixity in time and space disturbed by the act of reading, by the rewritings of the text and by implication the provisionality of textuality itself. Each band of the text occupies a different time-band and place as well as expressing different voices, each "talking back" to one another. The model of talkback radio, where strong opinions are expressed and commentary from listeners is invited, could indeed be seen as analogous to the structure of this text. It could also be argued that talkback radio represents a democratization of accessibility to the expression of ideas, echoed in the text's multi-vocal form.

Yet this very accessibility disturbs the borderline between what is private and what is public, hidden and "hacked into." The state of surveillance characterized by national watchfulness in a time of "terror" is replicated on the personal level in the text by the invasion of JC's private financial computer files by Alan's spyware and by the possibility that Alan posits to Anya that John has been writing about her "in secret." Additionally, it becomes clear that Alan has been going through Anya's files behind her back and has been using his spyware to access JC's computer, "poking around among his private thoughts" (DBY, 97). Thus the unanswered questions posed by the writer in the opinion, "On Democracy" — "Who serves whom? Who is the servant, who the master?" (DBY, 15) — are seen to invade all aspects of the text. The textual implications of this question give rise to further questions — what authority does the text have? What is the demarcation line in this text between the writer/secretary/reader? What is the relationship between Coetzee the writer and JC the writer (the teasing similarities and differences dotted cunningly throughout the text)? How does this destabilize the text itself and the reading process? It is, of course, my argument that the border itself performs this disruption, ostensibly trying to close off one segment of text, one voice from the other, but instead lending itself to being breached, in much the same way as national borders are breached by "illegal arrivals" (DBY, 94). The unsettling nature of the reading process itself — instigated largely by the text's own typographic borders — is thus analogous both to historical processes of settlement and to attempts to control and police the borders of the modern state.

And, characteristically, Coetzee the writer has anticipated a response to JC the writer-figure's opinions, incorporating within the text a critique of his credentials to "pronounce judgement on us" (DBY, 81), couched in the usual clichés of the host culture defending itself against criticism by migrants and voiced in the text by Alan

— "He doesn't understand Australian politics . . . If he wants old-fashioned politics . . . he should go back to Africa. He will be completely at home there" (DBY, 82). But, to return to Aileen Moreton-Robinson's words I quoted previously: "Who calls Australia home is inextricably connected to who has possession." Coetzee's text shows a strikingly incisive understanding of how borders are "simultaneously social, cultural and psychic . . . places where claims to ownership . . . are staked out, contested, defended, fought over"[29] during a period of Australia's history that posed just such political and ethical choices both for the state and for individual citizens within it. These are, indeed, the choices that are posed also for the reader, who has to make similar decisions, not just by working out how to read the text but also by pondering on the authorship and authority of its component parts. In disturbing the surface of textual stability and implicating the reading process itself, Coetzee deploys what David Attwell has called a "defamiliarization of place,"[30] taking on his Australian citizenship and the responsibilities it entails by engaging critically with a particularly "bad year" in Australia's history.

NOTES

1 J. M. Coetzee, *Doubling the Point: Essays and Interviews*, ed. David Attwell (Cambridge: Harvard University Press, 1992), 394.

2 J. M. Coetzee, "Another chapter for Nobel winner . . ." www.citizenship.gov.au/should_become/personal-stories/coetzee.htm/ (accessed 2 May 2009).

3 Jacques Derrida, "Living on: Border lines," in *The Derrida Reader: Between the Blinds*, ed. Peggy Kamuf (New York: Columbia University Press, 1991), 257.

4 A more detailed version of this discussion of borders in relation to *Slow Man* appears in Sue Kossew, "Border Crossings: Self and Text," in *J. M. Coetzee in Context and Theory*, eds. Elleke Boehmer, Robert Eaglestone and Katy Iddiols (London: Continuum, 2009): 60–70.

5 Coetzee, *Doubling the Point*, 205.

6 Edward Said, "Reflections on Exile," in *Reflections on Exile and Other Essays* (Cambridge: Harvard University Press, 2000), 185.

7 Said's phrase is "to practice *a paradoxical mode of thought*" and appears in Edward Said, *Humanism and Democratic Criticism* (New York: Columbia University Press, 2004), 83. Cited in Stathis Gougouris, "The Late Style of Edward Said," in *Edward Said and Critical Decolonization*, ed. Ferial J. Ghazoul (Cairo and New York: American University in Cairo Press, 2007), 42.

8 Stathis Gougouris, "The Late Style of Edward Said," 42.

9 Bill Ashcroft, *Postcolonial Transformations* (London and New York: Continuum 2001), 162, 181.

10 Edward Said, *On Late Style: Music and Literature against the Grain* (New York: Pantheon Books, 2006), 17.

11 It is interesting to note that Coetzee has, of course, used Cavafy's poem, "Waiting for the Barbarians," as the title of his earlier novel of that name.

12 Said, *On Late Style*, 148.

13 David Attwell, "Coetzee's Estrangements," *Novel: A Forum on Fiction* 41.2/3 (2008): 233.

14 J. M. Coetzee, *Diary of a Bad Year* (Melbourne: Text Publishing, 2007), 22, original emphasis. Hereafter abbreviated as DBY.

15 Jane Poyner, *J. M. Coetzee and the Idea of the Public Intellectual* (Athens, OH: Ohio University Press, 2006), 24.

16 Stephan Meyer and Thomas Olver, "Zoë Wicomb Interviewed on *Writing and Nation*," *Journal of Literary Studies* 18.1/2 (June 2002): 183.

17 See Paul White's introduction to *Writing Across Worlds: Literature and Migration*, eds. Russell King, John Connell and Paul White (London and New York: Routledge, 1995), 15.
18 Aileen Moreton-Robinson, "I still call Australia Home: Indigenous Belonging and Place in a White Postcolonizing Society," in *Uprootings/Regroundings: Questions of Home and Migration*, eds. Sara Ahmed, Claudia Castañeda, Anne-Marie Fortier and Mimi Sheller (Oxford and New York: Berg, 2003): 27–8.
19 Edward Said, *Representations of the Intellectual: The 1993 Reith Lectures* (New York: Vintage Books, 1996), 36.
20 J. M. Coetzee, *Slow Man* (Milson's Point, NSW: Random House Australia/Knopf, 2005), 197. Hereafter abbreviated as SM.
21 Paul Carter, *Living in a New Country: History, Travelling and Language* (London: Faber, 1992), 121, 120.
22 Carter, *Living in a New Country*, 115, original emphasis.
23 Coetzee, *Doubling the Point*, 393–4.
24 Carter, *Living in a New Country*, 115.
25 "Aussie laws 'like apartheid'," SAPA, 24 October 2005, 12:09, www.news24.com/News24/World/News/0,9294,2-10-1462_1822133,00.html (accessed 2 January 2010).
26 Coetzee, *Doubling the Point*, 342. Coetzee says of the apartheid regime: "The whites of South Africa participated, in various degrees, actively or passively, in an audacious and well-planned *crime* against Africa" (my emphasis).
27 Cited in Kevin O'Gorman, "Jacques Derrida's philosophy of hospitality," *The Hospitality Review* 8.4 (2006): 54.
28 Jacques Derrida, "Hostipitality," *Angelaki: Journal of the Theoretical Humanities* 5.3 (2000): 3–18. Cited in O'Gorman "Jacques Derrida's philosophy of hospitality," 51. It is, of course, significant that Anya "had been in the hospitality industry" (DBY, 12).
29 Avtar Brah, *Cartographies of Diaspora: Contesting Identities* (2nd ed. London: Routledge: 2002), 198.
30 Attwell, "Coetzee's Estrangements," 242.

CHAPTER 9

The Melancholy Ape

Coetzee's Fables of Animal Finitude

Chris Danta

A HESITATION BEFORE DEATH

Early on in the first of his fictional memoirs, *Boyhood: Scenes from Provincial Life*, J. M. Coetzee recounts a dramatic incident in which he almost drowns while on a scout camp near the Breede River in the Western Cape Province of South Africa. On the third day of the camp, all the new cadets (or "tenderfeet," as they are called) are required to swim across the river and back. Despite not actually knowing how to swim, the young Coetzee manages to splash his way across the river once, but then becomes exhausted on the return leg. As his head starts to dip under the water, a vision comes to him of his mother and brother reading the official letter telling of his death. The next thing he knows he is back on the riverbank, having been pulled to safety by his troop leader Michael.

In thinking back over this incident in the weeks that follow, Coetzee is overcome with admiration for the heroism of the older boy Michael, but also with the feeling of his own existential insignificance. Indeed, the two things go together: Michael's heroism only serves to expose Coetzee's sense of personal negligibility.

> Each time it strikes him how wonderful it is that Michael should have noticed — noticed him, noticed he was failing. Compared with Michael (who is Standard Seven and has all except the most advanced badges and is going to be a King's Scout) he is negligible. It would have been quite appropriate for Michael not to have seen him go under, even not to have missed him until they got back to camp. Then all that would have been required of Michael would have been to write a letter to his mother, the cool, formal letter beginning: "We regret to inform you . . ."
>
> From that day onward he knows there is something special about him. He should have died but he did not. Despite his unworthiness, he has been given a second life. He was dead but is alive.[1]

It is hard to read this passage — with its focus on unworthiness and self-erasure — without being reminded of Coetzee's great literary forbear, the Czech writer Franz Kafka. In an interview with David Attwell in *Doubling the Point*, Coetzee freely admits his debt to Kafka: "I acknowledge [the impact of Kafka on my fiction] . . . with what I hope is the proper humility. As a writer I am not worthy to loose the latchet of Kafka's shoe."[2] Kafka was a master of the rhetoric of self-deprecation and once famously described himself in his *Diaries* as "a hesitation before birth."[3] Rather than a hesitation before birth, Coetzee might have accounted for his own feeling of negligibility in the wake of his near-death experience by calling himself "a hesitation before death."

The thought of death is never very far away in Coetzee — and I think the Breede River incident in *Boyhood* helps us to understand why that is. When the young Coetzee is pulled out of the water by Michael, a second life opens up for him that takes place between the thought of his imminent death — of his mother and brother reading the formal letter beginning "We regret to inform you . . ." — and death itself. "He should have died but he did not. Despite his unworthiness, he has been given a second life. He was dead but is alive." Coetzee imbues his account of the near-death experience with theological overtones. In presenting his rescue as the receipt of an unmerited favour, he invokes the theological notion of grace: "The free and unmerited favour of God as manifested in the salvation of sinners and the bestowing of blessings."[4] Michael is also the name of an archangel in the Christian, Jewish and Islamic traditions. In Hebrew, the name Michael means, "Who is like God." Despite these teasing allusions to theological frameworks of meaning, it is a boy scout ("who is Standard Seven") and not an archangel who delivers Coetzee to safety on the bank of the Breede River. Coetzee's unmerited reprieve from death thus remains a moment of secular grace.

I take Coetzee's near-death by drowning to be not just a life-changing event, but also a fiction-changing event. If this incident has a reality beyond the pages of *Boyhood* (as I'm supposing it does), then it helps us to see why Coetzee's central characters are constantly burrowing into that melancholy space between the thought of their own death and death itself. It also reveals one of the organizing tropes of Coetzee's fiction to be that of a second life opening up within the first. This is how Paul Rayment, the central protagonist of *Slow Man*, reflects upon his near-fatal bicycle accident:

> If this does not amount to a big moment, a Copernican moment, then what does? The greatest of all secrets may just have unveiled itself to him. There is a second world side by side with the first, unsuspected. One chugs along in the first for a certain length of time; then the angel of death arrives in the person of Wayne Blight or someone like him. For an instant, for an aeon, time stops; one tumbles down a dark hole. Then, hey presto, one emerges into a second world *identical with the first*, where time resumes and action proceeds . . . except that now one has Elizabeth Costello around one's neck, or someone like her.[5]

Rather than archangel Michael, Coetzee here invokes the angel of death. But the angel of death is given the decidedly human form of the (aptly named) teenage hoon Wayne Blight, whose car knocks Rayment off his bicycle on Magill Road in Adelaide at the start of *Slow Man* in the terrible accident that leads to Rayment's right leg being amputated above the knee. Rayment's revelation in the passage above is of death as an almost-imperceptible transformation of his former life: "a mere hiccup in time after which life goes on as before."[6] The second life that opens up for him within the first, once he has tumbled down the dark hole of near-death, is not a higher life but rather a hesitation before death, a fall back into "a second world *identical with the first*, where time resumes and action proceeds."

Despite their frequent ruminations about the afterlife, Coetzee's characters cleave to the mundane with animal-like determination. Immediately after his "Copernican moment," Rayment thinks to himself, "*I want my old life back, the one that came to an end on Magill Road*."[7] He resents being thrust by his creator Elizabeth Costello into the ever-narrowing and agonistic space between the thought of death and death itself. But he does not seek to transcend his predicament by experiencing the afterlife in a genuinely theological way. The same can be said for the central protagonist of *Age of Iron*, Elizabeth Curren, who learns at the beginning of this novel that she is dying of cancer. For Curren, the experience of terminal cancer becomes a second life within the first. At one point in her long love letter to her adult daughter in America, she writes: "My daughter is my first child. She is my life. This [cancerous growth] is the second one, the afterbirth, the unwanted."[8] A second child, a second life, unwanted afterbirth. But even as her illness makes her contemplate "the other side," at no point does Curren give up on this life. "Yet this first life," she writes, "this life on earth, on the body of earth — will there, can there be a better? Despite the glooms and despairs and rages, I have not let go of my love of it."[9]

A passage from *Boyhood* helps us to see how Elizabeth Curren here probably speaks for J. M. Coetzee when she cleaves lovingly to the glooms and despairs and rages of the mundane. In this passage, which exhibits a gentle but grim kind of humour, the young Coetzee attests to being unable to listen to the account of Jesus' resurrection in Luke 24 being read out aloud in class.

> Though he himself is an atheist and has always been one, he feels he understands Jesus better than Mr Whelan does . . . At least Jesus did not pretend to be God, and died before he could become a father. That is Jesus' strength; that is how Jesus keeps his power.
>
> But there is one part in Luke's gospel that he does not like to hear read. When they come to it, he grows rigid, blocks his ears. The women arrive at the sepulchre to anoint the body of Jesus. Jesus is not there. Instead they find two angels. "Why seek ye the living among the dead?" say the angels: "He is not here but is risen." If he were to unblock his ears and let the words come through to him, he knows, he would have to stand on his seat and shout in triumph. He would have to make a fool of himself forever.[10]

Coetzee here wants Jesus the mortal man, not Jesus the immortal Son of God. For the young atheist, the power Jesus retains — even over God — is the power he achieves in death, by dying. Coetzee's heretical step is thus to separate Jesus from God, the mortal from the immortal: "At least Jesus did not pretend to be God, and died before he could become a father."

In *Boyhood,* it is almost as if Coetzee is suggesting that God is jealous of Jesus for leading a mortal life. In *Elizabeth Costello: Eight Lessons*, Coetzee's fictional alter ego Costello explicitly entertains this possibility of an immortal being jealous of a mortal in the context of Greek mythology, when she muses to herself that it is our death-bound subjectivity that makes us sexually attractive to the gods.

> In marking us down for death, the gods gave us an advantage over them. Of the two, gods and mortals, it is we who live the more urgently, feel the more intensely. That is why they cannot put us out of their minds, cannot get by without us, ceaselessly watch us and prey on us . . . Inventors of death; inventors of sex tourism too. In the sexual ecstasies of mortals, the *frisson* of death, its contortions, its relaxings: they talk about it endlessly when they have had too much to drink — who they first got to experience it with, what it felt like. They wish they had that inimitable little quiver in their own erotic repertoire, to spice up their couplings with each other. But the price is one they are not prepared to pay. Death, annihilation: what if there is no resurrection, they wonder misgivingly?[11]

This passage achieves its considerable power by introducing limits where we thought there were none. It shows Costello entering imaginatively into the apparently unlimited being of the Greek gods only to discover the limit of that particular mode of being. Costello's act of the sympathetic imagination has the effect of reversing traditional theological reasoning: rather than the gods being inscrutable to humans, it is we humans who prove inscrutable to the gods. As Costello concludes her heretical line of speculation: "We think of them as omniscient, these gods, but the truth is they know very little, and what they know know only in the most general ways."[12] The gods may retain power over humans — indeed, to the extent of becoming so-called sex tourists. But insofar as the thought of death remains foreign to them, they cannot really know what it is like to be human. In this sense, death becomes the truly anthropomorphic thought, the thought the gods themselves cannot bear to entertain, the thought that makes them stop up their ears like the young Coetzee about to hear the story of Jesus' resurrection read out in class: "Death, annihilation: what if there is no resurrection, they wonder misgivingly?"

OF GODS, HUMANS AND ANIMALS

In a recent article on *Elizabeth Costello*, Michael Valdez Moses points out something that most reviewers of this novel have missed: while "the work is concerned with human beings and animals (and their fraught relations) . . . the work of the rigorously sceptical and secular Coetzee is similarly concerned with the divine; it is a work populated by the gods, who are everywhere present." "What are we to make of Coetzee's tripartite division of his fictional universe into gods, men, and animals," Moses goes on to ask, "and in particular of his unexpected and seemingly anachronistic and unfashionable concern with the divine?"[13] Coetzee's tripartite division of his fictional universe into gods, men and animals begins to make sense, I would suggest, when we see how he uses it to explore the problem of finitude. Coetzee does not so much anthropomorphise the gods in *Elizabeth Costello* as measure them according to the anthropomorphic thought of finitude. For him, to be a god is to lack a sense of finitude and, for this reason, to desire its vicarious experience.

We might see Coetzee's ironic presentation of the Greek gods in *Elizabeth Costello* — as beings that desire mortals but not mortality — as yet another facet of his critique of the notion of individual resurrection. The young Coetzee of *Boyhood* finds the idea of Jesus' resurrection so preposterous as to be laughable. In his touching essay "On the Afterlife," the protagonist of *Diary of a Bad Year*, JC, responds to the problem more earnestly and maturely: "It is surprising that the notion of an individual afterlife persists in intellectually respectable versions of Christianity. It so transparently fills a lack — an incapacity to think of a world from which the thinker is absent — that religion ought simply to note such incapacity as part of the human condition and leave it at that."[14] The point here is that human beings have an incorrigible tendency to anthropomorphise the afterlife by imagining themselves persisting in it as individuals (Jesus' resurrection being, from this perspective, both the most elaborate manifestation and the most elaborate justification of such anthropomorphism). At the end of his essay, JC (the initials, coincidentally, not just of John Coetzee but also of Jesus Christ) tries to correct what he sees as the mistake of Christianity by promoting a non-anthropomorphic version of the afterlife: "The persistence of the soul in an unrecognizable form, unknown to itself, without memory, without identity," he writes, "is another question entirely."[15]

Rather than an afterlife, this perhaps more closely resembles an "afterdeath" — a mere prolongation of the dissolution of personal identity that can be thought to take place in the moment of death, a death without any of the human machinery of illumination: consciousness, memory, identity.

JC's formulation of an utterly impersonal afterlife once again shows the thought of death trumping the thought of life in Coetzee. There is a sense in which Coetzee pits a Kafkaesque rhetoric of self-erasure against the Christian doctrine of individual afterlife. "Even I, who live on shores where the waters swallow grown men, where life-expectancy declines every year, am having a death without illumination," writes Elizabeth Curren to her daughter in *Age of Iron*.

> Do I wish death upon my grandchildren? Are you, at this very instant, flinging the page away from you in disgust? *Mad old woman!* are you crying out? . . . By no means do I

> wish death upon them . . . But the wings you have tied on them will not guarantee them life. Life is dust between the toes. Life is dust between the teeth. Life is biting the dust.
> Or: life is drowning. Falling through water, to the floor.[16]

The predominance of water and drowning imagery here reminds us not just of the Breede River incident in *Boyhood*, but also of the poetic last pages of *Foe* in which an unnamed first-person narrator describes descending into the sunken wreck of Cruso's ship and discovering along with the bloated corpses of Cruso and Susan Barton the merest signs of life coming from Friday.[17] In *Age of Iron*, Curren writes so morbidly about her two grandchildren in America, "whose life-expectancy is seventy-five and rising,"[18] because she has recently borne witness to the premature and pointless deaths of her two surrogate grandchildren in South Africa, her housekeeper Florence's son Bheki and his troubled friend Johannes. The death of those children she has known naturally inflects her thinking about the life of those children she has not.

Coetzee's protagonists often come to express solidarity with various marginalized others by avowing the thought of an un-illuminated death. Coetzee's second fictional memoir, *Youth*, ends on a truly bathetic note, with the twenty-four-year-old Coetzee in London imagining his fellow computer programmer and social outsider, Ganapathy, who does not like cooking and so only eats bananas, absurdly dying from self-imposed malnutrition:

> He and Ganapathy are two sides of the same coin: Ganapathy starving not because he is cut off from Mother India but because he doesn't eat properly, because despite his M.Sc. in computer science he doesn't know about vitamins and minerals and amino acids; and he locked into an attenuating endgame, playing himself, with each move, further into a corner and into defeat. One of these days the ambulance men will call at Ganapathy's flat and bring him out with a sheet over his face. When they have fetched Ganapathy they might as well come and fetch him too.[19]

As with Elizabeth Curren's real and adopted grandchildren, here we have the strange twinning of mortal misfits. So strong is Coetzee's identification with Ganapathy's incapacity to live that he becomes his colleague's twin not only in life but also in death. According to Walter Benjamin in his influential essay "The Storyteller," "the reader of a novel actually does look for human beings from whom he derives the "meaning of life." Therefore he must, no matter what, know in advance that he will share their experience of death: if need be their figurative death — the end of the novel — but preferably their actual one."[20] Instead of human beings from whom we might derive the meaning of life, what Coetzee gives us at the end of *Youth* is the truly grim prospect of two un-illuminated deaths for the price of one.

THE ZOOMORPHIC THOUGHT OF DEATH

Earlier, I called death the truly anthropomorphic thought because Coetzee presents it as being anathema to the gods. This designation is quite useful in the context of Elizabeth Costello's discussion of the relation between the human and the divine because anthropomorphism was originally the theological sin of presenting the divine in human form. But it is inaccurate insofar as it utterly ignores the third component of Coetzee's fictional universe: animals. In the context of what Coetzee has to say about the fraught relations between humans and animals, death is more properly called the zoomorphic than the anthropomorphic thought. Coetzee's gods treat the thought of death as a kind of epistemological no-man's-land. They prefer to physically trespass upon rather than mentally occupy the territory of mortals. Coetzee's animals, by contrast, share our lot to the extent that they share our awareness of finitude. A most remarkable passage in *Boyhood* concerns the foreknowledge sheep on the Coetzee family farm display of their impending deaths in Cape Town abattoirs.

> Sometimes when he is among the sheep — when they have been rounded up to be dipped, and are penned tight and cannot get away — he wants to whisper to them, warn them of what lies in store. But then in their yellow eyes he catches a glimpse of something that silences him: a resignation, a foreknowledge not only of what happens to sheep at the hands of Ros behind the shed, but of what awaits them at the end of the long, thirsty ride to Cape Town on the transport lorry. They know it all, down to the finest detail, and yet they submit. They have calculated the price and are prepared to pay it — the price of being on earth, the price of being alive.[21]

This passage is the complement — the twin, if you like — of the one I have quoted from *Elizabeth Costello* about the sexual proclivities of the gods. Whereas death proves too high a price for the gods to pay, the sheep "have calculated the price and are prepared to pay it — the price of being on earth, the price of being alive."

A crucial point to make about Coetzee's fictional universe is that he extends the thought of death — or the awareness of mortality — to other animals besides the human. Amongst the various marginalized others with whom Coetzee's protagonists express solidarity by avowing the thought of an un-illuminated death we must include animals. As Louis Tremaine notes, there is "an unmistakable and ever more insistent pattern in Coetzee's fiction, from his earliest to his most recent work, a pattern of incorporating animals as narrative elements associated with suffering and death and, especially, with the question of the foreknowledge of impending death."[22] Derek Attridge argues similarly that, "the most powerful writing in the novel [*Disgrace*] involves the relation not to animal life but to animal death."[23] If (as Elizabeth Costello says) the gods know what they know only in the most general ways because they refuse to accept the full consequences of finite embodiment, then animals know what they know in the most particular — which is to say, embodied — ways. Death is more truly the zoomorphic than the anthropomorphic thought because we must turn away from the gods and towards the animals in order to acquire knowledge of it. This is something that the main protagonist of *Disgrace*, David Lurie, comes to realize when he goes to help Bev Shaw euthanize unwanted dogs in the Animal Welfare clinic in Grahamstown after being dismissed from his university position in Cape Town for sexual misconduct. In a passage that seems directly informed by the one I just quoted from *Boyhood*, Lurie observes the condemned dogs in the clinic sensing their own fate.

> His whole being is gripped by what happens in the theatre. He is convinced the dogs know their time has come. Despite the silence and the painlessness of the procedure, despite the good thoughts that Bev Shaw thinks and that he tries to think, despite the airtight bags in which they tie the newmade corpses, the dogs in the yard smell what is going on inside. They flatten their ears, they droop their tails, as if they too feel the disgrace of dying; locking their legs, they have to be pulled or pushed or carried over the threshold. On the table some snap wildly left and right, some whine plaintively; none will look straight at the needle in Bev's hand, which they somehow know is going to harm them terribly.[24]

As Raimond Gaita comments upon this passage in his book *The Philosopher's Dog*:

> This is knowledge in the shadow of death, and is, moreover, practical knowledge ascribed because of the way the animals behave in the face of danger. My preparedness to concede that dogs may know they are about to die in circumstances such as Coetzee describes or that cats do when, as they say, they go off to die, is a function of the fact that in those circumstances an animal's intelligence is entirely active, its understanding entirely practical.[25]

Gaita wants to distinguish between a practical and a reflective understanding of death. He thinks that animals are sometimes aware of their mortality but never to the extent that they actually wonder when they are going to die or entertain thoughts of the afterlife. The upshot of his argument is that humans come to enjoy a double intellectual and emotional advantage over other creatures in relation to death: they sense the pathos not only of their own finitude but also of the finitude of other animals. "Often, when I look at [my dog] Gypsy now," writes Gaita, "I am pained by the knowledge that she has not much longer to live. For me, the pathos of her condition is increased by the fact that she does not know that she must die."[26]

Gaita does not believe his position to conflict with Coetzee's: "The pathos that informs my sense of Gypsy as a mortal creature who does not know that she will die," he writes, "does not, I think, conflict with anything I have quoted from Coetzee or with anything I have elaborated in exposition of what I believe to be its philosophical basis."[27] But I disagree. I think Gaita entirely misses the point of Coetzee's fiction when he uses it to develop a distinction between a practical and a reflective understanding of death. Rather than sharply distinguishing between animal and human, Coetzee's novels constantly show humans and animals exchanging identities. One of the important ways in which the animal functions in Coetzee is as a catalyst for metamorphic desire. "He wants to be a creature of the desert, this desert, like a lizard,"[28] writes Coetzee in *Boyhood*. Perhaps nowhere is Coetzee's deconstruction of the distinction between human and animal put more sharply or more succinctly than in the following paragraph from *Age of Iron* in which Elizabeth Curren describes having to shed her humanness in the face of her present difficulties: "Man, I thought: the only creature with part of his existence in the unknown, in the future, like a shadow cast before him. Trying continually to catch up with that moving shadow, to inhabit the image of his hope. But I, I cannot afford to be man. Must be something smaller, blinder, closer to the ground."[29] The first two sentences of this passage echo Gaita's position that what distinguishes human beings from other creatures is their ability to project themselves into the future, into the unknown, and thus (for example) reflect upon the fact of their mortality. But the next two sentences qualify the exuberant humanism of the previous two. Curren's point is that one cannot afford to be a humanist — or inhabit the image of one's hope — when one is cast (as she is in this novel) into the existential and political shadow of death.

When Curren writes that rather than inhabiting the image of her hope or being "man," she must "be something smaller, blinder, closer to the ground," what comes to mind is a small animal — something on four legs rather than two. Perhaps she is thinking of a mole or the mole-like creature that narrates Kafka's story, "The Burrow," a text about which Coetzee has written an essay.[30] She might even be referring here to the vagabond Vercueil's dog. Whatever the case may be, Curren is imagining herself shedding her humanness — becoming smaller, becoming animal, becoming in Gaita's terms a more practical and a less reflective intelligence. Moreover, she is conceiving of this transformation from a reflective into a practical intelligence in positive rather than negative terms. Already in Elizabeth Curren, then, we perceive the lineaments of the deconstructive claim Coetzee later voices through Elizabeth Costello that "reason may be not the being of the universe but on the contrary merely the being of the human brain."[31]

In *The Philosopher's Dog*, Gaita mistakes the kind of knowledge on offer in Coetzee, which is precisely knowledge in the shadow of death, knowledge about our finitude that comes to us specifically from other animals. What Gaita ignores in the passage he cites from *Disgrace* is that David Lurie feels practically implicated in the deaths of the unwanted dogs. Lurie is not sensing the pathos of their deaths at this moment in the novel, if this means he is sensing something that they are incapable of sensing. Rather he is feeling the "disgrace of dying" — or the prospect of an un-illuminated death — along with them. Like Elizabeth Curren in *Age of Iron*, he is in the process of transforming from a reflective into a practical intelligence, from "man" into "something smaller, blinder, closer to the ground." These dogs, whose marginalization within human society mirrors his own in certain respects, serve to trigger within him the metamorphic desire to become-animal. As Lurie reflects after taking it upon himself to incinerate all the dog corpses from the Animal Welfare clinic: "A dog-man, Petrus once called himself. Well, now he has become a dog-man: a dog undertaker; a dog psychopomp; a *harijan*."[32] *Harijan* — meaning "child of God" — is the name Gandhi gave to individuals at the bottom of the Hindu caste system in India in preference to "untouchable." In *Disgrace*, Coetzee shows both humans and animals becoming *harijans* or "untouchables." Here, then, is why his protagonist feels he must accompany the euthanized dogs from the Animal Welfare clinic to the anthracite-fuelled incinerator at the Settlers Hospital: It is finally by touching their "untouchable" corpses that the socially disgraced Lurie enters fully into the "disgrace of dying" with these dogs.

When Gaita writes that the pathos of his dog Gypsy's condition is heightened by the fact that she does not know that she is going to die, he makes the pathos of death an exclusively human emotion. But Coetzee does not grant humans such an emotional advantage over other animals. In his fiction, he shows both humans and animals responding affectively to the thought of their own death. Perhaps nowhere is this fact better illustrated than in a remarkable scene from the third of his fictional memoirs, *Summertime: Scenes from Provincial Life*, in which Coetzee likens himself to a baboon experiencing "evening melancholy" as he watches the sun set on the family farm with his favourite cousin Margot.

> "Have you read the book by Eugène Marais about a year he spent observing a baboon troop? He writes that at nightfall, when the troop stopped foraging and watched the sun go down, he could detect in the eyes of the older baboons the stirrings of melancholy, the birth of a first awareness of their own mortality."
>
> "Is that what the sunset makes you think of — mortality?"
>
> "No. But I can't help remembering the first conversation you and I had, the first meaningful conversation. We must have been six years old. What the actual words were I don't recall, but I know I was unburdening my heart to you, telling you everything about myself, all my hopes and longings. And all the time I was thinking, *So this is what it means to be in love!* Because — let me confess it — I was in love with you. And ever since that day, being in love with a woman has meant being free to say everything on my heart."
>
> "Everything on your heart . . . What has that to do with Eugène Marais?"
>
> "Simply that I understand what the old male baboon was thinking as he watched the sun go down, the troop leader, the one Marais was closest to. *Never again*, he was thinking: *Just one life and then never again. Never, never, never.* That is what the Karoo does to me too. It fills me with melancholy. It spoils me for life."[33]

The book Coetzee speaks of here is Eugène Marais's 1937 ethological study *The Soul of the Ape*, an account of three years that Marais spent with a troop of chacma baboons (*Papio Ursinus ursinus*) in the Transvaal in South Africa. In Chapter 5 of this work, Marais discusses Hesperian depression — or depression that relates to the setting of the sun. The idea here is that human emotion is tidal in character and reaches its greatest ebb with the approach of darkness each day. A primitive or superstitious fear of the dark is one possible explanation for this onset of evening melancholy. As Marais notes: "The Boers explain the condition, as might be expected, on more abstract grounds. The coming of the night suggests the approach of death; the utter futility of human life; the distressing certainty of the end of all things; and the helplessness and paltriness of man."[34]

In observing the chacma baboons, Marais discovers that they too suffer from Hesperian depression:

> In few phases of behaviour did our troop of baboons appear to us more human-like, than in the unquestionable expression of this "evening melancholy." . . . With the setting of the sun and the first deepening of the shadows a singular transformation came over the entire scene. Silence fell upon them gradually. The "talking" ceased. The little ones crept cuddlingly into the protecting arms of their mothers . . . The older ones assumed attitudes of profound dejection, and for long intervals the silence was unbroken except for the soft whimpering complaints of the little ones and the consoling gurgling of the mothers. And then from all sides would come the sound of mourning, a sound never uttered than on occasions of great sorrow — of death or parting. I do not think there is any possibility of mistaking the state of mind which determines this behaviour — even by one not well acquainted with the character and ways of the animal.[35]

It is not hard to see why Coetzee is drawn to this moment in Marais's book. It shows the animal occupying the agonistic space between the thought of death and death itself that he usually reserves for his own protagonists. It provides evolutionary evidence for humans and other animals sharing not just a sense of finitude, but also an affective reaction to that finitude. Finally, it demonstrates an evolutionary connection between the thought of personal mortality and the emotion of melancholy. Given all this, it is unsurprising that Coetzee explains the baboons' evening melancholy to his cousin in the abstract manner of the Boers, as "the birth of a first awareness of their own mortality."

The scene from *Summertime* shows Coetzee becoming-animal or, more precisely, becoming-melancholy-ape: "'I understand what the old male baboon was thinking as he watched the sun go down,'" he says to his cousin, "'the troop leader, the one Marais was closest to. *Never again*, he was thinking: *Just one life and then never again. Never, never, never.* That is what the Karoo does to me too. It fills me with melancholy. It spoils me for life.'" Marais never mentions a favourite old male baboon, the troop leader to whom he was closet, in *The Soul of the Ape*. Coetzee presumably fabricates this detail in order to personalize and intensify his cross-species identification with the evening melancholy of the chacmas.[36] As it happens, this act of metaphorical identification is entirely lost on Margot: "She still does not see what baboons have got to do with the Karoo or their childhood years, but she is not going to let on."[37] Like Raimond Gaita, Margot maintains a stricter distinction between humans and animals than does her cousin; her cousin, she later reflects obviously still a little dumbfounded by the claim, "who believes that even baboons, as they stare out over the veld, are overcome with *weemoed* [melancholy]."[38] But whether or not it is understood, Coetzee's expression of animal melancholy in *Summertime* serves to deconstruct the distinction Gaita develops in *The Philosopher's Dog* between a practical and a reflective understanding of death by invoking the imperative to shed one's humanness — even if only momentarily — and become-animal.

BECOMING-ANIMAL / BECOMING-MORTAL

In *Summertime* Margot struggles to understand her cousin's metamorphic identification with animals because she fails to grasp that, for Coetzee, animals help us to come to terms with our own mortality. It is important to realize that Coetzee needn't have spoken so esoterically to her about Hesperian depression in baboons. To avoid confusion, he might have done away with the cross-species comparison and simply invoked the tidal character of human emotion. But as it has become increasingly apparent since the publication of *Disgrace*, Coetzee wants to express the thought of death in zoomorphic rather than anthropomorphic terms. Becoming-animal is for him tantamount to becoming-mortal, since it serves to convey one into that melancholic narrative space between the thought of death and death itself.

If writing is a metamorphic process in Coetzee — a matter of becoming-woman or becoming-animal — the transformation into woman or animal is at the same time a performance of mortality. In becoming the dying letter-writer Elizabeth Curren or the ageing novelist and animal activist Elizabeth Costello or the melancholy African ape, Coetzee demonstrates the same point: that animal finitude is the basis for any act of literary metamorphosis. According to Gilles Deleuze in his essay "Literature and Life":

> Writing is inseparable from becoming: in writing, one becomes-woman, becomes-animal or vegetable, becomes-molecule to the point of becoming-imperceptible . . . Becoming does not move in the opposite direction, and one does not become Man, insofar as man presents himself as a dominant form of expression that claims to impose itself on all matter, whereas woman, animal, or molecule always has a component of flight that escapes its own formalization.[39]

As we've seen, Coetzee's fictions certainly confirm this idea that writing is a transformative experience through which the writer moves away from the figure of the major (Man) towards the figure of the minor (woman, animal, molecule). This is their straightforwardly or explicitly political dimension.

But along with the *Realpolitik* of becoming-woman or becoming-animal, Coetzee's fictions are also concerned with something else that we might call the spiritual politics of animal finitude. Again, some of Deleuze's remarks in "Life and Literature" are illuminating in this regard. "One becomes animal all the more when the animal dies," writes Deleuze:

> And contrary to the spiritualist prejudice, it is the animal who knows how to die, who has a sense or premonition of death. Literature begins with a porcupine's death,

> according to [D. H.] Lawrence, or with the death of a mole in Kafka: "our poor little red feet outstretched for tender sympathy." As [Karl Philipp] Moritz said [in "Anton Reiser"], one writes for dying calves. Language must devote itself to reaching these feminine, animal, molecular detours, and every detour is a becoming-mortal.[40]

As I've been arguing in this chapter, it is possible to see Coetzee's work as an attempt to overcome the spiritualist prejudice that animals do not know how to die or do not have a premonition of death. In showing us how to die, Coetzee's animals are part of a broader critique he carries out in his fiction of the theological notion of an individual afterlife. For Deleuze in the passage above, every becoming-animal is a becoming-mortal. Coetzee expresses the connection between these two concepts more causally than Deleuze. For Coetzee, there can be no genuine transformation without the possibility of death, no becoming-animal without the thought of finitude.

To the extent that Coetzee's human protagonists dissociate themselves from the immortality of the gods and the idea of an individual afterlife in order to come to terms with the mortality that they share irremediably with other creatures, I think we can understand Coetzee as writing fables of animal finitude. A few of Coetzee's critics have discussed his work in relation to the fable, notably Graham Huggan and Laura Wright. As Wright observes, in Coetzee's fiction "'fable' takes on its more original meaning as a tale that employs animal characters to teach a moral."[41] On my reading, the moral of Coetzee's animal fables is not the sort we are likely to come across in Aesop or La Fontaine. Indeed, rather than in those by Aesop or Jean de La Fontaine, the moral of Coetzee's fables is most neatly put at one point in the Bible by the author of the book of Ecclesiastes: "Man's fate is like that of the animals; the same fate awaits both: As one dies, so dies the other. All have the same breath; man has no advantage over the animal" (3.19).[42]

Despite his obvious sensitivity to the question of animal suffering, Coetzee remains skeptical about the capacity of human beings to enter imaginatively or sympathetically into the lives of other animals. As he commented in an interview with the Swedish paper *Djurens Rätt* [Animal Rights] in May 2004:

> There is a strong argument to be made that it is impossible for a human being to inhabit the consciousness of an animal, whereas through the faculty of sympathy (fellow-feeling) it is possible for one human being to know quite vividly what it is like to be someone else . . . If indeed it is impossible — or at least very difficult — to inhabit the consciousness of an animal, then in writing about animals there is a temptation to project upon them feelings and thoughts that may belong only to our human mind and heart."[43]

Coetzee is clearly mindful of the dangers of anthropomorphism. Rather than produce fables in the traditional sense by granting human speech and human reason to other animals, he prefers to show us the metamorphic moment of identification between human and animal that enables the fable to take place. As Michel Serres observes in his work *The Parasite*: "What would fable be without metamorphoses? Men must be changed into animals with a wave of the magic wand. And how can that be? The secret of the fable is metamorphosis in the fable. It has to do with a miracle of hospitality."[44] For Serres, the fabulous transformation of the human being into an animal signals the hospitality of the human to the animal: the becoming-host of the human body. In temporarily becoming host to the fabulous animal, the human is (in Deleuze and Guattari's terms) deterritorialized: it loses its ontological specificity as it merges with its surroundings and becomes (in Elizabeth Curren's terms) "something smaller, blinder, closer to the ground."

We might read Coetzee's metamorphic identification with the fictitious troop leader of the baboons in *Summertime* as an instance of becoming-fabulous-animal. As Coetzee stares out onto the Karoo at sunset, he momentarily feels in his body something akin to the evening melancholy of the chacma baboons observed by Eugène Marais. This act of becoming-animal in turn mediates his emotional relation both to Margot and the Karoo: "'This place wrenches my heart,' he says [to her], 'It wrenched my heart when I was a child, and I have never been right since.'"[45]

By far the most spectacular instance of becoming-fabulous-animal in Coetzee occurs in *Elizabeth Costello* when Costello attests to a metamorphic form of identification with the protagonist of Kafka's story "A Report to an Academy," the fabulous ape Red Peter. A number of times in this novel, Costello says — without meaning to be ironic — that she feels a bit like Red Peter. "I am not a philosopher of mind," she demurs at one point, "but an animal exhibiting, yet not exhibiting, to a gathering of scholars, a wound, which I cover up under my clothes but touch on in every word I speak."[46] Here she alludes to the bullet injury Red Peter sustains when he is attacked and captured at a watering hole in the Gold Coast by a hunting expedition from the company of the famous German animal trader, Carl Hagenbeck. Red Peter is in fact shot twice in the attack — once in the cheek ("a slight wound; but it left a large, naked, red scar which earned me the name of Red Peter") and once in the groin ("a severe wound . . . the cause of my limping a little to this day").[47]

Why does the ageing writer Elizabeth Costello identify so strongly with Red Peter? Why does she allow her ageing body to become metamorphic host to the wounded body of the fabulous animal? As I intimated earlier, I think it has to do with her performance of mortality. Costello says she feels like Red Peter because she takes him to embody the zoomorphic thought of death. Like Coetzee's fables of animal finitude, "A Report to an Academy" is self-reflexively concerned with the metamorphic moment of identification between human and animal that makes the form of the fable possible. It tells of how the ape Red Peter becomes human by comically imitating certain defining cultural practices of Western Europeans such as shaking hands, drinking schnapps, smoking cigars and saying "Hallo!" "With an effort which up till now has never been repeated," Kafka's ape dutifully reports to the academy, "I managed to reach the cultural level of an average European. In itself that might be nothing to speak of, but it is something insofar as it has helped me out of my cage and opened a special way out for me, the way of humanity."[48] Rather than a choice, becoming-human was for Red Peter a matter of life and death: "I said to myself: do your utmost to get onto the variety stage; the Zoological gardens [in Hamburg to which he was being transported by the Hagenbeck company] means only a new cage; once there, you are done for."[49] Given the stakes, Red Peter was forced to pay a high price for becoming-human: the birth of the human in him came at the cost of the death of the animal. As the story opens, he claims he can no longer satisfy the academy's request to give an account of the life he formerly led as an ape: "my memory of the past," he says, "has closed the door against me more and more . . . To put it plainly . . . your life as apes, gentlemen, insofar as something of that kind lies behind you, cannot be further removed from you than mine is from me."[50]

Having begun this chapter by comparing Coetzee to Kafka, it is perhaps fitting that I end it by observing that Red Peter's report to the academy circumscribes the same melancholic narrative space between the thought of imminent death and death itself as Coetzee's fictions. When Red Peter stops being an ape and becomes a human being, a second life opens up for him within the first. But what he demonstrates through his report is that his human afterlife is not a transcendence of his animal life. Rather, "the way of humanity" is a way out, a wholly practical means of escape from the threat of imminent death. It doesn't matter in the end whether one becomes animal or whether one becomes human; the basis of fabulous metamorphosis remains the zoomorphic thought of death. In this respect, Kafka's Red Peter and Coetzee's Elizabeth Costello are in fact two sides of the same coin. For Red Peter, the dying body of the animal opens up the possibility of a strategic form of hospitality towards the human. For Elizabeth Costello, the perspective is reversed and it is the dying human body that allows for a form of melancholic and metamorphic identification with the animal.

NOTES

1 J. M. Coetzee, *Boyhood: Scenes from Provincial Life* (Harmondsworth: Viking, 1997), 16–7.
2 J. M. Coetzee, *Doubling the Point: Essays and Interviews*, ed. David Attwell (Cambridge: Harvard University Press, 1992), 199.
3 Franz Kafka, *The Diaries of Franz Kafka 1910–1923*, ed. Max Brod (London: Vintage, 1999), 405.
4 *Oxford English Dictionary*, 2nd ed., s.v. "Grace," def. 11a.
5 J. M. Coetzee, *Slow Man* (London: Viking, 2005), 122, original emphasis.
6 Coetzee, *Slow Man*, 123.
7 Coetzee, *Slow Man*, 123, original emphasis.
8 J. M. Coetzee, *Age of Iron* (London: Secker & Warburg, 1990), 75.
9 Coetzee, *Age of Iron*, 11–12.
10 J. M. Coetzee, *Boyhood: Scenes from Provincial Life* (Harmondsworth: Viking, 1997), 142.
11 J. M. Coetzee, *Elizabeth Costello: Eight Lessons* (Sydney: Vintage, 2003), 189.
12 Coetzee, *Elizabeth Costello*, 189.
13 Michael Valdez Moses, "'King of the Amphibians': *Elizabeth Costello* and Coetzee's Metamorphic Fictions," *Journal of Literary Studies* 25.4 (2009): 36.
14 J. M. Coetzee, *Diary of a Bad Year* (Melbourne: Text, 2007), 126.
15 Coetzee, *Diary of a Bad Year*, 126.
16 Coetzee, *Age of Iron*, 179, original emphasis.
17 J. M. Coetzee, *Foe* (London: Penguin, 1986), 155–7.

18 Coetzee, *Age of Iron*, 179.
19 J. M. Coetzee, *Youth* (London: Vintage, 2003), 169.
20 Walter Benjamin, *Illuminations: Essays and Reflections*, ed. Hannah Arendt, trans. Harry Zohn (New York: Schocken Books, 1968), 101.
21 Coetzee, *Boyhood*, 102.
22 Louis Tremaine, "The Embodied Soul: Animal Being in the Work of J. M. Coetzee," *Contemporary Literature* 44.4 (2003): 595.
23 Derek Attridge, *J. M. Coetzee and the Ethics of Reading: Literature in the Event* (Chicago: University of Chicago Press, 2004), 185.
24 J. M. Coetzee, *Disgrace* (London: Vintage, 2000), 143.
25 Raimond Gaita, *The Philosopher's Dog* (Melbourne: Text, 2007), 71.
26 Gaita, *The Philosopher's Dog*, 67.
27 Gaita, *The Philosopher's Dog*, 70.
28 Coetzee, *Boyhood*, 83.
29 Coetzee, *Age of Iron*, 155.
30 First published as "Time, Tense, and Aspect in Kafka's 'Der Bau'" in *Modern Language Notes* 96 (1981), Coetzee's essay is reprinted as "Time, Tense, and Aspect in Kafka's 'The Burrow'" in *Doubling the Point*, 210–32.
31 Coetzee, *Elizabeth Costello*, 67.
32 Coetzee, *Disgrace*, 146.
33 J. M. Coetzee, *Summertime: Scenes from Provincial Life* (North Sydney: Knopf, 2009), 96–7, original emphasis.
34 Eugène Marais, *The Soul of the Ape/The Soul of the White Ant*, trans. Anthony Blond (Harmondsworth: Penguin, 1989), 105.
35 Marais, *The Soul of the Ape*, 107-8.
36 The protagonist's invocation of a favourite animal is a minor but fascinating theme of Coetzee's fiction. Along with the example from *Summertime* I have just cited, I can immediately think of two others. In *Dusklands*, Jacobus Coetzee describes the behaviour of a small black beetle, of which "he has always been fond" (96). *Disgrace* ends with David Lurie about to euthanize a three-legged dog that "he has come to feel a particular fondness for" (214–15).
37 Coetzee, *Summertime*, 97.
38 Coetzee, *Summertime*, 141.
39 Gilles Deleuze, "Literature and Life," in *Essays Critical and Clinical*, trans. Daniel W. Smith and Michael A. Greco (London and New York: Verso, 1998), 1.
40 Deleuze, "Literature and Life," 2.
41 Laura Wright, *Writing "Out of All the Camps": J. M. Coetzee's Narratives of Displacement* (New York: Routledge, 2006), 15.
42 The Holy Bible, New International Version (Grand Rapids, Michigan: Zondervan Publishing House, 1984). I pursue the connection of this biblical passage to both Coetzee's and Kafka's fiction in my essay "'Like a dog . . . like a lamb': Becoming Sacrificial Animal in Kafka and Coetzee," *New Literary History* 38.4 (2007): 723–39.
43 "Animals, Humans, Cruelty and Literature: A Rare Interview with J. M. Coetzee," by Henrik Engstrom. *Satya*. May 2004. www.satyamag.com/may04/coetzee.html (accessed 18 November 2008).
44 Michel Serres, *The Parasite*, trans. Lawrence R. Schehr (Minneapolis and London: University of Minnesota Press, 2007), 99.
45 Coetzee, *Summertime*, 97.
46 Coetzee, *Elizabeth Costello*, 70–1.
47 Franz Kafka, "A Report to an Academy," in *The Basic Kafka*, ed. Erich Heller (New York: Washington Square Press, 1979), 246–7.
48 Kafka, "A Report to an Academy," 254.
49 Kafka, "A Report to an Academy," 253.
50 Kafka, "A Report to an Academy," 245–6.

CHAPTER 10

Silence as Heterotopia in Coetzee's Fiction

Bill Ashcroft

In *Diary of a Bad Year* the protagonist tells Anya why he no longer writes novels. Writing a novel, he says, is like carrying the world around on your back for three years. The weight of Coetzee's novels comes not from their structural demands, the need for an interesting narrative, the need to say something. It comes from the novelist's exhausting need to relinquish authority. We get a glimpse of this in the chapter "The Gate" in *Elizabeth Costello*. When Elizabeth Costello is asked to articulate her beliefs before she can pass through she says: "I am a writer . . . It is not my profession to believe, just to write. Not my business. I do imitations, as Aristotle would have said."[1]

What must it be like to have no beliefs? Surely Coetzee believes that people should not mistreat, slaughter and eat animals? Doesn't *Diary of a Bad Year* itself express opinions about the state of the world that may well come from beliefs? Despite the Kafkaesque dystopianism of "The Gate," then, Elizabeth Costello's position as a secretary of the invisible, her rigorous refusal to have beliefs of her own, is what I would call utopian. We might say that she occupies a space of possibility, a silence that, paradoxically, the writer can only achieve in the writing. This silence is, on one hand, the silence of the author ceding authority to his fiction, and on the other the horizon of that fiction's possibilities. In a curious way this absence of opinions is the strongest opinion possible about the authority of the text. Elizabeth Costello might appear to signify a change of direction taken by Coetzee in Australia. But she is in fact an extension of the agonism that pervades his writing. Coetzee has always resisted the temptation to be the dictator, resisted the authority of the author, although it begins to take real shape from the writing of *Foe*.

My argument here is that this is an extension of the anti-imperial critique of his writing — he resists what may be the ultimate imperialism, the empire of the author's voice. The form this takes in his later writing is the abjection of the narrative voice, which might be said to be, particularly in the "autobiographical novels," the voice of the author. But it occurs most significantly in the spaces of silence. Silence in Coetzee has been the focus of some debate. Benita Parry condemns it as the silence of the white writer in Africa, a now somewhat out-of-date opinion. Derek Attridge on the other hand sees silence operating in the realm of canonicity itself, exposing both the necessity and difficulty of genuine structural change in a country like South Africa.[2] Meanwhile, Coetzee remains silent. My interest in this topic comes from my investigation of utopianism in post-colonial writing. On the face of it Coetzee's writing doesn't appear exactly full of hope, but it generates a form of agonism that depends upon and curiously enforces the utopian function of writing. This agonism is much like that shown by Foucault, in *The Thought from Outside*, when he rejects any form of resistance that would replace one system with another:

> Anyone who attempts to oppose the law in order to found a new order, to organize a second police force, to institute a new state, will only encounter the silent and infinitely accommodating welcome of the law.[3]

Coetzee similarly refuses any thought of a system to replace the various dimensions of imperialism that are critiqued in his work. The thing those imperialisms share is their own sense of utopia — whether of social order, civilizing mission, or a commonwealth — utopias realized archetypically in *Robinson Crusoe*. But the utopianism that emerges, paradoxically, from his critique of imperial utopias may be best understood in the context of the utopian function of literature itself, a function elaborated most famously by Ernst Bloch.

Bloch insists that the orientation towards the future, the "Not-Yet-Become" is intrinsic to human beings.[4] Humanity *requires* utopian vision in order to imagine and thus affect the future. "Primarily," he says, "everybody lives in the future, because they strive . . . Function and content of hope are experienced continuously, and in times of rising societies they have been continuously activated and extended."[5] This realm of the possible, the realm of utopia is preeminently the realm of literature. Literature, according to Bloch, is inherently utopian because its *raison d'être* is the imaging of a different world. "It is utopia in the very precise sense that its connection to this reality is like that of fulfillment to lack"; its temporal point of reference is the future, and to Bloch "literary activity becomes a special form of dream work."[6] This doesn't mean, of course, that literary works are inevitably optimistic or even hopeful but that their orientation to the future gives shape to the possibilities conceived in the human imagination. We begin to see the importance of silence in the fact that didacticism is the enemy of these possibilities.

The question then is: How can Coetzee's silence be seen as in some way utopian? I have no doubt he would reject this suggestion. But how can post-colonial texts maintain a sense of the possibility of liberation, a sense of hope, how can they maintain their emancipatory potential yet avoid the temptation to editorialize? This is the same kind of question as asking how the author can disavow authority. To understand this I want to utilize Foucault's conception of *heterotopias*, which we first glimpse in his Introduction to *The Order of Things* when he famously discusses the bizarre taxonomy mentioned by Borges. A year later, in the essay "Of Other Spaces," he explains that heterotopias, unlike utopias, are real sites. Society designates sites for work, for recreation, for rest, for education, for transportation, and so on. But Foucault is interested in "counter-sites," places positioned on the outside of cultural space, irrelevant to the practical functioning of everyday life. Cemeteries, gardens, theatres, ships, brothels, vacation camps — like Borges' fabled taxonomy, there is no way to find a common locus for them. These are real places but "absolutely different" from other sites: not utopias but "heterotopias" and they emerge when the *site* comes to dominate the idea of social space.

This discussion "Of Other Spaces" occurs in the context of the transformation of space in human history. In the Middle Ages space was a hierarchic ensemble of places: sacred places and profane plates; protected places and open, exposed places; urban places and rural places; and celestial places opposed to the terrestrial place. It was this complete hierarchy, this opposition, this intersection of places that constituted what could very roughly be called medieval space: the space of emplacement, which was itself sacred in conception. Galileo opened up this localization of space, desanctifying it to make it one of extension: a thing's place was no longer anything but a point in its movement. Today the *site* — which can be defined by relations of proximity between points or elements — has been substituted for extension.

LANGUAGE AND HETEROTOPIA

Given the very strong identification of heterotopias as real *sites* it is fascinating that Foucault describes the disturbance they create, in the Preface to *The Order of Things*, not in terms of space, or proximity or orientation, but in terms of language. Heterotopias "undermine language, because they make it impossible to name this *and* that, because they shatter or tangle common names, because they destroy 'syntax' in advance." Utopias "permit fables and discourse: they run with the very grain of language and are part of the fundamental dimension of the *fabula*." This is why, in Bloch's terms, literature is utopian. Heterotopias, on the other hand (such as those to be found so often in Borges),

> . . . are disturbing, probably because they secretly undermine language, because they make it impossible to name this *and* that, because they shatter or tangle common names, because they destroy "syntax" in advance, and not only the syntax with which we construct sentences but also that less apparent syntax which cause words and things (next to and also opposite one another) to "hold together." This is why utopias permit fables and discourse: they run with the very grain of language and are part of the fundamental dimension of the *fabula*; heterotopias (such as those to be found so often in Borges) desiccate speech, stop words in their tracks, contest the very possibility of grammar at its source; they dissolve our myths and sterilize the lyricism of our sentences.[7]

It is this function that immediately captures our attention: heterotopias "desiccate speech, stop words in their tracks, contest the very possibility of grammar at its source; they dissolve our myths and sterilize the lyricism of our sentences."

Heterotopias disrupt the order of things in their function as "counter-sites." Foucault locates their disruption in the *heteroclite*: in such a state things are laid," "placed," "arranged" in sites so very different from one another that it is impossible to find a place of residence for them, to define a *common locus* beneath them all. The nature of heterotopias is therefore characterized by various kinds of disjunction, transition, even oxymoron and tautology. The heterotopia thus throws language into a space of transition — heterotopias being liminal or transitional have a transitive effect on language. This is perhaps most clearly epitomized in the heterotopia *par excellence*, Foucault's final example in "Of Other Spaces" — the ship:

> The ship is a floating piece of space, a place without a place, that exists by itself, that is closed in on itself and at the same time is given over to the infinity of the sea and that, from port to port, from tack to tack, from brothel to brothel, it goes as far as the colonies in search of the most precious treasures they conceal in their gardens, you will understand why the ship has not only been for our civilization, from the sixteenth century until the present, the great instrument of economic development . . . but has been simultaneously the greatest reserve of the imagination.[8]

The ship is the transitional heterotopia that moves between heterotopias: the brothel; the colony; the garden, all of which, though sites, are themselves transitional spaces. If we take the island as the primary locus of utopia, as it is for Thomas More and Daniel Defoe, the ship becomes the primary metaphor of the heterotopia because it is the image *par excellence* of transition.

If heterotopias disrupt language, if they have a very clear impact on our grammar and syntax, what relationship do they have with literature, the utopian space of the possible? If the colonial utopia is symbolized by Robinson Crusoe's island, the post-colonial heterotopia hinges on the metaphor of the ship, on change and movement, on transformation and ambivalence. This is perhaps why Coetzee's *Foe* concludes in the strangely transformative heterotopia of the sunken ship, a site where speech is finally and utterly "desiccated" — "stopped in its tracks."

The difficulty is that the distinctive feature of heterotopias is that they are *real* places opposed to the imaginary place of utopia — counter sites that mirror at least the idea of the utopian. Owing to their capacity for disruption, in particular, their capacity to disrupt language and representation itself, post-colonial heterotopias are most often critical and contestatory. In this respect because post-colonial representations of colonized life are "counter sites," they may be seen to be almost always heterotopic. The relationship between utopia, with its sacred imaginary, and heterotopia, with its sacred trace, is comprehensively embodied, for Foucault, in the metaphor of the mirror, which is both imaginary and real.

> The mirror is, after all, a utopia, since it is a placeless place . . . But it is also a heterotopia in so far as the mirror does exist in reality, where it exerts a sort of counteraction on the position that I occupy . . . The mirror functions as a heterotopia in this respect: it makes this place that I occupy at the moment when I look at myself in the glass at once absolutely real, connected with all the space that surrounds it, and absolutely unreal, since in order to be perceived it has to pass through this virtual point which is over there.[9]

This combination of the absolutely real and absolutely unreal is present in a heterotopia that performs the disruptive function better than any other, a space that "destroys syntax in advance," particularly that syntax that causes words and things to hold together. More than any other it "desiccates speech, stops words in their tracks," it "dissolves our myths and sterilizes the lyricism of our sentences." This is the heterotopia of . . . silence.

THE HETEROTOPIA OF SILENCE: J. M. COETZEE'S *FOE*

Silence is not, of course, a *site* in any but the most metaphorical sense. But we might consider it a *space* — a space in and between languages — and a *horizon* — the horizon to which all language is directed. It is perhaps at its most disruptive, rebellious and illicit when it appears as a space in literature. In its "absent presence," silence, like the mirror, is the meeting point of the utopian and the real. It is utopian because it may be taken to be the absolute space of possibility, but as a site, or subject in literature, it is real, a heterotopia that disrupts the very idea of the possibility of representation.

The relation between silence and writing is of course a profound contradiction that is expressed in an interesting way by Agamben who says that the unstable and unfamiliar, as well as the possible, is actively produced and changed in the process of writing and reading.[10] What is expressed in writing is "an absolute writing that no one writes: a potential to be written." Here he is no doubt alluding to Benjamin's idea of *reine sprache* — ideal language — the unachievable horizon of all speech.[11] But Agamben goes further: not only does writing bring into presence that which exists, it may bring into the region of possibility that which is yet to exist. He stresses that "pure actuality, that is, the actuality of an act, is (also) pure potentiality, that is, potentiality of a potentiality."[12] I would suggest that "pure actuality," the potentiality of a potentiality, dwells in . . . silence; the space of possibility that the author opens up by refusing authority. Silence is at the centre of writing because it is writing's horizon, the realm of absolute possibility. "To write is to surrender to the interminable,"[13] says Blanchot, and, for Coetzee, this means surrendering authority.

This is why there is no writer I know who is harder on his characters, particularly those characters whom we might associate with the author — Jacobus Coetzee in *Dusklands*, David Lurie in *Disgrace*, the central characters of *Boyhood*, *Youth* and

Summertime, the testy narrator in *Diary of a Bad Year*, or even Elizabeth Costello, both tired and tiresome in those moments when she is most clearly ventriloquizing Coetzee's beliefs. Why does he do this? How is he *brave* enough to do this? It is partly because he requires, in fact insists, that his characters at least appear beyond his control — have a life of their own. This interpenetration of fictional and real that seems to characterize his work in the later work begins in earnest in *Foe*. David Malouf once said that everything that happens in a story is absolutely real at the moment of writing, and this is true of Coetzee and his characters. In this way silence, which is manifested as a refusal of the authority of the text, is a kind of power at the same time as it is a form of effacement.

Silence is most, if not completely, understandable in the context of language, which assumes a central importance in modernity because language now, above all, becomes the field of action for the operation of power — the capacity to change people's actions, to transform the future. In his paean to the technology of printing in *The Storm*, Daniel Defoe extolled its capacity to permanently inscribe speech as "the greatest improvement of its Kind in the World," conveying its contents "for Ages to come, to the Eternity of mortal Time."[14] Writing was also the key feature of Crusoe's colonization of the island. Thus taking control of time, through writing, language becomes the field of the possible because it becomes the field of representation rather than *presentation*. If language as a representational tool, a method of organizing time, becomes critical in modernity, silence is disruptive because it is oriented to *space* — a space within language itself that continually questions its (imperial) confidence in the efficacy and veracity of communication.

Silence features in Coetzee's fiction, *and* his criticism. At the end of a discussion of the South African farm novel, in which he notes the genre's pervasive silences, he asks a possibly unanswerable question:

> Is it a version of utopianism (or pastoralism) to look forward (or backward) to the day when the truth will be (or was) what is said . . . when we will hear (or heard) music as sound upon silence, not silence between sounds?[15]

Hearing music as "sound upon silence, not silence between sounds" presents a silence that is both ambivalent and real, both possibility and disruption. This ambivalent mirroring of the utopian and heterotopian is the function of silence in J. M. Coetzee's *Foe* which seems to be the very embodiment of the agonism of "writing back."

In many respects, particularly in the author's attempt to disavow authority, Coetzee's later, "Australian" texts are a continuation of his whole oeuvre. But there is a pivotal moment in his writing when silence dominates — a moment that explains why silence pervades his later work, and that is *Foe*. But seeing silence as a heterotopia, a site rather than a location, explains also, I think, why no concept of *place* can be found in his later work. A specious explanation might be that moving to Australia, Coetzee moved away from a place with which he was familiar and which appeared, almost inevitably, in his work. But once silence becomes the heterotopic site of the author's freedom, *place* as either extension or location is rendered unnecessary. In a metaphoric sense the ship remains the dominant site of Coetzee's fiction.

Foe is a novel about the silences, the unspoken, concealed at the heart of the story of *Robinson Crusoe*. Near the end of the novel, the author, Foe, says to Susan Barton, "In every story there is a silence, some sight concealed, some word unspoken . . . Till we have spoken the unspoken we have not come to the heart of the story."[16] The silence at the heart of *Robinson Crusoe,* a founding myth of the civilizing mission, is Friday, whose silence both conceals and resists, but more importantly opens up a utopian horizon over which the authorial voice of that mission has no control.

It is the place and the function of this silence, rather than the imperial narrative of *Robinson Crusoe,* to which *Foe* is writing back, the gap between what "really" happens, or might have happened, and the story the writer is moved to write — the silence, we might say, at the heart of the imperialism of the text. It is preeminently concerned with the relationship between the writer, the writing and the world. In this regard it is plunging past the colonial allegory of Robinson Crusoe's story to the heart of canonicity itself. And yet the novel goes still further again, questioning the very gap between the "real" and the written, exploring the nature of writing and that supremacy of narrative in the apprehension of "real" things. While it is about writing it is also about the voice, while it is about the function of narrative it is also about who has the right to speak, while it examines the creation of otherness this is also more than the otherness of race; it is the otherness that exists at the very heart of writing. Ultimately, this silence lies at the heart of language itself. But, for the writer, silence is the space of an ethical choice, the choice to withhold the authority of the author's voice, to withhold the imperial principle on which *Robinson Crusoe*, for instance, depends.

This makes *Foe* a post-colonial "writing back" like no other, because it is not merely responding to the imperial utopia with a counter narrative, nor is it only responding to the canon with the idea of silence as some kind of *aporia* at the heart of Empire. Silence is a real site that is at the same time the utopian space of possibility. Silence is the space that turns the certainties of modernity — certainties that are critical to the civilizing mission — inside out. In this way, although *Foe* tells a very different story, an untold story that might have been re-fabricated by Defoe into *Robinson Crusoe,* it is a story with silence at its heart, because within that silence dwell the multiple possibilities of the story. Coetzee's engagement with writing, with the ethics and power of the writer, and ultimately with the power of the story over events, meets the *idea* of *Robinson Crusoe* at its most significant point: the point at which it becomes a story at all.

Writing is one of the most significant features of colonial control. Its capacity to make narrative permanent, its capacity to objectify events, to give a simulacrum of the real, to install the simulacrum of space and time themselves, lie at the heart of its imperial power. Robinson Crusoe's discovery of writing implements, navigational instruments and books — key technologies of modernity — revealed them to be crucial in the colonial process, quite simply for their power over events, their power as a metonym of Providential direction, their power to organize space (through maps, naming and description of the island) and time (through Crusoe's chronology, his history). His further cause, to write a journal that might never be read, was to enable "Reason to dominate Despondency" as he puts it.[17] Reason, an ambivalent word, which to Defoe suggested both sanity and logical order, was a crucial accompaniment to Religion in the establishment of a civilized and civilizing presence on the island. On the contrary, Cruso, in *Foe*, is not so much lacking in reason as having allowed it to go dormant through a lack of writing's utility in providing his life with either a past or, consequently, a future.

The most obvious "absences" from *Robinson Crusoe* in the story of *Foe* — the arrival of a woman on the island, the lethargy that dominates Cruso's life, Friday's muteness and the complete absence of a text — are immediately apparent. But in order to set up the sense of the imperial power of narrative, to destabilize Defoe's story, *Foe* opens with a series of reversals from the original story that make it very clear how much this novel relies on the fame of *Robinson Crusoe*, and the reader's familiarity with that particular island utopia, to enable the space of writing's silences to unfold. The first absence that strikes us is the absence of the "desert island" paradise. The island in *Foe* is no paradise, no "desert isle" but stinking and insect infested, "a great rocky hill with a flat top, rising sharply from the sea on all sides except one, dotted with drab bushes that never flowered and never shed their leaves" (F, 7). We remember here that Robinson Crusoe's first encounter with the island was with a virtual wasteland. The island became a utopian space through reason, religion and the technologies of European modernity. Susan Barton finds no technology, no initiative, no human speech, and above all, no wreck. There are no goats but a tribe of apes; there is nothing to eat on the island but fish and a kind of sea lettuce; Cruso lives in a flimsy structure of poles and reeds; he makes no attempt to teach Friday more than the most rudimentary words of English. These absences are significant because they are all metonymic of the disruptive *silence* that *Foe* exposes at the heart of the imperial story.

WRITING'S ABSENCE AND COLONIAL LACK

Above all, Cruso has no writing supplies and shows no interest at all in recounting his story. Indeed, when Susan tells him the story of her adventures she tries to extract from him some narrative of his arrival and life on the island; "But the stories he told me were so various, and so hard to reconcile one with another, that I was more and more driven to conclude age and isolation had taken their toll on his memory, and he no longer knew for sure what was truth, what fancy" (F, 11–12). Cruso shows no interest in narrative, nor can he impress any particular narrative as authoritative since he has no writing implements with which to construct a story, nor, in fact does he see the need for any. This is probably the most critical reversal of all. Not only does Robinson Crusoe's story rely on the permanence of writing, but the story itself cannot exist without narrative, without being told.

The absence of writing would mean the impossibility of empire. Without writing there can be no permanent story, no objectifying of space and time, no history, no geography, no utopian reorganization of the world. Without writing there can be no imagined triumph of civilization. But that is exactly the point of the story of *Foe*. Far from "civilizing" the island, Cruso has capped his lethargy, his unconcern for his own story, his tedious life, his lack of interest in tools, with a monumental and all consuming work of futility — the construction of terraces to grow crops for which there is no seed, no harvest, no buyer and ultimately, no need. There is possibly no more telling deconstruction of the colonial process than these terraces, which are, in point of fact, a parody of the civilizing mission — an attempt to turn the island into an agricultural site, and potentially, an agricultural society. Their complete futility, their reliance on the arrival of future occupants with bags of seed, seems to dismantle the triumphal project of the *mission civilsatrice* quite comprehensively. What is he digging but a kind of grave for the arrogant conviction and self-aggrandizement of agricultural society? Nothing could be more alien to the life of the island than these futile terraces, turning the island into virtual waste space. How different are these terraces, we are compelled to ask, from the equally alien apparatus of the colonial civilizing mission?

Yet the terraces are the legacy Cruso will leave behind, and to him more significant than any journal. "Cruso kept no journal," says Susan Barton, "perhaps because he lacked paper and ink, but more likely, I now believe, because he lacked the inclination to keep one, or, if he ever possessed the inclination, had lost it" (F, 16). She is persistent in her attempts to persuade him of the benefits of such a journal — as a memory and memorial, to give events their particularity, to set his own story apart from the stories of other shipwrecks, and most significantly, to explain the techniques and solutions of the very little industry he did display. But the greater her importuning, the greater his defiance: "I will leave behind my terraces and walls," he said. "They will be enough. They will be more than enough" (F, 18). Cruso displays the very opposite of the industrious puritan piety of Defoe's hero. Yet his futile terraces are a perfect metaphor for the colonial inscription on the palimpsest of place.

Cruso's is therefore a story that would not exist except for the retelling by Susan Barton, but it is *her* story first and foremost. "It is a story you should set down in writing and offer to the booksellers," urges the captain who rescues the castaways, "There has never before, to my knowledge, been a female castaway of our nation" (F, 40). At this point, Cruso having died aboard ship, the real story of *Foe* begins. For Susan realizes that a story might pass well enough "but what little I know of book-writing tells me its charm will quite vanish when it is set down baldly in print. A liveliness is lost in the writing down which must be supplied by art and I have no art" (F, 40). She is unimpressed by the captain's suggestion that the book-sellers will find someone to "set her story to rights," because if she cannot vouch for the truth of it what would be the worth of it? Here we begin an excursion into the relationship between the subject and her author Mr Foe, an author who is the foe to the truth, an elusive and unsatisfactory combatant, but one who is ultimately, along with the book-sellers, in control of the story. For as Susan recognizes later: "he has the last word who disposes over the greatest force" (F, 124). This statement is a cunning allusion to Foucault's equation of Power/Knowledge and goes right to the heart of the imperial power of writing, exposing the importance of narrative as both the exemplar and realization of its power.

The question is, of course: Where is the truth of the story if it must be fashioned by art into a narrative? And how can she vouch for the truth of the story if Friday cannot speak? Clearly, Friday represents more than the absence of the black or colonized voice in the canonical story. He stands for the absence of finality, the impossibility of finality in the narrative itself. Friday's tongue-less mouth is the *aporia* of narrative, the point at which all narrative contradicts its object to tell a truth. And as such, despite, or because of, his silence, he is the centre of the story. Such an *aporia* undermines the narrative of Robinson Crusoe's civilizing mission just as resolutely as Cruso's terraces. It is not only the story of colonialism that is called into question but also *story* itself. But teleology, perhaps even time itself, is what the "colonial story," the civilizing mission, is all about and Coetzee brilliantly connects the space of silence at the heart of the story with the absence at the heart of colonialism.

Coetzee is a master of allegory, and the story of Susan Barton's attempts to find the elusive and mostly absent Mr Foe in order to tell her story, is an allegory of the distance that lies between the story and "what happened," or, to be more precise, between the author's story — the one that receives the imprimatur of publication — and Susan Barton's version of her life on the island. The novel divides these stories into sections of the novel. The first section (F, 1–45) is Susan Barton's story "The Female Castaway." This is the story that she hands over to Foe: "I have set down the history of our time on the island as well as I can, and enclose it herewith" (F, 49). The second story (F, 47–111) the account of Foe's absence, is the journal record of Susan's letters to the absent author, both sent and unsent, while she and Friday squat in his house left empty when he fled from the bailiffs. This episode includes Susan's vain search to find passage for Friday back to Africa. The third (F, 113–52) is the story of Susan's eventual discovery of Foe and of his "theft" of her "true" story from her. Susan becomes Foe's sexual partner, his muse and his interlocutor as she discovers the difference between her story and the narrative that needs to be written if the story is to be published. The fourth story (F, 152–7) is the narrative of another voice, an author who comes across a pile of papers beginning "At last I could row no further . . ."; this is the most mysterious story, the account of the absence embodied in Friday's mouth.

TRUTH, ABSENCE AND LANGUAGE

Each of these stories is significant, each plays a contrapuntal tune upon the theme of authorship, but the most poignant, and the longest, is the second story of the author's absence, for this is the allegory of the futile struggle of "truth" to find its way to the author and thus to the story. From the beginning this truth is ambiguous. The account begins with the plea for the author to return the *substance* of the truth to Susan's true story:

> Return to me the substance I have lost, Mr Foe: that is my entreaty. For though my story gives the truth, it does not give the substance of the truth . . . To tell the truth in all its substance you must have quiet, and a comfortable chair away from all distraction, and a window to stare through; and then the knack of seeing waves when there are fields before your eyes, and of feeling the tropic sun when it is cold; and at your fingertips the words with which to capture the vision before it fades. I have none of these, while you have all.
>
> (F, 51–2)

The truth is not a simple thing but must be returned to its substance in the story by means of the imagination and by imagery, without which it is a hollow shell of the truth. The question of the substance, or *substantiality* of the characters themselves, is one that haunts the novel as it haunts all Coetzee's work in which the border between the narrative and that which lies outside it is continually ruptured. If the story can be truer than the truth, by providing the substance, at what point, we might ask, does the substance become imaginative excess; does truth become fiction? Or is all truthful narrative a fiction simply because it is a story?

Susan's vision of the island is the substance that can be given reality in narrative, but in her letters it becomes clear that the story of Cruso's un-enterprising and uneventful life is not a truth that will bear the telling.

> "You remarked it would have been better had Cruso rescued not only musket and powder and ball, but a carpenter's chest as well, and built himself a boat. I do not wish to be captious, but we lived on an island so buffeted by the wind that there was not a tree did not grow twisted and bent."
>
> (F, 55)

We can see the traces of *Robinson Crusoe* creeping into the less eventful account given by Susan Barton, and indeed, see it take over her story. Here is the beginning of a narrative that did not occur, for the musket, the carpenter's chest and the implements of writing, as well as many other details of a more interesting story will indeed appear. This "more interesting story" — the story that became *Robinson Crusoe* — confirms that imperial expansion begins as discourse, a discourse that the material developments of that imperialism bring to reality, a discourse without which those material developments would not have their particular character.

For both imperial control and its post-colonial contestation the story, particularly literature, conceives possible futures before they take place.

A significant aspect of that imperial story is the spread of language and Friday's language learning also comes to usurp Elizabeth's story. Defoe's Robinson Crusoe began to teach Friday the language:

> . . . in a little Time I began to speak to him, and teach him to speak to me; and first, I made him know his Name should be *Friday*, which was the Day I sav'd his Life; I call'd him so for the Memory of the Time; I likewise taught him to say *Master*, and then let him know that was to be my Name.[18]

Yet no such thing occurred on Susan Barton's island. "Cruso would not teach him," says Susan, "because, he said, Friday had no need of words. But Cruso erred. Life on the island, before my coming, would have been less tedious had he taught Friday to understand his meanings" (F, 56).

This teaching of language, both spoken and written, is a key feature of the "civilizing" process, something Susan Barton realizes later when she attempts to teach Friday:

> I tell myself I talk to Friday to educate him out of darkness and silence. But is that the truth? There are times when benevolence deserts me and I use words only as the shortest way to subject him to my will. At such times I understand why Cruso preferred not to disturb his muteness. I understand, that is to say, why a man will choose to be a slaveowner.
>
> (F, 60–1)

The slippage between education and slavery is a telling one. Susan says to Foe later, "If Friday is not mine to set free whose is he?" (F, 99). The maternal task of teaching Friday the colonizing language, to free him, to "educate him out of darkness and silence" exposes the dominance of vision, the idea central to European modernity, that to speak and thus to understand, is to *see*. Silence is therefore threatening to the civilizing mission because it is the equivalent of darkness, primitiveness and with primitiveness, unbridled sexuality, hence Susan's suggestion of the link between the tongue and the penis (F, 119). Relentlessly, Friday's silence, by drawing Susan into the belief that he should be *given* a voice, draws her into the heart of the imperial story.

AUTHORSHIP

Susan, like her story, living impoverished in Foe's empty house, writing to Foe but unable to reach him, represents the truth of events that lack the force to make it through to the publishable narrative. The ironic reversals and absences from *Robinson Crusoe* in Susan Barton's story suggest the extent to which hers and

Friday's stories will be silenced. If Foe cannot be found, Susan must take over the burden of the story. "But what shall I write?" she asks. "The island is not a story in itself," declares Foe (F, 117). The story must be structured and his is a five-part structure: "the loss of the daughter, the quest for the daughter in Brazil; abandonment of the quest, and the adventure of the island; assumption of the quest by the daughter, and the reunion of the daughter with her mother" (F, 117). Four of these five parts revolve around the daughter, who forms no part of Susan's story. What is Foe doing? More pertinently, what point is Coetzee's novel making? In taking Susan's story away from her so comprehensively Foe is demonstrating not just the slippage between "reality" and narrative, but the way in which the story enters into and controls the real. This is precisely what occurs in the colonial story. The narrative of empire materially determines the course of real events.

But here the theme is one to which Coetzee returns in later novels: the intrusion of the "real" world into the story and its disruption of the authority of the text. While living in Foe's house, Susan discovers a strange girl watching the house. "She stands across the street for hours on end, making no effort to conceal herself" (F, 72). The girl, although Susan doesn't realize it, is the early intrusion of Foe's five-part narrative into Susan's story — both her story on the island and her story in England. But this does not dim the apparent reality of the child and her emotional attachment to the mother, which leads her to weep uncontrollably when Susan claims not to know her. This bizarre occurrence can only be understood later when we see Foe taking Susan's story away from her to build the story around the daughter. This girl, who doesn't know Foe and yet who claims to be Susan's daughter, is the metonymic intrusion of narrative into the real, the silencing of the real. For it is the daughter around which Foe will construct his story, much to Susan's dismay.

The radical consequence of this daughter, who intrudes into Susan's life as the figure of narrative's ability to materially affect "real" events, is that Susan finds herself becoming a story. She knows that if she protests that she has never seen this girl before, Foe will merely say she has forgotten. For he has the "force" to have the last word:

> . . . if I were merely a receptacle ready to accommodate whatever story is stuffed inside me, surely you would dismiss me, surely you would say to yourself, "This is no woman but a house of words, hollow, without substance"?
>
> (F, 131)

The irony of that word "substance" is that it is precisely the "substance" of the truth that Susan has asked the author, Foe, to "return" to her story (F, 51–2). But the substance of truth may be usurped by the excess of narrative imagination — Susan is in peril of becoming a story herself, a "house of words."

> "I am not a story, Mr Foe. I may impress you as a story because I began my account of myself without preamble, slipping overboard into the water and making out for the

> shore. But my life did not begin in the waves. There was a life before the water . . . All of which makes up a story I do not choose to tell."
>
> (F, 131)

Susan is indeed a figure in a story, who is "spoken" by J. M. Coetzee, but the larger question here appears to be: where is the dividing line between truth and narrative? Or is narrative (even the "truest" narrative) by its nature a story with beginning, middle and end and therefore always a fiction?

Susan's struggle with Foe over her story has been a struggle over the truth. Despite her perplexity at the way in which the truth of her story is being usurped she is committed to Foe: "Would I be here," she asks, "if I did not believe you to be my intended, the one alone intended to tell my true story?" In this respect Susan is Foe's muse, "a goddess, who visits poets in the night and begets stories upon them." As Foe's muse, Susan is like the mother in Foe's parable who handed her child over to another. "The Muse is both goddess and begetter. I was intended not to be the mother of my story, but to beget it. It is not I who am the intended, but you" (F, 126). In this formulation, the author is not the begetter but the midwife of the story.

FRIDAY'S SILENCE

But it is Friday's silence that occupies the heart of the novel. Friday has had his tongue cut out, according to Cruso, by slave traders. But even that is contentious, and Susan wonders whether Cruso himself has committed the act. Friday can neither talk nor learn the language and from very early in Susan's vain attempts to contact Foe Friday problematizes the telling of her story. For:

> What we can accept in life we cannot accept in history. To tell my story and be silent on Friday's tongue is no better than offering a book for sale with pages in it quietly left empty. Yet the only tongue that can tell Friday's secret is the tongue he has lost!
>
> (F, 67)

Susan clings to the idea that she might educate Friday into "the magic of words" (F, 58), a magic that enables Mr Foe to know Friday though he has not met him. Not only does the book empty out, or contract space in this way by offering knowledge without proximity, but it abolishes time, producing an existence that is permanent, extending beyond the life it records. The story of the island, no matter how permanent it is rendered by printing, will be no story without Friday's account. As a heterotopia Friday's silence is deeply problematic because while it is the space of possibility, it is also real, and it "desiccates speech, stops words in their tracks, contests the very possibility of grammar at its source; dissolves our myths and sterilizes the lyricism of our sentences" to quote Foucault.

When Foe criticizes Susan's story as bland and unappetizing she replies that if the story seems stupid it is because it doggedly holds its silence.

> "The shadow whose lack you feel is . . . the loss of Friday's tongue . . . The story of Friday's tongue is a story unable to be told, or unable to be told by me. That is to say, many stories can be told of Friday's tongue, but the true story is buried within Friday, who is mute. The true story will not be heard till by art we have found a means of giving voice to Friday."
>
> (F, 117–18)

"Till by art we have found a means of giving voice to Friday" — this statement is the core of the dilemma of silence. It links the two themes of the novel: the silence at the heart of the story, and the capacity of colonial power to give, to *ascribe*, a story to Friday. "Friday," says Susan, "he is what I make of him . . . a child waiting to be born" (F, 121). He will be born by means of the voice, through which he will also come into the light and be able to *see*. Like Caliban, the language he is taught by Miranda will enable him to *know who he is*. Whatever he does his story will be told. In this way Susan confirms the colonizing impetus that works through her philanthropic intentions, the imperial power that is strangely synonymous with the power of the author.

But the story composed by imperial power, a power by means of which the world's story itself can be written, is a story that is empty at its heart, because the mute subject of its power, the silent and unteachable Friday, defies narrative. In Susan's terms, he refuses to be born. From the point of view of the Grand Narrative of civilization, the heterotopia of Friday's silence is an emptiness that cannot be filled, an absence, an *aporia*. But as a possibility that cannot be controlled by the author, Friday's silence is unlimited.

Friday's silence is the crucial figure at the heart of the story, because for Foe, "till we have spoken the unspoken we have not come to the heart of the story . . ." (F, 141). The heart of the story could just as well be called the eye of the story or the mouth and listening to it but the imperative of the author is clear: "'We must make Friday's silence speak, as well as the silence surrounding Friday'" (F, 142). It is quite clear how very differently Foe and Susan approach this task. For Susan it is a matter of making Friday speak. But Friday's open mouth stands for the silence, as Foe understands, lying at the heart of writing. The eye of the story is the wreck itself, the eye that will read the truth written. Susan has the desire to communicate, like the craving of a lover for a response from the loved one kissed. But perhaps Foe is more prescient, although his interest is in the attractiveness of the story, because the truth of the wreck is the dead eye of writing.

Nevertheless Foe encourages Susan to teach Friday to write, which she attempts with unexpected results. Friday draws eyes attached to feet. "But as there are many kinds of men," says Foe "so there are many kinds of writing. Do not judge your pupil too hastily. He too may be visited by the Muse" (F, 147). However, the ultimate achievement of Susan's teaching is to discover Friday writing the letter *o*

— the sign of his tongueless mouth, of zero, of silence. The achievement of writing is merely to confirm writing's impotence against his mute unapproachable resistance. In its elliptical way, this is possibly the most damaging "writing back" performed by any post-colonial text, because it prefigures the resistance of the colonized to writing itself.

The concluding "story" of the novel, the short excursion of "the author" — Coetzee (?) — into the world of Susan and Foe, is a conclusion that confirms this resistance to finality and to the heart of the story ever being spoken. The watcher searches the room in which Susan Foe and Friday are sleeping, and enters the story told by Susan that he finds on the table. "With a sigh, making barely a splash, I slip overboard . . .." Friday is found at the heart of the story, within the wreck that symbolizes the central absence of all narrative:

> But this is not a place of words. Each syllable, as it comes out, is caught and filled with water and diffused. This is a place where bodies are their own signs. It is the home of Friday.
>
> (F, 157)

It is a home of silence, the ultimate resistance to language. But it is also the home of endless possibility, as Friday's mouth opens: "From inside him comes a slow stream, without breath, without interruption" (F, 157). This is the stream of possible words emitted from his silence, bubbles like 'O's flowing "up through his body and out upon me." This continual stream is the silence that generates all story, the silence that cannot be spoken, the heart from which all narrative emerges.

Friday's silence can be seen to signify many things (if we want to busy ourselves filling the silence). It is the resistance to the linguistic program of the civilizing mission; it is the silence at the heart of the imperial story; it is the postmodern refusal of narrative closure. But since Coetzee's arrival in Australia it has become clearer that silence has always embodied an ethical choice for the author. This is not a political or morally prescriptive choice and may or may not refer to Coetzee the immigrant South African writer. But it is the ethical choice to refuse to control the heart of the story, as Foe would wish. This is far from easy when issues of justice and freedom cry out for attention as they do in post-colonial writing. But it is the choice to allow the fullest possibility of the text to open up beyond the author's control. This involves walking a tightrope between two extremes: on one extreme lies a didacticism that can become moralistic, tendentious and unrelenting . . . with nothing that is not editorialized; on the other extreme lies an aesthetic and distanced prose that refuses to have anything to say. But by refusing to make Friday's silence speak Coetzee allows it to open up the utopian horizon of possibility. Silence then becomes the ship, the mirror, the partially desacralized space of heterotopia. In the end, this is the site of an ethical choice, a choice to let the silence speak.

NOTES

1 J. M. Coetzee, *Elizabeth Costello: Eight Lessons* (Milsons Point, NSW: Knopf, 2003), 194.
2 Derek Attridge, *J. M. Coetzee and the Ethics of Reading: Literature in the Event* (Chicago: Chicago University Press, 2004), 228.
3 Michel Foucault, *Maurice Blanchot, the Thought from Outside* (New York: Zone Books, 1990), 38.
4 Ernst Bloch, *The Principle of Hope*, trans. Neville Plaice, Stephen Plaice and Paul Knight (Minneapolis: University of Minnesota Press, 1995), 13.
5 Bloch, *The Principle of Hope*, 4.
6 Ernst Bloch, *The Utopian Function of Art and Literature: Selected Essays*, trans. Jack Zipes and Frank Mecklenberg (Minneapolis: University of Minnesota Press, 1989), 7, 10.
7 Michel Foucault, *The Order of Things: an Archeology of the Human Sciences* (London: Tavistock, 1970), xviii.
8 Michel Foucault, "Of Other Spaces," *Diacritics* 16 (Spring 1986): 27.
9 Foucault, "Of Other Spaces," 24.
10 Giorgio Agamben, *Potentialities: Collected Essays in Philosophy*, ed. and trans. D. Heller-Roazen (Stanford: Stanford University Press, 1999), 68–9.
11 Walter Benjamin, "The Task of the Translator," in *Illuminations*, trans. Harry Zohn (New York: Schocken, 1969), 92.
12 Agamben, *Potentialities*, 216.
13 Maurice Blanchot, *The Space of Literature*, trans. A. Smock (Lincoln: University of Nebraska Press, 1982), 27.
14 Daniel Defoe, *The Storm* (London: Penguin, 2005; 1704), 23.
15 J. M. Coetzee, *White Writing: On The Culture of Letters in South Africa* (New Haven: Yale University Press, 1988), 81.
16 J. M. Coetzee, *Foe* (Harmondsworth: Penguin, 1986), 141. Hereafter abbreviated as F.
17 Daniel Defoe, *Robinson Crusoe*, ed. Michael Shinagel (New York: Norton, 1994; 1719), 49.
18 Defoe, *Robinson Crusoe*, 149.

Bibliography

Adorno, Theodor W. *Aesthetic Theory*. trans. C. Lenhardt, eds. Gretel Adorno and Rolf Tiedemann. London: Routledge and Kegan Paul, 1984.

—— *Kierkegaard: Construction of the Aesthetic*. trans. and ed. Robert Hullot-Kentor. Minneapolis: University of Minnesota Press, 1989.

Agamben, Giorgio. *Potentialities: Collected Essays in Philosophy*. ed. and trans. D. Heller-Roazen. Stanford, California: Stanford University Press, 1999.

—— *Nudities*. trans. David Kishik and Stefan Pedatella. Stanford, California: Stanford University Press, 2011.

Ashcroft, Bill. *Postcolonial Transformation*. London and New York: Routledge, 2001.

Attridge, Derek. *J. M. Coetzee and the Ethics of Reading: Literature in the Event*. Chicago and London: University of Chicago Press, 2004.

Attwell, David. *South Africa and the Politics of Writing*. Berkeley: University of California Press, 1993.

—— "South African Literature in English." *The Cambridge History of African and Caribbean Literature*. eds. F. Abiola Irele and Simon Gikandi. Vol. 2. Cambridge: Cambridge University Press, 2004: 504–29.

—— "Coetzee's Estrangements." *Novel: A Forum on Fiction* 41:2/3 (2008): 229–43.

—— "Mastering Authority: J. M. Coetzee's *Diary of a Bad Year*." *Social Dynamics* 36:1 (2010): 214–21.

Augé, Marc. *Non-Places: Introduction to an Anthropology of Supermodernity*. trans. John Howe. London: Verso, 2008.

Badiou, Alain. *Ethics: An Essay on the Understanding of Evil*. trans. Peter Hallward. London: Verso, 2001.

—— *Handbook of Inaesthetics*. trans. Alberto Toscano. Stanford, California: Stanford University Press, 2005.

—— *Conditions*. trans. Steven Cocoran. London: Continuum, 2008.

Bakhtin, Mikhail. *Problems of Dostoevsky's Poetics*. trans. Caryl Emerson. Minneapolis: University of Minnesota Press, 1984.

Balzac, Honoré de. *Lost Illusions*. trans. Herbert J. Hunt. London: Penguin, 1971.

Beckett, Samuel. *The Unnamable*, London: Picador, 1979.

Benjamin, Walter. *Illuminations: Essays and Reflections*. ed. Hannah Arendt, trans. Harry Zohn. New York: Schocken Books, 1968.

Bergson, Henri. *Creative Evolution*. trans. Arthur Mitchell. Mineola: Dover, 1998.

Blanchot, Maurice. *The Space of Literature*. trans. Ann Smock. Lincoln: University of Nebraska Press, 1982.

—— *The Unavowable Community*. trans. Pierre Joris. Barrytown, New York: Station Hill, 1988.

—— *The Work of Fire*. trans. Charlotte Mandell. Stanford, California: Stanford University Press, 1995.

Bloch, Ernst. *The Utopian Function of Art and Literature: Selected Essays*. trans. Jack Zipes and Frank Mecklenberg. Minneapolis: University of Minnesota Press, 1989.

—— *The Principle of Hope*. trans. Neville Plaice, Stephen Plaice and Paul Knight. Minneapolis: University of Minnesota Press, 1995.

Boehmer, Elleke, Katy Iddiols, and Robert Eaglestone. eds. *J. M. Coetzee in Context and Theory*. London: Continuum, 2009.

Brah, Avtar. *Cartographies of Diaspora: Contesting Identities*. London: Routledge, 2002.
Bréhier, Émile, ed. *La théorie des incorporels dans l'ancien stoïcisme*. Paris: Librairie philosophique J. Vrin, 1997.
Buning, Marius. "The 'Via Negativa' and its first stirrings in *Eleutheria*." in Beckett and Religion/ Beckett/Aesthetics/Politics, *Samuel Beckett Today/Aujourd'hui* 9, eds. Marius Buning, Matthijs Engelberts and Onno Kosters, with guest editors, Mary Bryden, Lance St John Butler, and Peter Boxall. Amsterdam: Rodopi, 2000: 43–54.
Bunn, David. "'Our Wattled Cot': Mercantile and Domestic Space in Thomas Pringle's African Landcapes." in *Landscape and Power*. ed. W. J. T. Mitchell. 2nd ed. Chicago: University of Chicago Press, 2002: 127–74.
Carey, Peter. *Illywhacker*. London: Faber, 1988.
— *True History of the Kelly Gang*. London: Faber, 2000.
— *My Life as a Fake*. London: Faber, 2003.
— *Theft*. London: Faber, 2006.
Carter, Paul. *The Road to Botany Bay*. London: Faber, 1987.
— *Living in a New Country: History, Travelling and Language*. London: Faber, 1993.
Clarke, Marcus. "Preface to Adam Lindsay Gordon's *Poems*." in *Empire Writing*. ed. Elleke Boehmer. Oxford and New York: Oxford University Press, 1998: 50–2.
Clough, Patricia Ticineto. "The Case of Sociology: Governmentality and Methodology." *Critical Inquiry* (Summer 2010) 36.4: 627–41.
Coetzee, J. M. *Dusklands*. New York: Penguin, 1974.
— *In the Heart of the Country*. London: Secker & Warburg, 1976.
— *Life and Times of Michael K*. London: Secker & Warburg, 1983.
— "The Great South African Novel." *Leadership SA* 4 (1983): 74–9.
— "J. M. Coetzee: Interview, by Folke Rhedin." *Kunapipi* 6.1 (1984): 6–11.
— *Foe*. London: Penguin, 1986.
— "The Novel Today." *Upstream* 6.1 (1988): 2–5.
— *White Writing: On the Culture of Letters in South Africa*. Chicago: University of Chicago Press, 1988.
— *Age of Iron*. London: Secker & Warburg, 1990.
— *Doubling the Point: Essays and Interviews*. ed. David Attwell. Cambridge: Harvard University Press, 1992.
— "Homage." *Threepenny Review* 53 (Spring 1993): 5–7.
— *The Master of Petersburg*. London: Secker & Warburg, 1994.
— *Boyhood: Scenes from Provincial Life*. Harmondsworth: Viking, 1997.
— *Disgrace*. London: Vintage, 2000.
— *Stranger Shores: Essays 1986–1999*. London: Secker & Warburg, 2001.
— *Elizabeth Costello: Eight Lessons*. London: Secker & Warburg, 2003.
— *Youth*. London: Vintage, 2003.
— *Waiting for the Barbarians*. London: Vintage, 2004.
— "Animals, Humans, Cruelty and Literature: A Rare Interview with J. M. Coetzee." By Henrik Engstrom. *Satya*. May 2004. www.satyamag.com/may04/coetzee.html (accessed 18 November 2008).
— *Slow Man*. London: Secker & Warburg, 2005.
— *Diary of a Bad Year*. Melbourne: Text, 2007.
— *Summertime: Scenes from Provincial Life*. North Sydney: Knopf, 2009.
— "Author Interview." www.randomhouse.co.uk/readersgroup/readingguide.htm?command=Search&db=/catalog/main.txt&eqisbndata=0099526832#interview (accessed 22 October 2009).
Coetzee, J. M. and David Attwell. "An Exclusive Interview with J. M. Coetzee." *Dagens Nyeter* (8 December 2003). www.dn.se/kultur-noje/an-exclusive-interview-with-j-m-coetzee-1.227254 (accessed 13 October 2009).
Danta, Chris. "'Like a dog . . . like a lamb': Becoming Sacrificial Animal in Kafka and Coetzee." *New Literary History* 38.4 (2007): 723–39.

Darian-Smith, Kate, Liz Gunner and Sarah Nuttall. eds. *Text, Theory, Space: Land, Literature and History in South African and Australia*. London: Routledge, 1996.
Defoe, Daniel. *Robinson Crusoe*. ed. Michael Shinagel. New York: Norton, 1994.
— *The Storm*. London: Penguin, 2005.
Deleuze, Gilles. *Essays Critical and Clinical*. trans. Daniel W. Smith and Michael A. Greco. London: Verso, 1998.
— *Desert Islands and Other Texts (1953–1974)*. ed. David Lapoujade, trans. Michael Taormina. New York: Semiotext(e), 2004.
Deleuze, Gilles and Félix Guattari. *What is Philosophy?* trans. Hugh Tomlinson and Graham Burchell. New York: Columbia University Press, 1994.
de Man, Paul. "The Rhetoric of Temporality," in *Critical Theory Since 1965*. eds. Hazard Adams and Leroy Searle. Tallahassee, FL: University Press of Florida, 1986: 199–222.
de Maupassant, Guy. "*Le Roman*." in *Novelists on the Novel*. ed. Miriam Allott. London: Routledge and Kegan Paul, 1959.
Derrida, Jacques. "Living on: Border lines," in *The Derrida Reader: Between the Blinds*. ed. Peggy Kamuf. New York: Columbia University Press, 1991.
— *Monolingualism of the Other, or, The Prosthesis of Origin*. trans. Patrick Mensah. Stanford, California: Stanford University Press, 1998.
— "Hostipitality." *Angelaki: Journal of the Theoretical Humanities* 5.3 (2000): 3–18.
— *Of Hospitality: Anne Dufourmantelle Invites Jacques Derrida to Respond*. trans. Rachel Bowlby. Stanford, California: Stanford University Press, 2000.
Derrida, Jacques, and Anne Dufourmantelle. *Acts of Religion*. ed. Gil Anidjar. New York: Routledge, 2002.
Dostoevsky, Fyodor. *Demons*. trans. Richard Pevear and Larissa Volokhonsky. London: Vintage, 1994.
Douglas, Paul. *Bergson, Eliot, and American Literature*. Lexington: University of Kentucky Press, 1986.
Duncan, Ian. "Narrative Authority in J. M. Coetzee's *Age of Iron*." *Tydskrif vir Letterkunde* 43.2 (2006): 174–85.
Emerson, Ralph Waldo. *Nature*. Boston: Beacon Press, 1985.
Faulkner, William. Nobel Prize Banquet Speech. 10 December 1950. http://nobelprize.org/nobel_prizes/literature/laureates/1949/faulkner-speech.html (accessed 10 January 2010).
Field, Andrew. *Nabokov: His Life in Art*. London: Hodder and Stoughton, 1967.
Fink, Hilary L. *Bergson and Russian Modernism 1900–1930*. Evanston, IL: Northwestern University Press, 1999.
Fletcher, Angus. *Allegory: The Theory of the Symbolic Mode*. New York: Cornell University Press, 1964.
Foucault, Michel. *The Order of Things: an Archeology of the Human Sciences*. London: Tavistock, 1970.
— "Of Other Spaces." *Diacritics* 16 (Spring 1986): 22–7.
— *Maurice Blanchot: the Thought from Outside*. New York: Zone Books, 1990.
— *The Government of Self and Others: Lectures at the Collège de France 1982–1983*. ed. Frédéric Gros, trans. Graham Burchell. Houndmills: Palgrave Macmillan, 2010.
Frye, Northrop. *Fearful Symmetry: A Study of William Blake*. Princeton: Princeton University Press, 1969.
— *The Bush Garden: Essays on the Canadian Imagination*. Concord: Anansi, 1995.
Gaita, Raimond. *The Philosopher's Dog*. Melbourne: Text, 2007.
Geertsema, Johan. "'We Embrace To Be Embraced': Irony in an Age of Iron." *English in Africa* 24.1 (1997): 89–102.
— "Irony and Otherness: A Study of Some Recent South African Narrative Fiction." Doctoral thesis. University of Cape Town, 1999.
Gildon, Charles. *The Life and Strange Surprising Adventures of Mr. D----- De F--, of London, Hosier, who has liv'd above fifty Years by himself, in the Kingdoms of* North *and* South Britain. *The various*

Shapes he has appear'd in, and the Discoveries he has made for the Benefit of his Country. In a Dialogue between Him, Robinson Crusoe, *and his Man* Friday. *With Remarks Serious and Comical upon the Life of Crusoe*. London: Printed for J. Roberts in Warwick-Line, 1719.

Gillies, Mary Ann. *Henri Bergson and British Modernism*. Montreal and Kingston: McGill-Queen's University Press, 1996.

Goldsworthy, Kerryn. "Fiction from 1900 to 1970." in *The Cambridge Companion to Australian Literature*. ed. Elizabeth Webby. Cambridge: Cambridge University Press, 2000: 105–33.

Gougouris, Stathis. "The Late Style of Edward Said," in *Edward Said and Critical Decolonization*. ed. Ferial J. Ghazoul. Cairo: American University in Cairo Press, 2007: 37–45.

Graves, Robert. *The Greek Myths*. Vol. 1. 2nd ed. Harmondsworth: Penguin, 1960.

Gray, Stephen. *Southern African Literature: An Introduction*. New York: Barnes and Noble, 1979.

Griffith, Michael. "William Blake and the Post-colonial Imagination in Australia." in *Literary Canons and Religions Identity*. eds. Erik Borgman, Bart Philipsen and Lea Verstricht. Farnham: Ashgate, 2004: 127–40.

Hage, Ghassan. *White Nation: Fantasies of White Supremacy in a Multicultural Society*. Sydney: Pluto. 1998.

Hassan, Andrew. *Sailing to Australia: Shipboard Diaries by Nineteenth-Century British Emigrants*. Manchester: Manchester University Press, 1994.

Healy, Chris. *From the Ruins of Colonialism*. Cambridge: Cambridge University Press, 1997.

Heaney, Seamus. *Preoccupations: Selected Prose 1968–1978*. London: Faber, 1980.

Heidegger, Martin. *Being and Time*. trans. John Macquarie and Edward Robinson. Oxford: Basil Blackwell, 1962.

Heyward, Michael. *The Ern Malley Affair*. London: Faber, 1993.

The Holy Bible. New International Version. Grand Rapids, MI: Zondervan Publishing House, 1984.

Hooper, Glenn. ed. *Landscape and Empire, 1720–2000*. Farnham, Surrey: Ashgate, 2005.

Huggan, Graham. *The Postcolonial Exotic: Marketing the Margins*. London: Routledge, 2001.

—— "'Greening' Postcolonialism: Ecocritical Perspectives." *Modern Fiction Studies* 50.3 (2004): 701–31.

—— *Australian Literature: Postcolonialism, Racism, Transnationalism*. Oxford and New York: Oxford University Press, 2007.

Kafka, Franz. *The Basic Kafka*. ed. Erich Heller. New York: Washington Square Press, 1979.

—— *The Diaries of Franz Kafka 1910–1923*. ed. Max Brod. London: Vintage, 1999.

King, Russell, John Connell and Paul White. eds. *Writing Across Worlds: Literature and Migration*. London and New York: Routledge, 1995.

Lawson, Henry. "The Bush Undertaker," in *The Anthology of Colonial Australian Gothic Fiction*. eds. Ken Gelder and Rachael Weaver. Melbourne: Melbourne University Press, 2007: 139–46.

Levin, David Michael. ed. *Modernity and the Hegemony of Vision*. Berkeley: University of California Press, 1993.

Levinas, Emmanuel. *Otherwise than Being or Beyond Essence*. trans. Alphonso Lingis. The Hague: Martinus Nijhoff, 1981.

Llewelyn, John. *Emmanuel Levinas: The Genealogy of Ethics*. London: Routledge, 1995.

Lowry, Elizabeth. "J. M. Coetzee's ruffled mirrors." *TLS*, 22 August 2007. http://entertainment.timesonline.co.uk/tol/arts_and_entertainment/the_tls/article2322205.ece (accessed 11 January 2010).

Macherey Pierre. *A Theory of Literary Production*. trans. Geoffrey Wall. London: Routledge Kegan Paul, 1985.

Marais, Eugène. *The Soul of the Ape / The Soul of the White Ant*. trans. Anthony Blond. Harmondsworth: Penguin, 1989.

Marais, Mike. "Coming into Being: J. M. Coetzee's *Slow Man* and the Aesthetic of Hospitality." *Contemporary Literature* 50.2 (2009): 27–98.

—— *Secretary of the Invisible: The Idea of Hospitality in the Fiction of J. M. Coetzee*. Amsterdam and New York: Rodopi, 2009.

McKeon, Michael. *The Origins of the English Novel: 1600–1740*. Baltimore: Johns Hopkins University Press, 1987.

Meyer, Stephan and Thomas Olver. "Zoë Wicomb Interviewed on *Writing and Nation*." *Journal of Literary Studies* 18.1/2 (June 2002): 182–98.

Miller, Christopher. *Blank Darkness: Africanist Discourse in French*. Chicago: University of Chicago Press, 1985.

Miller, J. Hillis. *On Literature*. London: Routledge, 2002.

Moore, Marianne. *Marianne Moore: Complete Poems*. London: Faber, 1984.

Moreton Robinson, Aileen. "I still call Australia Home: Indigenous Belonging and Place in a White Postcolonizing Society," in *Uprootings/Regroundings: Questions of Home and Migration*. eds. Sara Ahmed, Claudia Castañeda, Anne-Marie Fortier and Mimi Sheller. Oxford: Berg, 2003: 23–40.

Morphet, Tony. "Two Interviews with J. M. Coetzee, 1983 and 1987." *TriQuarterly* 69, 1987: 454–64.

Moses, Michael Valdez. "'King of the Amphibians': *Elizabeth Costello* and Coetzee's Metamorphic Fictions." *Journal of Literary Studies* 25.4 (2009): 25–38.

Mulhall, Stephen. *The Wounded Animal: J. M. Coetzee & the Difficulty of Reality in Literature & Philosophy*. Princeton and Oxford: Princeton University Press, 2009.

Nabokov, Vladimir. *Strong Opinions*. New York: Vintage, 1990.

—— *Despair*. London: Penguin, 2000.

Nietzsche, Friedrich. *Human, All Too Human: A Book for Free Spirits*. trans. R. J. Hollingdale. Cambridge: Cambridge University Press, 1986.

Novak, Maximilliam E. *Daniel Defoe: Master of Fictions*. Oxford: Oxford University Press, 2001.

O'Gorman, Kevin. "Jacques Derrida's philosophy of hospitality." *The Hospitality Review* 8.4 (2006): 50–7.

The Oxford English Dictionary. 2nd ed. 1989.

Payne, Michael and John Schad. eds. *life. after. theory*. London: Continuum, 2003.

Poyner, Jane. *J. M. Coetzee and the Idea of the Public Intellectual*. Athens, OH: Ohio University Press, 2006.

Ravindranathan, Thangam. "*Amor Matris*: Language and Loss in J. M. Coetzee's *Age of Iron*." *Safundi: The Journal of South African and American Studies* 8.4 (2007): 395–411.

Said, Edward. *Representations of the Intellectual: The 1993 Reith Lectures*. New York: Vintage Books, 1996.

—— *Reflections on Exile and Other Essays*. Cambridge: Harvard University Press, 2000.

—— *On Late Style: Music and Literature against the Grain*. New York: Pantheon Books, 2006.

Schaffer, Kay. *Women and the Bush: Forces of Desire in the Australian Cultural Tradition*. Cambridge: Cambridge University Press, 1988.

Schreiner, Olive. *The Story of an African Farm*. Oxford: Oxford University Press, 1998.

Serres, Michel. *The Parasite*. trans. Lawrence R. Schehr. Minneapolis: University of Minnesota Press, 2007.

Shakespeare, William. *Hamlet, Prince of Denmark*. ed. Philip Edwards. Cambridge, Cambridge University Press, 1989.

Shulevitz, Judith. "Who Cares?" (review of *Diary of a Bad Year*). *Slate*, 10 December 2007. www.slate.com/id/2179374/pagenum/all/ (accessed 11 January 2010).

Siddhartha, Deb. "Señor Year" (review of *Diary of a Bad Year*). *Bookforum*, December/January 2008. www.bookforum.com/inprint/014_04/1385 (accessed 11 January 2010).

Sidney, Sir Philip. *The Defence of Poesy*. ed. Lewis Soens. Lincoln: University of Nebraska Press, 1970.

Taylor, D. J. "Codes for the enigma of survival" (review of *Slow Man*). *Independent*, 2 September 2005. www.independent.co.uk/arts-entertainment/books/reviews/slow-man-by-j-m-coetzee-505074.html (accessed 11 January 2010).

Thorold, Alan and Richard Wicksteed. "Grubbing for the Ideological Implications: A Clash (More or Less) with J. M. Coetzee." *Sjambok*, n.d.: 3–5.

Tremaine, Louis. "The Embodied Soul: Animal Being in the Work of J. M. Coetzee." *Contemporary Literature* 44.4 (2003): 587–612.

Tsiolkas, Christos. *Dead Europe*. Melbourne: Vintage, 2005.

Uhlmann, Anthony. "Negative Allegory: Buning on Allegory and the *Via Negativa*," in *Where Never Before: Beckett's Poetics of Elsewhere, "Samuel Beckett Today/Aujourd'hui."* ed. Sjef Houppermans et al. Amsterdam: Rodopi, 2009.

— "Deleuze, Ethics and Ethology," in *Deleuze and Ethics*. eds. Daniel W. Smith and Nathan Jun. Edinburgh: Edinburgh University Press, forthcoming 2011.

Watt, Ian. *The Rise of the Novel*. Berkeley: University of California Press, 1957.

White, Patrick. *Voss*. London: Vintage, 1994.

— *The Tree of Man*. London: Vintage, 1994.

— "The Prodigal Son." 3 November 2008. http://arts.abc.net.au/white/titles/other/whitespeaks.html (accessed 3 November 2008).

White, Richard. *Inventing Australia: Images and Identity 1688–1980*. Sydney: Allen and Unwin, 1981.

Wilkes, G. A. "Patrick White's *The Tree of Man*," in *Ten Essays on Patrick White*. ed. G. A. Wilkes. Sydney: Angus and Robertson, 1970: 21–33.

Williams, Mark. *Patrick White*. London: Macmillan, 1993.

Winton, Tim. *Dirt Music*. London: Picador, 2004.

— *Breath*. London: Picador, 2008.

Wright, Laura. *Writing "Out of All the Camps": J. M. Coetzee's Narratives of Displacement*. New York: Routledge, 2006.

Zimmerman, Everett. "Defoe and Crusoe." *ELH* 38.3 (1971): 377-396.

Žižek, Slavoj. *Welcome to the Desert of the Real*. London: Verso, 2002.

— *Violence*. London: Verso, 2007.

Zola, Emile. "The Experimental Novel," in *The Nineteenth Century Novel: A Critical Reader*. ed. Stephen Regan. London: Routledge, 2001: 104–16.

Index

Lightning Source UK Ltd.
Milton Keynes UK
UKOW07f1844200215

246608UK00005BA/148/P

9 781623 569587